Screening Genders

Rutgers Depth of Field Series

Charles Affron, Mirella Jona Affron, Robert Lyons, Series Editors

————

Richard Abel, ed., Silent Film

John Belton, ed., Movies and Mass Culture

Matthew Bernstein, ed., Controlling Hollywood: Censorship and Regulation in the Studio Era

John Thornton Caldwell, ed., Electronic Media and Technoculture

Angela Dalle Vacche, ed., The Visual Turn: Classical Film Theory and Art History

Robert Eberwein, ed., The War Film

Peter X Feng, ed., Screening Asian Americans

Krin Gabbard and William Luhr, eds., Screening Genders

Marcia Landy, ed., The Historical Film: History and Memory in Media

Peter Lehman, ed., Defining Cinema

Peter Lehman, ed., Pornography: Film and Culture

James Naremore, ed., Film Adaptation

Stephen Prince, ed., The Horror Film

Stephen Prince, ed., Screening Violence

Ella Shohat and Robert Stam, eds. Multiculturalism, Postcoloniality, and Transnational Media

J. David Slocum, ed., Terrorism, Media, Liberation

Valerie Smith, ed., Representing Blackness: Issues in Film and Video

Janet Staiger, ed., The Studio System

Virginia Wright Wexman, ed., Film and Authorship

Alan Williams, ed., Film and Nationalism

Linda Williams, ed., Viewing Positions: Ways of Seeing Film

Barbie Zelizer, ed., Visual Culture and the Holocaust

Edited and with an Introduction by
Krin Gabbard and William Luhr

Screening Genders

Rutgers
University
Press
New Brunswick,
New Jersey and
London

Library of Congress Cataloging-in-Publication Data

Screening genders / edited and with an introduction by Krin Gabbard and William
Luhr.
     p. cm. — (Rutgers depth of field series)
  Includes bibliographical references and index.
  ISBN 978-0-8135-4339-0 (hardcover : alk. paper)
  ISBN 978-0-8135-4340-6 (pbk. : alk. paper)
 1. Sex role in motion pictures.   I. Gabbard, Krin.   II. Luhr, William.
  PN1995.9.S47S37 2008
  791.43'6552—dc22

                                    2007044900

A British Cataloging-in-Publication record for this book is available from the British
Library.

Visit our Web site: http://rutgerspress.rutgers.edu

Manufactured in the United States of America

To our colleagues and friends at the
Columbia University Seminar on Cinema
and Interdisciplinary Interpretation

Contents

GAY, STRAIGHT, QUEER, AND BEYOND

GENDERING GENRE

Acknowledgments

Our thanks go first to the colleagues who have made such valuable contributions to this volume. We are grateful to Charles Affron, who gave us the idea for this book, and to the staff at Rutgers University Press for making it happen. Special thanks to Jennifer Albanese for her valuable assistance in preparing the manuscript. Pamela Grace has been a patient and supportive colleague throughout the process, and our sincere thanks go to her.

William Luhr wishes to thank the New York University Faculty Resource Network, along with Chris Straayer, Bill Simon, and Robert Sklar of the Department of Cinema Studies, who have been invaluable in providing research help and facilities, as have Charles Silver, Steve Higgins, and the staff of the Film Study Center of the Museum of Modern Art. Generous assistance has also come from the members of the Columbia University Seminar on Cinema and Interdisciplinary Interpretation, particularly my truly remarkable co-chair, Krin Gabbard, as well as David Sterritt and Christopher Sharrett. Thanks also to Robert L. Belknap, director of the University Seminars, and the Seminar Office's essential staff, Alice Newton and Michelle Salerno. At Saint Peter's College, gratitude goes to the President, Eugene Cornacchia, Academic Dean Marylou Yam, Bill Knapp, and the staff of Information Technologies, Frederick Bonato and the members of the Committee for the Professional Development of the Faculty, Lisa O'Neill, director of the Honors Program, Jon Boshart, chair of the Fine Arts Department, John M. Walsh, Mrs. Barbara Kuzminski, Thomas Kenny, David Surrey, David X. Stump, SJ, Oscar Magnan, SJ, and Leonor I. Lega for generous support, technical assistance, and research help. As always, I am deeply indebted to my father, Helen and Grace; Walter and Richie; Bob, Carole, Jim, Randy, Roger, Judy, and David.

Krin Gabbard also thanks the director, staff, and participants at the Columbia University Seminar on Cinema and Interdisciplinary Interpretation, especially Christopher Sharrett. William Luhr has been the ideal co-chair as well as co-author. He has been tirelessly helpful in both situations, always pulling me along and keeping me up to speed. I don't know how I could have done any of this without him. At SUNY Stony Brook, I thank President Shirley Kenny, Dean James Staros, and my chair, Robert Harvey. I am also grateful for the support I regularly receive from my Stony Brook colleagues Jackie Reich, Adrian Perez-Melgosa, Ira Livingston, Neda Astanasoski, Román de la Campa, E. Ann Kaplan, Peter Manning, Adrienne Munich, and James Rubin. Without the daily efforts of Mary Moran-Luba, the extraordinary woman who runs the departmental office, completing this book would have been impossible. Victoria Judd and Alinda Askew have also been an essential part of my working life at Stony Brook. I deeply regret that, for the first time, neither of my parents will read a book with my name on it. Two extraordinary people, Lucina Paquet Gabbard and Glendon Gabbard, passed away in 2006 and 2007. Anything that is good about me comes from them. (See the second film still in our Introduction.) Happily, I still live with a beautiful and compassionate woman, my wife Paula.

Screening Genders

Krin Gabbard and William Luhr

Introduction

Today, any understanding of how masculinity and femininity are constructed is almost impossible without reference to the Hollywood cinema. Surprisingly, a real interrogation of this relationship did not begin until the 1970s, just as academic film studies was coming of age. In its earliest incarnations film studies drew from literary analysis, with its attendant issues of narrative structure, thematic unity, textual analysis, and authorship. But it soon sought to distinguish itself from literary studies by looking to other fields, such as art history, anthropology, psychological theories of perception, and semiotics. The discipline endeavored to further differentiate itself by concentrating on distinctive elements not available to narrative forms like the novel or drama. Film studies eventually came into its own with the advent of structuralism and poststructuralism. One of many approaches that had been largely ignored earlier, gender studies suddenly became a hot topic. In the early twenty-first century, gender is one of the central concerns in the still-growing and increasingly interdisciplinary field of cinema studies. Today, film scholars are much more likely to engage with feminist analysis, the problematization of masculinity, queer theory, and transgender issues than with questions of authorship or the aesthetics of the moving image.

As E. Ann Kaplan's essay in this volume illustrates, gender studies emerged within the larger context of what may be termed empowerment or identity studies. Formalist studies of texts focused upon relationships within the texts themselves and showed little interest in extra-textual issues such as the historically specific social and sexual identity of the author. During that moment, questions about the author's identity were seen as potentially reinforcing social prejudices. So, to classify a work as created by a member of a marginalized group, such as an African American, a woman, or a gay or lesbian, might have been considered an attempt to imply that the work itself was therefore marginal, agenda-driven, or somehow inferior. Times have changed. More recently, explorations of the racial identity of Spike Lee and Oscar Micheaux, the closeted lesbianism of Dorothy Arzner, and the homosexuality of George Cukor, Andy Warhol, James Whale, and R. W. Fassbinder have offered valuable insights into their works.

Much of this began with the influence of psychoanalysis and feminism upon film studies. As Marxism had shown that the social class of a person is profoundly important, a fundamental tenet of feminism (indeed, all gender studies) is that the gender and psychological makeup of a filmmaker, an actor, or an audience member is as important as the historical moment and social class of that individual. With the work of theorists such as Laura Mulvey, E. Ann Kaplan, Steve Neale, Lucy Fischer, Linda Williams, and Constance Penley, gender studies began to change minds about cinematic meaning and reception.

Once feminism had become established, the field of gender exploration broadened. If it was important to study femininity, it was also important to study masculinity, since neither exists in isolation and each often defines itself in relation to the other. Furthermore, masculinity is hardly a simple proposition. Pee-Wee Herman, Tom Hanks, Denzel Washington, and Brad Pitt are all men, but they are very different kinds of men. When scholars such as Richard Dyer, Dennis Bingham, Peter Lehman, Robert Sklar, and Steve Cohan began parsing the differences among men as feminists had earlier done for women, they opened the door to related fields such as masculinity and queer studies.

These explorations delved not only into specific character images, such as "tough guy," "glamour girl," or "sissy," but also the ways in which gender issues inflect genre and subjectivity in reception. Why are genres such as melodrama considered "women's" films and others, such as the Western or combat film, considered "male action genres"? Most genres establish strong presumptions about what constitutes masculinity or femininity, and those presumptions differ with the genres. A central male character in a Western, for example, is likely to shoot someone and engage in a fistfight before the film ends; this is not likely to happen with a man in a musical or romantic comedy. Furthermore, the film industry has always operated upon gender presumptions about the likely tastes of their audiences when constructing films. An understanding of what this means and how it interfaces with social norms has been aided by reception studies and explorations of spectatorship. Do women see films in different ways than men? In the 1970s feminists argued that spectatorship was tightly gender-specific, but only a few years later a new wave of feminist theorists argued that there are many ways in which women, or in fact the same woman, can respond to a film. A woman might identify with the heroine at one point in a film but with a male character at another. Their gender does not necessarily determine the responses of all women at all times. Their reactions are also affected by a film's style, narrative structure, ideology, and the charisma of the actors, among other factors. Furthermore, such responses can change over time, just as genre norms change over time. A film or a character with which a woman may have identified strongly at one point in her life might, at a later point, seem silly or uninteresting to the same person. David Lugowski notes in his essay in this volume that, as the field has grown, it has increasingly discarded ahistorical, universalizing, and Eurocentric presumptions about gender and investigated increasingly diverse and polymorphous models.

Gender studies now has its own conferences, journals, and a substantial list of books devoted to the topic. Groups such as gays, lesbians, and transgendered people have emerged from the shadows and are now bringing their own unique sensibilities to the center of the discipline. The purpose of this volume is to outline, contextualize, and demonstrate some of the major approaches that have emerged from the meeting of cinema and gender studies.

————

A crucial discovery of the field is that gender is performative and not "natural." How many little girls and boys have learned how to dress, to groom themselves, to walk, stand, and talk from the movies? How many people have patterned themselves after attributes of movie stars, and how many people evaluate others by those same criteria? They often think that they are "improving" themselves or making themselves more masculine or more feminine without realizing that they are simply engaging in a performance of gender. Furthermore, their choices of traits that they wish to either acquire or erase reveal value-laden cultural presumptions that result from complex negotiations among sociocultural norms, personal imperatives, and value-encoded media representations. And these things change over time. An August 2006 AOL News headline read "Church Fires Teacher for Being Female." The story revealed that, although a woman had taught Sunday School at the First Baptist Church in Watertown, New York, for fifty-four years, a new biblical interpretation adopted by the church prohibited women from teaching men. Hence she was fired for her gender. Although this anecdote comes from outside of the world of film, it has countless parallels with the acceptance or rejection, and in many cases acceptance and then rejection, of gender images in the history of film. Many notions of what masculinity "is" and what femininity "is" have been drawn from movies and in turn have influenced the ways in which subsequent movies have been crafted.

In this regard, no player in the long history of the cinema has been as important as John Wayne in showing men what it means to be masculine. Although regularly regarded as the prototypical "man's man," his masculinity was carefully crafted and geared to the gender imperatives of his era. In fact, Wayne's career as a featured actor began when the director Raoul Walsh noticed the grace with which a young stage hand named Marion Morrison was moving scenery. He soon cast the renamed "John Wayne" in *The Big Trail* (1930), the film in which the actor began to craft the character he would play for the rest

John Wayne at the beginning of a long career. Jerry Ohlinger's Movie Materials Store.

of his life—a shy but purposeful cowboy who, if provoked, would not hesitate to wreak righteous violence.[1]

For many years now, the term *John Wayne* has constantly recurred in even the most informal discussions of gender, and his star image is unequaled in potency and longevity. In 1948 he began a remarkable twenty-six-year period during which, with one exception, he appeared in distributors' listings of the ten most popular film stars (and among the top four for nineteen of those years). Now, thirty years after his death, he still regularly appears in listings of the top-ten most popular movie stars. For generations, he has stood as a dominating ideal for American masculinity.

This remarkable appeal is directly related to the moment in which he consolidated his star image, the post–World War II era. His image involved a particular kind of postwar American masculinity, one defined by the challenges of the World War II military, still fresh in popular memory, as well as by the mythic status of the frontier American West.

The generation that fought World War II was highly anxious about the erosion of individuality and masculine vitality in the postwar era. Many felt that, in the aftermath of a globally empowering victory, they were losing control of their lives. One manifestation of this anxiety was the pervasive image of the doomed, impotent, and demoralized man in the films noirs of that era that helped define its deepest fears. Another manifestation was the growing concern among parents that they were losing control of their own children, the rebellious teenagers of the 1950s. A widely publicized masculine fear involved losing individuating potency and becoming simply a "number," an "organization man," a corporate "man in a gray-flannel suit."

Although wartime military life had stressed regimentation and submission to authority, for many it also signified a masculine proving ground, a valorizing test by fire. Wayne's contemporary military roles in films such as *Flying Tigers* (1942), *Back to Bataan* (1945), *They Were Expendable* (1945), *Sands of Iwo Jima* (1949), *Operation Pacific* (1951), and *Flying Leathernecks* (1951) presented him as heroic even though he wore a uniform like others around him and submitted to regimentation. In a popular joke in postwar military life that indicated the appeal of his persona, John Wayne movies were called "training films." Wayne's military image, then, defined heroism despite regimentation for a generation fearful of losing its identity in an increasingly corporate culture. At precisely the same time, however, his Western persona worked in the opposite way. A fantasy of masculine potency, that persona presented him as a man alone in an idealized past, totally unregimented, self-sufficient, and self-determining. This persona coped not with an oppressive, depersonalizing social structure, as many in the 1950s saw their era, but instead with an unformed social system open to grand possibilities for the righteous and the strong. His image as a man among men in the days when "men were men" provided a resonant point of identification for men concerned about their own potency. Both of Wayne's personae spoke resonantly to the anxieties of 1950s masculinity.

Wayne was consolidating his image as *the* Western star when the Western itself occupied its cultural peak, and the genre incorporated strong gender presumptions. When Gary Cooper was unable to attend the 1953 Oscar ceremony to receive his Best Actor award for the Western *High Noon* (1952), Wayne, considered a Western star of comparable stature, was selected to accept it for him. Extraordinarily popular in Hollywood, the Western also dominated prime-time television throughout the late 1950s. The 1959 season opened with twenty-seven Westerns in prime time, constituting nearly one-fourth of prime-time programming. In January 1959, eight of the top ten rated programs were Westerns.

After the 1950s, however, as American culture changed, so also did the popular response to Wayne's star image. In the 1950s the masculinity he represented was attuned to mainstream culture, respected by young and old alike; by the 1970s, however, the growing youth culture considered his brand of postwar masculinity reactionary. A popular bumper sticker of the time read "John Wayne for Secretary of Defense." Satirically invoking Wayne's screen image as a man of righteous violence, the slogan also linked him with the government then embroiled in the unpopular Vietnam War. Wayne himself was outspoken in his support of that government and that war. Many in the younger generation of the 1970s who protested the actions of a government sending young people to die also viewed Wayne's masculinity as detrimental to national ideals. Ron Kovic's book, *Born on the Fourth of July*, chronicles the transformation of his young, idealistic patriotism into an embittered critique of dominant American ideology after he was paralyzed by a devastating wound in Vietnam. In the book, he recalled idolizing Wayne as a youth but summarized his subsequent sense of betrayal when he said, "I gave my dead dick for John Wayne."

Wayne never participated in World War II, the one that should have been *his* war. Although Wayne and director John Ford had a long and fortuitous association, it did not stop Ford from mocking Wayne as a draft-dodger. Ford, who had served in the war, expressed his disdain most provocatively when he told Wayne that he was a "sissy."

Ford was not the only one to see Wayne as something other than a heterosexual paragon. Perhaps because of cultural shifts, perhaps not, Wayne was being associated with homosexuality as early as the 1960s. In *Midnight Cowboy* (1969), Joe Buck (Jon Voigt) comes to New York City from Texas in full Western regalia hoping to make a living as a male prostitute. The streetwise New Yorker Rico Rizzo (Dustin Hoffman) assures him that he'll have no luck with wealthy New York women if he dresses as a cowboy. "That's faggot stuff," he insists. Joe Buck replies incredulously, "John Wayne. Are you goin' to tell me he's a fag?" Although Rizzo does not reply, his point is that the exaggerated manliness projected by Wayne—and perhaps even the softer, graceful side of his persona—may have more appeal to gay men than to heterosexual women.

In the French farce, *La Cage aux folles* (1978), a gay nightclub owner Renato (Ugo Tognazi) urges his highly effeminate lover Albin (Michel Serrault) to comport himself in a more masculine fashion, specifically by suggesting that he walk like John Wayne. In the corresponding scene in *The Birdcage* (1996), an especially faithful American remake of *La Cage aux folles*, the humor hits a bit closer to home. When Robin Williams urges Nathan Lane to imitate John Wayne ("You're a big fan, right?"), Lane does his own impression of the famous walk. He then looks at Williams plaintively, lamenting that it was no good. But Williams says, "Actually, it's perfect. I just never realized that John Wayne walked like that." (In his essay in this collection, David Lugowski refers to Wayne's walk as "determined and macho, but oddly uneven and sexy.") At least as early as the 1990s, Wayne's masculine performativity had been so widely accessed that it could be the occasion for jokes. In the twenty-first century, we can look back on what was supposedly Wayne's "natural" masculinity and see it in fact as a highly mannered assemblage of gestures that now show their age. Perhaps for similar reasons, the Western itself, once the most protean of Hollywood genres, has now declined precipitously in popularity.

———

Movies have not only constructed gender images; they have also erased many aspects of gender identity. Patricia Mellencamp's essay in this volume addresses the virtual invisibility of women over sixty in significant roles in film history. (Consider the scene from *Prelude to a Kiss*, released in 1992, with two young stars and two elderly actors in romantic postures. Such posturing is normal in romantic films for young actors but very seldom seen with actors over fifty. As people with active romantic lives, they are virtually invisible.)

In many ways this invisibility is related to the absence of African Americans in significant roles in Hollywood films prior to the 1970s and Vito Russo's "big lie" of classical Hollywood films asserting that lesbians and gay men simply did not exist. Such people exist in the world, just not in the world of film, and gender studies helps us understand why. The career of Joan Crawford is an illuminating example of a performer who embodied various feminine types throughout her career, often finding success where few women of a certain age dared to tread. Unlike John Wayne's masculinity, however, Crawford's feminine performativity has not aged well, and her appeal is now highly specialized. The various stages of her career do not reflect her "natural" aging process but rather a series of carefully crafted but dated and transparent postures.

Although Crawford played a number of ingénues in films such as *The Unknown* (1927), she soon became emblematic of the roaring 20s as a flapper in *Our Dancing Daughters* (1928). She even appeared posing sensuously on calendars and worked as a pin-up girl *avant la lettre*. Perhaps her most sexually provocative role was in *Rain* (1932), when she played Sadie Thompson, a prostitute who seemed beyond redemption, at least until the closing moments of the film.

Meg Ryan with Glendon Gabbard and Alec Baldwin with Lucina Paquet Gabbard in Prelude to a Kiss *(1992). Twentieth Century-Fox.*

It is a commonplace that, reflecting the sexism in our culture, female stars seldom survive beyond forty while male stars go on forever. Wayne played lead roles until his death, but Crawford repeatedly made major adjustments to her aging. Although MGM fired Crawford for being too old at thirty-seven in 1943, she came back as a strong, middle-aged, middle-class woman in the extremely popular film noir, *Mildred Pierce* (1945). An actress considered too old to go on playing flappers, energetic romantic heroines, and prostitutes now appeared as a devoted mother prepared to sacrifice her own life to protect her daughter from a murder charge. She went on to spend much of the 1940s and early 1950s playing highly sexualized but older and often betrayed women. She even allowed her star image to assume grotesque proportions when she went toe-to-toe with another female force of nature, Mercedes McCambridge, in *Johnny Guitar* (1954). Nevertheless, by the 1960s, she could still be sexualized, even appearing in a tight-fitting leotard in *The Caretakers* (1963).

Her image reached something of a nadir in *Whatever Happened to Baby Jane?* (1962) in spite of the fact that the film was a box office hit. She played a successful actress whose career ended after a crippling accident. The film begins with Crawford's aging character living in isolation as an invalid with a mad sister, the former child star Baby Jane, played with scenery-chewing excess by Bette Davis. In most scenes, Crawford has little to do except look pitiful or

Joan Crawford in Johnny Guitar *(1954). Republic Pictures. Jerry Ohlinger's Movie Materials Store.*

scream and cower at Baby Jane's assaults. Most memorably, she lifts the lid off a plate to discover that Jane had prepared a dead rat for her dinner. In her years of playing gray grotesques, Crawford was not always the victim. In *Strait-Jacket* (1964) she played an axe-murderer.

Crawford died in 1977 and was fast fading from memory when her daughter published a notorious memoir, *Mommie Dearest,* in 1979. Crawford, at least in the characterization of Christina Crawford, was no heroine, not even a Mildred Pierce. Played with enormous eyebrows and strained facial expressions by Faye Dunaway in the 1981 film, Crawford became more monstrous than even Baby Jane. Today, regardless of the longevity of her earlier career and her moving performances in films such as *Grand Hotel* (1932), when the name Joan Crawford is uttered, someone will surely screech "No more wire hangers!!!," evoking her shrill characterization in *Mommie Dearest.* Whether as the willful heroine in shoulder-padded dresses or the caricature portrayed by Dunaway, Crawford, like Greta Garbo, Judy Garland, Ethel Merman, and a handful of other divas from golden ages past, has become a gay icon.

Now an essential part of the discipline, queer studies has given us tools to understand the coded signals of the old subculture of closeted gays and lesbians when censorship forbade their overt representation on film. Thanks to the work of queer theorists such as Richard Dyer, Jane Feuer, Chris Straayer, Alexander Doty, Judith Mayne, and David Lugowski, we now understand the special appeal of Crawford, Garbo, Garland, and the rest as well as the astonishing gay popularity of films such as *Breakfast at Tiffany's*, *Meet Me in St. Louis*, *Queen Cristina*, and of highly stylized genres such as the musical and the melodrama. Before they moved into the mainstream, gays and lesbians constituted a professoriate in exile, poring over a canon of films, decoding dialogue and performance strategies, and finding pleasures that were previously unknown to straight practitioners of cinema studies. They continue to provide valuable insights into contemporary film where, although homosexual images are not only permitted but also commonplace, they continue to engage complex representational strategies that are not prominently "marked" as gay but that diverge in significant ways from the "straight" and "normal."

Such investigations have helped erode simplistic binary notions of gender, in movies as well as in social existence, and they open up wider categories. Human behavior has long had strong sexual coding attached to it—men are active and women are passive; men like machinery and weapons and women like decorative objects; men like to drink heavily and fight and women like to cook and crochet. But our culture has recently opened up space in which men who enjoy cooking or the ballet and women who enjoy fast cars or contact athletics can be considered men and women not in "danger" of crossing over to the "other" side and becoming gay. And if they are gay, must gay men have limp wrists and gay women bull necks? Furthermore, gender studies has shown that categorizations such as masculine, feminine, gay, straight, and transgendered are themselves profoundly limited and in need of constant exploration and revision. A twenty-one-year-old lesbian Hispanic woman from Seville and a fifty-five-year-old gay Latina from Mexico City may have very little in common. The same might be true of a straight, blonde wealthy male from London and a dark-haired, working-class white male from Detroit. Many traditional and oppressive gender presumptions, like racial presumptions, are crumbling. However, many are still firmly in place and need investigation.

————

This volume opens with two long essays. The first, by E. Ann Kaplan, traces the history of and significant milestones in gender studies in film; the second, by Lucy Fischer, shows how this history and the methods it spawned may be applied to a single film, the critically acclaimed *Magnolia* (1999). These are followed by eight shorter essays that develop more specialized approaches and include issues of race, class, nationality, religious belief, age, and queerness.

An underlying premise of this book is that the study of gender is inseparable from a raft of other concerns. In her interrogation of Marcello Mastroianni's reputation as a "Latin Lover," for example, Jacqueline Reich is as sensitive to postwar Italian identity and social class as she is to the actor's masculine presentation; in fact, she considers them inseparable. Comparably, Chris Holmlund shows in her essay on Pam Grier that a full accounting of the actress's career and persona must involve more than just how she performs her gender identity; it must also include her self-presentation as a woman of color, as an aging actress, and as a defining figure in a number of film genres, most strikingly her crucial role in the "blaxploitation" cinema of the 1970s. Jerry Mosher looks to film noir to trace the history of the "fat heavy," a recurring figure whose gender presentation was negatively marked by an excess of body weight. Kathleen Rowe Karylyn is also concerned with gender and genre in her argument that romantic comedy provides a space where transgressive women can resist masculine authority without experiencing the suffering usually inflicted on them in melodrama. In addition to providing an essential history of gay and queer cinema studies, David Lugowski considers the many reasons why gay men—himself included—are enchanted with Ginger Rogers.

Robert T. Eberwein finds surprisingly vivid representations of alternative sexualities in films about military life that, on the one hand, dealt with largely single-sex institutions and, on the other, with the cultural need to disavow homosexuality. Patricia Mellencamp explores the representation of women over sixty, a group traditionally excluded from central roles, especially when sexual desire is involved, even though the social reality is something else altogether. When films have presented such women in central roles, they have often rendered them monstrous, as with Joan Crawford and Bette Davis in films such as *Whatever Happened to Baby Jane?* The most severe critique of traditional assumptions about gender is offered by Chris Straayer in her insightful discussion of two independent films, one featuring a bearded lesbian, the other a transgendered lesbian. Both films force viewers to think long and hard about the question, "What is a woman?"

————

This book is ambitious in its engagement with recently developed approaches to cinema and covers a variety of historical moments as well as an array of cinemas—Hollywood, independent, avant-garde, and the European art film. We realize, however, that no book can cover everything. "Had we but world enough and time," other areas to which we would have liked to devote more space include Asian, African, and Latin American cinema, silent cinema, genres such as science fiction and pornography, questions of institutional censorship, and much more. We had hoped to cover some of these areas, but we were not always able to commission essays that did exactly what we wanted them to do. In other cases we had to choose among a number of excellent essays that addressed similar concerns. We know that a good deal of material is missing, and we encourage others to continue this endeavor. We are, however, proud of the essays we have collected here and feel that they provide a substantial engagement with the field.

NOTE

1. Some observations on the cultural significance of John Wayne's career in this essay draw upon previously published material, including Gabbard in Kimmel and Aronson 2004, II: 819–921; Luhr 2004, 75–90; and Willis 1997.

The Subject of Gender

E. Ann Kaplan

A History of Gender Theory in Cinema Studies

At least in Anglo-American culture, the emergence of women's liberation movements in the late 1960s and early 1970s marked the first stirrings of a critical gender consciousness. Betty Friedan's *The Feminine Mystique* (1963) set the stage for liberation movements by detailing middle-class women's isolation, even oppression, within the suburban household, but women's roles in the antinuclear movements, such as the Aldermaston marches in the United Kingdom or SANE (Students Against Nuclear Energy) in the United States, also led to the development of women's liberation movements in the mid-1960s within diverse social sectors. The fact that a movement was widely perceived as socially progressive did not mean that it was so in all areas. Many women involved in progressive causes during the era began to see significant gender inequities within them. For example, women within the male-dominated Students for a Democratic Society (SDS) resisted their relegation to food preparation and child care and argued for the inclusion of women's rights in the SDS agenda. Women within The New University Community (NUC), a faculty wing of SDS, pressured the organization to address issues such as discriminatory employment practices, unfair divorce laws, and medical and biological issues specific to women. Independent Marxist-feminist groups emerged along with so-called radical feminists, often linked to lesbian-centered groups. Protests and demonstrations on behalf of women's rights regarding sexual choice, day care, and equality in the workplace generated widespread publicity for women's liberation. Such activities gradually increased public awareness of and involvement in debates about feminist issues. At the same time, academics in fields such as history, literature, and film, sensitive to the neglect of female perspectives within mainstream academic research, began to explore scholarly approaches to these issues within their disciplines, Indeed, these two faces of feminism can hardly be separated: academic women often actively worked for social change in relation to a whole range of women's issues, while activist women often enjoyed the support of universities in furthering their ends.

Women film scholars were among the first to reject the traditional male-centered perspectives in academia and, with Copernican force, to reverse the position from which texts were approached to engage a female-centered one. *Sexual Politics*, Kate Millett's forceful critique of misogyny in the male-centered modern novel and of Freud's male-centered psychoanalytic theories, galvanized the literary scene in 1969. As less vitriolic literary critics such as Susan Cornillion-Koppelman and Mary Ferguson followed Millett's work, many women film scholars eagerly seized the baton. Meanwhile, in the wake of research by scholars such as Louis Althusser, Roland Barthes, and Jacques Lacan, theorists (especially in England) introduced structuralist approaches. Some feminist film theory also embraced Neo-Marxism, structuralism, and psychoanalysis long before these approaches entered feminist literary analyses. Feminist scholars had a profound impact on cinema studies. They looked at the representation of women on film and brought attention to the utter neglect of female directors in male scholarship. They revolutionized film scholarship.

Three main strands (often mixed in actual practice) emerged early on in feminist film theory: (1) "archival" and historical approaches, (2) sociological role-focused approaches, and (3) what has been called cine-psychoanalysis. A certain coherence within the limited frame of 1970s and 1980s feminist film research centered around the concept of the gendered gaze of the camera, but from the start sociological perspectives were crucial. Early gay/lesbian scholarship focused on stereotypes, the politics and ideology regarding lesbians (in the context of radical feminist analyses), and "camp" sensibility and style. Several alternate perspectives developed in the 1990s as a result of changing political, social, and intellectual contexts, including the waning of feminism as a widespread activist movement. One of these was the flood of research by minority and "Third World" women (itself a problematic and much debated term). Other alternate perspectives included masculinity studies and queer cinema studies. Largely inspired by feminist theory, both mounted serious challenges to concepts basic to feminist film theories, producing by the turn of the millennium their own growing subfields. Finally, new interdisciplinary fields emerged such as visual studies or digital media. While related to film studies, these fields necessitated the broadening out of somewhat narrow gaze-related theories to consider historical, technological, and institutional contexts given short shift in cine-psychoanalysis. At the same time, second-wave feminist theorists were themselves revising gaze theories.

From Archival Research to Cine-Psychoanalysis

In tandem with contemporary scholarship in history and literature, early women film scholars strove to discover forgotten filmmakers—forgotten because most male film critics and scholars (who mainly wrote and studied film before the 1960s) were not interested in women directors as such. The two women studio directors of the sound era, Dorothy Arzner and Ida Lupino, were the first to be studied because their films were in distribution, but foreign women directors, like Mai Zetterling, also gained attention at this time. Later, feminists took considerable interest in silent Hollywood women directors and producers, such as Lois Weber and Mary Pickford. (In recent years, intensive international study of the many roles of early women in cinema has been undertaken by the Women Film Pioneers Project.)

Sociological analysis of women in film soon followed. In the early 1970s, three influential books on women and film emerged at nearly the same time, all adopting a sociological and role-focused analysis: Molly Haskell's *From Reverence to Rape* (1973), Marjorie Rosen's *Popcorn Venus* (1972), and Joan Mellen's *Women and Their Sexuality in the New Film* (1974). Of these, Haskell's volume, drawing upon her vast knowledge of Hollywood as an institution and of movies themselves, has had the most lasting impact. Her witty, penetrating look at the shabby treatment of women on and off the screen came out of her profound understanding of how men, especially Americans, felt threatened by women, and her intense appreciation of female actresses and their performances. Haskell importantly points out the irony that the Production Code, along with the Depression, "brought women out of the bedroom and into the office" (1987, 30). She argues that female actresses of the 1930s and 1940s (such as Rosalind Russell, Katharine Hepburn, and Joan Crawford) offered images of intelligence, forcefulness, and personal power, far surpassing roles of actresses in later films. Male directors who "integrate women into the flow of life" (to use Haskell's term) enjoyed the spunky, smart women who challenge the hero. Critiquing as too hasty early feminist film analysis, Haskell defines herself as a film critic first and a feminist second, hoping to offer "the wholeness and complexity of film history" (1987, 38).

Academic feminists embraced Haskell's book even though, in their frustration with sociological and role analyses, they were moving beyond her approach. Arguably, the next generation of women film scholars turned to metaphysics/semiotics/psychoanalysis, hoping to transcend the limitations of studies focusing on individual actresses and women's roles in cinema: the comparison of cinema images with women in lived reality seemed merely to critique the current gendered organization or to expand it by, for instance, insisting on more male involvement in domesticity. The new scholars hoped instead to discover the root cause of why women were given secondary status in Hollywood and society in the first place. Laura Mulvey's groundbreaking essay, "Visual Pleasure and Narrative Cinema" (1975), rapidly took hold as exemplary of such a new approach. Mulvey's polemical contribution isolated three related "looks" in Hollywood cinema and argued that all of these were male. The first of these was the look of the camera (mainly operated by men) in the pro-filmic studio site; the second was the look of the spectator that of necessity followed the camera's masculine gaze; and the third was the dominating look of male characters within the filmic narrative, depriving women of agency and subjectivity. Mulvey used the work of Freud and Lacan in theorizing the cinematic gaze, arguing that, in film viewing, the screen paralleled Lacan's mirror phase in which the child mis-recognized himself as more coordinated and graceful than he actually was. Cinema was set up so that men could identify with the idealized male hero within the symbolic order imaged in the narrative, while women were left to identify with figures relegated to inferior status and silenced. Mulvey would later write that women could only enjoy mainstream cinema by becoming masochists, that is, identifying with the suffering women, or by becoming "transvestites" and adopting a male perspective.

Mulvey was one of the first to appropriate psychoanalysis as a political weapon to demonstrate how the patriarchal unconscious has structured film form. Her vivid language contributed to the essay's influence, as when she writes, "Woman's desire is subjugated to her image as bearer of the bleeding wound: she can exist only in relation to castration and cannot transcend it." Man, she argued, can live out his fantasies by "imposing them on the silent image of woman still tied to her place as bearer, not maker, of meaning" (2000, 39–41).

In the wake of Mulvey's deliberately polemical essays, feminist scholarship developed certain tropes and conventions in relation to a "male" gaze and the "three looks" that Mulvey outlined. At the same time, British and U.S. TV studies influenced psychoanalytic feminist film theory: writers such as Tania Modleski and Charlotte Brunsdon persuasively argued that the different medium of TV necessitated different theories of the spectator/screen relationship. These theories were appropriated by film studies, expanding the rather rigid theoretical presumption of just one "male" gaze. Reaction against the notion of a monolithic male position also provoked scholars in masculinity and queer studies to identify the many different ways in which subjects, regardless of their sexuality and gender, can look at images of men and women.

Mulvey's essay was often misread as presenting a depressing description of woman's fate rather than as a call to action. Mulvey in fact believed that psychoanalytic theory could advance the understanding of the position of women and thereby enable women to move forward. Her concern with challenging the pleasures of Hollywood cinema centered upon its reliance on voyeurism—the male gaze at the woman deprived of agency. Her polemical call "to free the look of the camera into its materiality in time and space and the look of the audience into dialectics and passionate detachment" (2000, 47) clearly related to her own burgeoning practice (together with Peter Wollen) as an avant-garde filmmaker. Mulvey was prepared to put into action what she was advocating in her essay.

Mulvey's article prompted a good deal of research, as well as intelligent critiques of her theories. E. Ann Kaplan's *Women and Film* (1983) sought to straddle some of the debates about feminist film theory in the 1970s. While ultimately seen as allied with the European psychoanalytic position, she both asked fundamental questions about that work and supported other, more sociological and historical positions. The book addressed why some women were strongly drawn to psychoanalysis and poststructuralism, arguing that pointing to social oppression per se did not begin to account for women's second-class status. Attention to language and the unconscious seemed to offer some hope of understanding what increasingly seemed a mystery that could not simply be explained with biological answers—namely, that the facts that women gave birth and were needed to care for children limited what they could achieve. Too many exceptions showed that women could overcome their biological roles; there had to be something deeper, something more difficult to change than social policies or cultural norms.

Later, David Rodowick pointed out that Mulvey did not attend to Freud's complex remarks about the contradictoriness of desire that "problematizes any strict binary distinction between 'maleness/femaleness' and activity/passivity" (1991). Over a series of seminal articles and books, Mary Ann Doane extended Mulvey's research in useful ways, following up questions that Mulvey only touched upon. For example, in her influential essay, "Woman's Stake: Filming the Female Body," Doane shifted the discussion by introducing the concept of the female body in its relation to psyche, as against the prior focus on image and psyche. She contrasted representation of the female body in Hollywood and in avant-garde cinema, and her shift to woman's different relation to language influenced later research. Shortly afterward, in an equally influential essay, "Film and the Masquerade," Doane contrasted male and female distance from the image. For the male, the distance between film and spectator must be maintained, whereas the female over-identifies with the image, obliterating the space between viewer and screen (Doane 1981) and producing a degree of narcissism. In developing her argument, Doane turned to new French feminisms, Freudian theories, and Joan Riviere's concept of the female masquerade. Through examining a photograph, "Un Regard oblique" by Doisneau, Doane provides an example of what it might mean to "masquerade" as a spectator. She concludes that there are three possible positions for the female spectator—the masochism of over-identification with the image, the narcissism involved in becoming one's own object of desire, and the possibility of cross-gender identification, as women choose to identify with the male hero. Doane objects to theories of repression because they lack feminine power. Women, she argued, need to develop a theory of spectatorship that will dislocate what male culture has constructed for them.

Doane's influence is evident in the mid-1980s *"Stella-Dallas"* debate, which drew increasing attention to largely neglected images of the mother in cinema. The debate dramatized differences emerging in feminist film theory: while E. Ann Kaplan had argued that filmic identification with the figure of Stella invited audiences to accept as proper her giving up of her beloved daughter, forgoing motherhood through her internalization of patriarchal familial norms, Linda Williams argued that the film invited audiences to share multiple points of view, and that Stella's actions could be seen as showing strength and agency. Responses in *Cinema Journal* (1984–1985) usefully debated some key assumptions in feminist film theory of the time. This debate also came when research on images of the mother in cinema were taken up in the analysis of melodrama by E. Ann Kaplan, in her *Motherhood and Representation* (1992), and in Lucy Fischer's work on cinematernity that significantly examines comedies, which had so often been ignored in feminist criticism. Christine Gledhill's 1987 edited volume, *Home Is Where the Heart Is: Studies in Melodrama and the Woman's Film*, brought together articles relevant to motherhood and melodrama. Meanwhile, proponents of object relations approaches such as Jackie Byers argued for their greater use in analyzing melodrama, while Gaylyn Studlar (1986) suggested that a focus on pre-oedipality made more sense than the conventional attention to oedipal scenarios. Studlar substitutes Gilles Deleuze's study of Sacher-Masoch's novels for Mulvey's Freudian/Lacanian framework, arguing that masochism can also ground narrative. Studlar, that is, replaces oedipal sadism with pre-oedipal pleasure in a symbiotic bond with the mother. For Studlar, "masochism is a 'subversive' desire that affirms the compelling power of the pre-oedipal mother" (Studlar 1988). These debates ultimately show that there was never any uniformity within cine-psychoanalysis about the gaze, or about what kind of psychoanalysis was most appropriate to cinematic modes. Additional productive "corrections" followed.

Gay/Lesbian Theory

Psychoanalytic film theories accommodated Cold War ideologies by looking back to Europe's nineteenth century and a world fixed on a framework in which communism versus capitalism was a subtext. Freud's theories enabled understanding of the neuroses produced in the nineteenth-century bourgeois family—itself the anchoring institution for the Industrial Revolution. In this light, the use of psychoanalysis in a critique of capitalist ideology made sense. In the years since 1989, U.S. culture and society have changed dramatically, as have international relations. It took the collapse of the Soviet Union to open space for rethinking imperialism, and it took the increased flows of peoples across borders and into the academy to encourage new perspectives, such as post-modernism and its related postcolonialism.

As cine-psychoanalytic theories began to gel into a rather formulaic mold, more resistances to gaze theories arose, in spite of efforts by scholars such as Mary Ann Doane and Joan Copjec to underscore the complexities and pene-trating questions that the theory involved, and in spite of Laura Mulvey's own continuing "corrections" to her polemical 1975 essay. Critics were particularly troubled by the dominance in these theories of French structuralism—Lacan-ian theories, Saussurian semiotics, and Althusserian Marxism—along with the obvious heterosexual foundation on which they were based.

Gay/lesbian approaches to film emerged earlier than many might recall. Richard Dyer's edited volume for the British Film Institute, *Gays and Film*, appeared in 1978 (reprinted in 1980), and Vito Russo's extensive study of gays in film, *The Celluloid Closet: Homosexuality and the Movies*, was published in 1981. Russo not only critiqued the oppressive image of gays in film; he chal-lenged gay and lesbian directors and actors to "come out of the closet," and give political dimensions not only to their sexuality but also to their very existence. Essays in Dyer's volume included discussion of stereotyping, pornography, defining a "gay" sensibility, politics and ideology, and gay film production. Car-oline Sheldon's essay in the volume, with its socialist-feminist orientation, briefly discusses problems with Freudian theory in regard to lesbianism before turning to other issues. At that time, gay and lesbian approaches avoided psy-choanalytic theory since Freud was hardly useful for understanding homosex-uality. At best, Freud argued for bisexuality as "normal," but it was clear that he had no sustained interest in homosexuality. Lesbian critics at first focused upon common lesbian stereotypes in Hollywood film and then explored lesbian interest in 1930s and 1940s films with strong female heroines as well as the bur-geoning production of films about lesbians by feminists like Jan Oxenberg, Sherrie Farrell, and Kate Millett. Meanwhile, Lucy Arbuthnot and Gayle Seneca anticipated later studies in their analysis of *Gentlemen Prefer Blondes*, focus-ing upon the implicitly lesbian bonding between Marilyn Monroe and Jane Rus-sell in that film.

The lack of work in this area until much later is strange since gay male filmmakers like Kenneth Anger, Andy Warhol, Paul Morissey, and later Isaac Julien, were actively producing gay images available for analysis. Despite Hober-man's 1983 volume on *Midnight Movies*, including discussion of these direc-tors' films, it took until 2002 (with Wheeler Dixon's *Experimental Cinema*) and years following for due attention to be given to these so-called underground, largely gay, directors.

Gay/lesbian studies often employed historical, aesthetic, and sociopolitical methodologies, illuminating same-sex desire where none had before been seen, or revealing homosexual relations within and outside the cinema that the films and film criticism did not fully declare (or care to detail). B. Ruby Rich, Sue-Ellen Case, and other gay women offered strong critiques of academic feminist film theory. Judith Mayne's research on Dorothy Arzner marked a major turning point in academic criticism. Mayne noted the irony that Arzner had become an icon for psychoanalytic structuralist theorists, like Claire Johnston, who nonetheless refused to "see" Arzner's obvious lesbianism (Mayne 1994). Patricia White's *The Uninvited* (1990) followed and greatly extended the notion of implicit lesbianism between female characters in Hollywood film (suggested by Arbuthnot and Seneca) in her complexly argued and illuminating volume.

Feminist Theory Takes on Race

In hindsight, a significant gap in early cine-psychoanalytic theories is that critics tended to assume an apparently monolithic "woman" who was really a white Western woman and neglected the specificity of minority and other marginalized women. These theories, then, operated not only upon a heterosexual bias but also a Eurocentric one.

Black and Latino studies were instituted in the 1980s as more minority students attended college and as debates about U.S. and international racism raged. Inspired work in feminist film and academic fields began to appear, led by African American critics and filmmakers such as bell hooks, Michele Wallace, Jacqueline Bobo, Julie Dash, and Manthia Diawara. In *Black Looks: Race and Representation*, for example, bell hooks critiques feminist theorists for their lack of attention to the specificity of race in film. Building on white feminists' gaze theories, hooks coins the term *the oppositional gaze* as she shifts the point of view to the gaze of the hitherto oppressed black subject, whose look at white culture had long been forbidden. The 1994 co-edited anthology, *Multiple Voices in Feminist Criticism*, highlighted political and social approaches in service of "a constructive feminist engagement with issues of diversity through essays that treat women as social and political entities defined not only by gender within patriarchy but also by other power relations." Many important studies of race and cinema from feminist perspectives followed in the late 1990s, much of it sparked by Paul Willemen and Jim Pines's co-edited collection, *Questions of Third Cinema* (1990), and by the work of Ella Shohat and

Robert Stam, in their *Unthinking Eurocentrism*, as well as that of E. Ann Kaplan in her *Looking for the Other: Feminism, Film and the Imperial Gaze.* Much of the recent research on World Cinema crosses national and racial borders to explore the intersection of cinematic themes, production, and exhibition in the complex new global realities of our era. To isolate just one set of studies, excellent research is being done by Asian and Asian American film scholars on women in Chinese, Japanese, Taiwanese, and many other cinemas.

A New Focus on the Male

Along with Richard Dyer's *Gays and Film* (1977), Steve Neale's influential 1983 article, "Masculinity as Spectacle," may be seen as initiating a focus on Hollywood masculinity even if critics did not immediately follow with extended studies of either masculinity in general or homosexuality in film. Vito Russo's *Celluloid Closet* (1981) was one of the few to pursue issues regarding male homosexuality in visual culture from a sociological and political perspective. Neale acknowledges the work done within the gay movement but stresses how the overwhelming focus on women in studies of gender and sexuality at the time neglected "the images and functions of heterosexual masculinity within mainstream cinema" (Neale in Kaplan 2000, 253). After briefly referring to Mulvey's theory of the male gaze, to the focus on male heroes among gay spectators, and to the subversive homosexual subtexts to Hollywood films identified by Dyer, Neale looks at "how heterosexual masculinity is inscribed, and the mechanisms, pressures and contradictions that inscription may involve" (254). The traditional disavowal of the erotic gaze at male figures served to prevent mainstream cinema from coming to terms with the male homosexuality it seeks to deny or denigrate. Alexander Doty's subsequent work was especially sensitive to how the queer identity of even mainstream performers such as Jack Benny could be "hidden in plain sight" from the American public.

While studies of gay and lesbian films were under way in the late 1980s, the first systematic studies of masculinity in mainstream movies coalesced around Paul Schrader's 1980 film, *American Gigolo*. At a 1988 meeting of the Florida State University Conference on Literature and Film, Peter Lehman, William Luhr, Patricia Mellencamp, Robert Eberwein, and Danae Clark explored the complex ways in which the film's male prostitute played by Richard Gere undermined notions of the traditional male hero. Conspicuously referred to as "Julie," Gere's character is frequently the object of the gaze. He even exposes his penis. In addition, he is employed by women; he is unable to outwit the patriarchs of the police force; and the ending, clearly drawn from

Bresson's *Pickpocket,* frames the face of the one woman who has actually loved him through prison bars. Gere's attractive male hero is in no way responsible for his own salvation, if that is indeed what it is.

Frank Krutnik's *In a Lonely Street: Film Noir, Genre, Masculinity* (1991) took on a subject that had long been central to the projects of feminist scholars, who regarded the femme fatale of film noir as a self-empowered individual but also as the embodiment of male paranoia toward women, especially after World War II, when notions of gender were being radically reshuffled. Krutnik, drawing upon Freudian feminist film theory and gay film studies, stresses Freud's concern with the "mastering plan" of patriarchal culture and the crucial role of sexed subjectivity within it. Following Juliet Mitchell, Krutnik explains how "the structuring components of familial positioning serve as a microcosm of the general ordering of patriarchal culture" (1991, 79). He notes how insecure the phallic regime of masculine identity actually is and categorizes the masochism evident in many films noirs as indicative of the male hero's desperate attempt to overthrow the authority of the paternal law and the determinacy of castration (1991, 85). Krutnik argues that the "tough" thrillers oscillate between, on the one hand, "the licit possession of masculine identity and desire required by the patriarchal cultural order," and, on the other hand, the unstable psychosexual status of the male subject-hero. Looking back to Richard Dyer's research, Krutnik reveals the anxiety of masculinity and normality in specific noir narratives.

Dennis Bingham identified the extent to which masculinity is essentially performative in *Acting Male* (1994). Steven Cohan looked at the question in greater detail in *Masked Men: Masculinity and the Movies in the Fifties* (1997). Cohan begins by considering the impact of World War II on conventional notions of American masculinity, since the war exposed the fragility of the border between heroism and brutality. In the postwar period, Cohan draws upon Kaja Silverman's insights to discuss "the loss of belief in the conventional premises of masculinity" (1992, 104). While the "manly art of boxing" had channeled male anger and frustrations before the war, the postwar era experienced widespread anxiety about the "feminizing" of men. Virility now became a "gender performance," one built on homosocial bonding that might slide into homosexual desire (1992, 106). One result is a group of violent action movies featuring what Cohan calls "tough guys" as psychopaths and, in support of his argument, he provides detailed studies of changes in the figures played by actors like Glenn Ford and Humphrey Bogart. Cohan ends his book with a chapter on how Rock Hudson, especially when playing "opposite" Tony Randall, was a much less closeted gay movie star than many might recall.

In *Running Scared: Masculinity and the Representation of the Male Body* (1993), Peter Lehman argues that the camera's fascination with female nudity and its simultaneous turning away from the male genital region mystifies masculinity, thus contributing to the power imbalances that always operate in the depiction of male and female bodies. Working primarily within a psychoanalytic model, Lehman traces the massive displacement of anxieties about the penis into all manner of cultural production, especially stories about men with disabilities, disfigurements, small bodies, and unconventional social roles. He is careful to distinguish the penis—what Lacan calls "the pound of flesh"—from the phallus, the grand signifier that has empowered men at the same time that it has alienated them from their own bodies. Pragmatically appropriating ideas from Freud, Lacan, Rodowick, Studlar, and Silverman, Lehman is especially critical of Mulvey's argument that only women can be held up as objects of display in dominant cinema. But his conviction that women and heterosexual men are capable of finding multiple levels of pleasures in looking at male bodies puts him in the dangerous position of claiming for straight men some of the same territory that had been staked out by feminists and queer theorists. Realizing that he can be accused of bringing straight male subjectivity back to the center it had occupied for much too long, Lehman assembles a range of texts to demonstrate the need to look at men with new critical paradigms. By no means, however, can he be associated with rearguard actions such as the mythopoetic men's movement: many of these back-to-"nature" types would remystify exactly what Lehman has sought to demystify.

Masculinity studies has continued to explore different genres and to rethink the many ways in which patriarchy has established itself in dominant cinema. Critics such as William Luhr, Thomas DePiero, and Robert Eberwein have uncovered profound veins of hysteria, masochism, and homoeroticism, even in films that have strived mightily to reinscribe masculine ideals. Yvonne Tasker historicized representations of masculinity, linking the hard bodies of Sylvester Stallone and Arnold Schwarzenegger to Ronald Reagan's macho swagger on the international stage in the 1980s. Chris Holmlund has considered the various solutions to problems created when a masculine icon such as Clint Eastwood begins to age at the same time that he plays characters for whom old age does not seem to matter.

Scholars in masculinity studies have also caught up with feminist scholars who moved beyond a focus on middle-class women in Anglo-American culture. Krin Gabbard has appropriated Eric Lott's work on nineteenth-century minstrelsy to consider white male fascination with black masculinity. Robyn Wiegman has traced the profoundly contested territory of African American masculinity in *Boyz N the Hood*. And many scholars have written about the prominent homoerotic subtexts amidst the macho theatrics in John Woo's Hong Kong action films.

A New Queer Cinema Studies

Queer cinema studies, like masculinity studies, built upon the contributions of feminist theorists. The field brings together and extends in new ways cine-psychoanalytic theories, "masculinity" studies, and work on film, race and ethnicity. Teresa de Lauretis' influential work on "sexual indifference" may be seen as one starting point for Queer Film Studies. While de Lauretis had long invoked cine-psychoanalysis as a foundation, she later profoundly interrogated psychoanalysis, working with Freud's and Luce Irigaray's theories, among others, in her "Sexual Indifference and Lesbian Representation" (1988), and in her later extended study, *Practices of Love*. Although De Lauretis' dense and carefully argued position defies summary, two points need to be emphasized. In her ground-breaking essay, De Lauretis states how "the first emphasis on sexual difference as gender (woman's difference from man) has rightly come under attack for obscuring other differences in women's psycho-social oppression." She notes the intimate relationship of sexual and social indifference in Western culture for centuries—a link that served to bolster colonial conquest and racist violence—before turning to examine lesbian representation through diverse struggles of lesbian writers and artists to demonstrate the linkage of the body to language and meaning.

Carol Clover, meanwhile, moved gaze theories forward—and perhaps feminism backward—in her ground-breaking 1992 study of the horror film, *Men, Women, and Chain Saws: Gender in the Modern Horror Film*. She argues that heroines in slasher films are "transformed males" (52), a strategy enabling the genre to provide a gender crossing that is liberatory for males. What looks like male-on-female violence stands in for male-on-male sex. Clover goes on to show, however, that this gender-game, once observed, applies to other kinds of film in which, perhaps in response to feminist agendas and analyses, males appropriate the female form for their own ends and desires, a process that challenges gender-specific theories of identification.

Rich and extensive studies "queering" cinema followed in the next decade, partly spurred by the AIDS crisis, seen by some as an integral component of these new developments. Between the mid-1980s and 2000, there was an explosion of gay/lesbian film festivals, prompting more research, criticism, and questioning of methods and categories. As early as 1980, Dyer had defended using the category *homosexuality*, despite notions (based on Michel Foucault's work) that the category seemed "to accept a purely historical division of sexuality into hard and fast categories which cut across the fluidity of human sexuality" (Dyer 1980, 4). His 1990 study, *Now You See It*, of films made by lesbians and gay men with explicitly lesbian themes and subject matter elaborates his position that there is no "untrammeled embodiment of an authentic homo-sexual experience stripped of social contamination" (Dyer 1990, 1). All such images of necessity exist within the practical exigencies of their specific social and historical reality.

Debates about the categories critics were employing in gay/lesbian film studies and about queer cinema continue. There is no room here to do justice to the complexity of theories and positions, since queer cinema studies has indeed developed into its own rich subfield, with productive debates as intense as those that once surrounded cine-psychoanalysis. Judith Halberstam's research has been particularly useful in pushing the envelope. Her *Female Masculinity* (1998) draws upon Michel Foucault's history of male sexuality to show how the category "lesbian" "constitutes a term for same-sex desire produced in the mid- to late twentieth century within the highly politicized context of the rise of feminism and the development of what Foucault calls a homosexual "reverse discourse"' (51). Her overall aim is to "produce a model of female masculinity that remarks on its multiple forms but also calls for new and self-conscious affirmations of different gender taxonomies" (1998, 9). She is interested in the multiple forms of gender variance that can be found in female masculinity. Her work is especially important for focusing on minority masculinities and femininities that "destabilize binary gender systems in many different locations" (29). A volume on *New Queer Cinema: A Critical Reader*, edited by Michele Aaron, details just how far scholarship on queer cinema has come, and also how intensely debated issues within the subfield currently are.

Some Conclusions

The directions in which gender studies in film research grew and changed, through its destabilization by questions raised by minority, gay, and Third World subjects, were also determined by dramatic changes in the world outside the academy, such as the fall of the Soviet Union, and the resultant introduction of new, but related, fields. Old secure binaries of feminist film theories that clearly emerged as solidly modernist began to erode. In this way, the "center" could not hold, and psychoanalytic theories and issues of the gaze began to be muted to a minor key. This is not to say that they disappeared. Psychoanalysis can be found in the "masculinity" studies that followed feminist film theory in the work of Steve Neale, Krin Gabbard, and Peter Lehman, and which is part of the shift from feminist film theory to gender studies in film. Approaches broadened to combine historical, sociological, psychological, and genre aspects in gender film studies, as in research by Miriam Hansen, Lucy Fischer, Annette

Kuhn, Janice Welsch, and many others. Miriam Hansen's study of gender in early American cinema brought feminist theory to silent cinema studies while also bringing new emphasis to concepts of the public sphere. Lucy Fischer's studies of women in film include her 2004 pioneering volume, *Designing Women: Cinema, Art Deco and the Female Form,* on the relationship between female figures in the art deco movement and ways actresses and film sets were fashioned in the 1930s and 1940s. Annette Kuhn's varied interests in women and cinema include cultural studies approaches such as her ethnographic study of cinema viewing practices through interviews with elderly London residents.

There is currently a solid body of research on the representation of genders, including feminist film theory, that has provided the firm grounding for much contemporary work by third-wave feminists, whose interest in cross-identification, transvestism, and transgender images is taking feminist work in new directions. Gender transformation has moved to the top of cinematic concerns. Psychoanalysis may not be the central focus of many studies, but it is now being revised to fit new family paradigms, digital media, and phenomena of late global capitalism. Other aspects of feminist film theory, even the issue of the "gaze," remain pertinent to recent studies. While the pioneers of feminist film theory have moved on to new topics because new areas of research have emerged with social, political, and intellectual developments, feminist film theory continues to be relevant to film scholarship and also continues to be taught in a variety of venues. Queer theory and masculinity studies continue to emerge, appropriating their methods from an eclectic range of disciplines, but still reflecting the theoretical breakthroughs that were essential to the feminist revolutions of the 1970s and 1980s.

Lucy Fischer

Theory into Practice:
En-Gendering Narrative in *Magnolia*

Masculine Feminine

Paul Thomas Anderson is out to prove the obvious: that we live in a chance universe, that coincidence and mishap play a larger role in our destinies than we like to think. In Magnolia *he intertwines four disparate (but equally glum) stories of people living in California's San Fernando Valley and shows how they touch—or fail to touch—one another in the course of a single, very long day.*
—Richard Schickel (1999, 37)

Magnolia *is operatic in its ambition, a great, joyous leap into melodrama and coincidence, with ragged emotions, crimes and punishments, deathbed scenes, romantic dreams, generational turmoil and celestial intervention, all scored to insistent music. It is not a timid film.*
—Roger Ebert (2000, C2)

These two reviews of *Magnolia* (one negative, one positive) seek, as such popular pieces do, to give the average reader a capsule summary of what the drama is about. Richard Schickel, who finds the film full of clichés, mentions the themes of mishap, chance, and emotional savagery. Conversely, Roger Ebert finds the film ambitious, with its motifs of death, romance, generational struggle, and faith. Indeed, similar issues were catalogued by numerous other newspaper and magazine pundits. However, what virtually all failed to see (despite Schickel's claim that *Magnolia* is "obvious") was that the film is a grand treatise on questions of gender. While the subject may not entirely have escaped the standard critic's view, it remained sufficiently below the surface to be generally ignored. It is precisely to excavate this theme that scholarly theories (previously discussed by E. Ann Kaplan) were formulated and injected into academic discourse. It is such conceptual frameworks that I bring to bear on my analysis of *Magnolia* to demonstrate how it simultaneously presents and critiques the operations of patriarchy.

Magnolia concerns a day in the lives of nine individuals who live in the San Fernando Valley. Magnolia is, in fact, the name of a street that transverses that section of Los Angeles. Paul Thomas Anderson hails from that area and wanted to make a film about it because, as he states, "no movies are made about the Valley" (2000, 198). The characters he follows are connected to one another through family, work, or happenstance. Broadcast executive Earl Partridge (Jason Robards), for instance, is the employer of quiz show host Jimmy Gator (Philip Baker Hall) and of the male nurse Phil Parma (Philip Seymour Hoffman) who tends to him during his illness. He is also the father of motivational speaker Frank T. J. Mackey (Tom Cruise). Some characters, however, meet solely by accident: Policeman Jim Kurring (John C. Reilly) encounters grown-up, ex-quiz-show star "Little" Donnie Smith (William H. Macy) when the latter commits a burglary. Some figures never cross paths but are allied through a mutual third party, as when Jim responds to a domestic complaint and meets Gator's daughter Claudia (Melora Walters). Several characters are dying and two more attempt suicide. Others seem equally distraught: Claudia is a drug addict, Frank is estranged from his father, and Jim experiences professional failure. Many undergo profound breakdowns: Earl's wife Linda (Julianne Moore) erupts in hysterical anger at a druggist and a lawyer; Jim cries when he loses his gun; Donnie drunkenly confesses his love to a bartender; Jimmy crumbles during a TV broadcast; Frank lashes out at a reporter and later sobs by his father's deathbed; finally, Stanley Spector (Jeremy Blackman), a young quiz kid, is incontinent during a show. Given this grim picture of home and work environments, we are not surprised when weather patterns in the region run amok and a shower of frogs falls from the sky.

Patriarchy

Patriarchy creates megapatterns that affect us all—even as we forge different individual choices within them.

—Gloria Steinem (1994, 11)

Clearly, on one level, *Magnolia* is a film about family. But gesturing toward feminist theory, we would be more precise to deem it a dissertation on patriarchy: a family, community, or society governed by men. As sociological analysis would indicate, the male characters hold the powerful positions in the drama: "Big" Earl Partridge (as his moniker would indicate) is a media mogul, and Jimmy Gator is the host of one of his successful productions. Conversely, all the assistants on the program are women: Cynthia (Felicity Huffman) tends to the game show contestants, and Mary (Eileen Ryan) is like a second wife to Jimmy—helping him dress, fixing his drinks, lending him a sympathetic ear. To invoke another male character, Frank Mackey is a popular infomercial star whose assistant Janet is heard only as a voice on the telephone.

Within the domestic scene, patriarchy also reigns supreme. Wives seem to be disempowered appendages to their husbands. Rose Gator (Melinda Dillon) is the type of suburban wife and mother documented by Betty Friedan in the 1960s, and Linda Partridge seems the trophy spouse of a wealthy, elderly man. Furthermore, the male heads of household have all misbehaved—lending credence to the notion that women are oppressed in conventional marriages. Earl cheated on his first wife and abandoned her and their son when she fell sick. Similarly, Jimmy confesses that he has had numerous mistresses.

Though female characters in *Magnolia* are demoralized by life in a patriarchal world, many of the men further encourage their figuration as "hysterics." Earl Partridge refers to Linda as "a little daffy" or "nuts"; when Jimmy Gator visits Claudia, he keeps telling her not to "go crazy." Significantly, she challenges his characterization of her: "Don't call me crazy!" she angrily retorts.

A vision of the dysfunctional patriarchal family seems inscribed from the outset in one of *Magnolia*'s opening framing stories in which a voice-over narrator informs us that Sydney Barringer, a teenage boy (troubled by his parents' ongoing marital discord), jumped off the ledge of his apartment building at the precise moment that his mother (on the third floor) fired a gun at his abusive father. The bullet killed Sydney, turning his suicide into a homicide—or, more precisely, conjoining the two. (Significantly, Richard Schickel saw this episode only as invoking the theme of "chance.") As though to extend the notion of fathers as odious patriarchs, when Frank Mackey is finally reunited with Earl Partridge, he calls his father a "prick" and, with his own masculine bravado, refuses to cry at his parent's imminent demise.

The "Feminized" Male

It may be that one of the appeals of [melodrama] for women is precisely its tendency to feminize the man, to complicate and destabilize his identity.
—Tania Modleski (1984, 25)

While early feminist critics (surveying diverse gender images in film) saw male and female characters as inhabiting oppositional roles, later scholars began to nuance such black-and-white polarities. Hence, authors like Tania Modleski (in speaking of Max Ophuls's *Letter From an Unknown Woman* [1948]) labeled the

Tom Cruise and Jason Robards in Magnolia *(1999). New Line Cinema. Jerry Ohlinger's Movie Materials Store.*

film's hero a "feminized male." In *Magnolia*, a work that has learned the lessons of sophisticated gender analysis (either genuinely or slyly), patriarchy is appropriately tempered and assaulted. Jimmy has been diagnosed with cancer and Earl is dying—hardly virile stances. On the latter's deathbed, Frank calls him a "cock-sucker" (thus impugning his heterosexuality). Jim (who holds a "macho" law enforcement job) drops his nightstick before entering Claudia's apartment and later loses his gun—all signs of professional incompetence. As psychoanalytic criticism has indicated, oedipal castration anxiety has inflected traditional film narrative and it is easy to read Jim's loss of his "tools" as symbolically related to that subterranean dynamic.

Beyond such Freudian symbols, Jim is feminized in a more positive sense, at least within the framework of object relations psychology, popularized in feminist film criticism through the work of Nancy Chodorow. In this regard, Jim is, to some degree, a nurturing figure who, upon meeting Claudia, recognizes her pain and makes an attempt to communicate with her and draw her out of her defensive shell. He also acts sympathetically (saying, "Be cool. Stay in school") to Dixon (Emmanuel L. Johnson), a young black rapper, and is compassionate when Donnie commits a burglary. These are caring interpersonal acts most often associated with women. While sensitive, Jim still remains a conventional male in some respects: when he enters Claudia's apartment (responding to a noise complaint), he is, clearly, attracted to her and stays longer than he should, fishing around for information as to whether she has a boyfriend. Later, we see them on a date, breaking the prohibition against police-victim fraternization.

The most positive "feminized male" in the drama is Phil Parma—Earl's nurse. First, his vocation is associated with women. Second, he goes beyond merely fulfilling his patient's medical needs by facilitating Earl's dying wish to be reunited with his prodigal son. At one point prior to that reunion, we are tempted to see Phil otherwise. He phones a market to order some food, and then sheepishly requests some "girlie" magazines like *Playboy, Penthouse,* and *Hustler.* We assume that he is seeking some male voyeuristic pleasure but, as it turns out, he has purchased these publications solely to look for Frank's ads for his "Seduce and Destroy" seminars that teach men how to "handle" women. Armed with that information, Phil calls Frank's assistant and convinces her to let Frank know that his father is dying. Significantly, in his hyper-masculine seminars, Frank completely demeans any notion of the "feminized male." One of his PowerPoint slides reads: "How to Fake Like You Are Nice and Caring."

According to Joanne Clarke Dillman, by populating its narrative with compromised male characters, "*Magnolia* disrupts the classic Oedipal patterning common to many mainstream films. The film repeatedly enacts a pronounced degree of male failure and what amounts to an indictment of the system of father rule" (2005, 144). There are, however, certain aspects of the work that qualify Dillman's view. First, despite the presence of "feminized" males and the film's skewering of patriarchs, it privileges men by the sheer number of them functioning as major characters (Phil, Donnie, Jim, Jimmy, Earl, Stanley, and, his father, Rick). Second, one might ask whether by populating *Magnolia* with nurturing men, the film eliminates this role for women— since none within the drama are remotely supportive.

Child Abuse

Abuse robs children of the opportunity to develop healthy, trusting relationships with adults, contributes to low self-esteem, and impairs healthy psycho-social development. Indeed, the effects of childhood abuse often last a lifetime.
—The National Council on Child Abuse and Family Violence
(Grapes 2001, 13)

What the framing story about Sydney Barringer foregrounds is the problem of child abuse within the traditional family. While, in that segment of the prologue, it is a boy who is the victim, much research has pointed to father/daughter incest as a major pathology throughout history, and one that survives today. As Susan Forward and Craig Buck write in *Betrayal of Innocence*: "Father-daughter cases are the ones which most often come to light and become the bases for the bulk of incest studies and statistics. Seventy-five percent of all reported incest cases involve fathers and daughters" (1978, 55). This topic is directly raised in *Magnolia* when we learn, toward the end, that Jimmy Gator has probably abused his daughter (and that his wife has, most likely, ignored the situation). It is, ostensibly, for this reason that Claudia has become a self-destructive drug addict incapable of forming meaningful relationships. Significantly, when asked about the genesis of *Magnolia*, Anderson states that he first imagined "the situation between Claudia and Jimmy" (2000, 198).

While father/daughter incest speaks to issues of perverse male *sexual* power, other instances of child abuse signal exploitation of a different order. Given that *Magnolia* is set in Los Angeles, it is not surprising to find in it examples of mistreatment relating to the entertainment industry. Anderson speaks of how the film concerns "what it means to grow up in L.A." (2000, 199). While the term *stage mother* exists in our lexicon, usually to indict the parents of such real-life stars as Judy Garland, there is no such label for the overly ambitious father of a talented youngster. Yet we see exactly this individual in *Magnolia*. Rick Spector (Michael Bowen), the dad of reigning child quiz show champion, Stanley, is a ruthless go-getter who treats his son as a money-making machine. While the other contestants are jaded child professionals (who speak of their publicists, agents, endorsements, etc.), Stanley is a quiet, unassuming, sensitive boy. When, under the pressure of competition and Cynthia's refusal to let him go to the bathroom, he soils his pants, his dad humiliates him before his peers, shouting, "Oh, Jesus. What the fuck? Why did you do this?" Almost immediately, Rick's attention turns to the competition, as he shouts at his son, "You're two fuckin' days from the record, get through this and I'll do anything for you, you just gotta get through this." Though Stanley initially proceeds with the broadcast, he later opts out, stating, "I don't want to play. I always play, I always answer the questions and I don't wanna do it anymore." Toward the drama's close, he calmly informs his dad that he needs to be nicer to him in the future.

In addition to a contemporary quiz kid, *Magnolia* also presents a past bearer of the crown: Donnie Smith. He now lives his life as a pathetic "has been"—a messed-up former child "star" like many who have crashed and burned in media culture. As Anderson notes, "It's the good old-fashioned study of a Gary Coleman or Jackie Coogan" (2000, 202). Significantly, one of the periodic weather forecasts that punctuate the narrative predicts trouble from El Niño, a California wind named for the Spanish word *boy* or *child*.

Finally, the film's catalogue of paternal child abuse includes Earl's mistreatment of his son. When Frank has his deathbed reunion with his father, he chastises him for having deserted his dying mother, leaving a traumatized child to oversee her illness. As revenge, in his official (but deceitful) bio, Frank claims that his father is deceased and his mother alive—inverting the facts.

Jeremy Blackman, Michael Bowen, and Felicity Huffman in Magnolia *(1999). New Line Cinema. Jerry Ohlinger's Movie Materials Store.*

The name of the quiz show Earl owns is "What Do Kids Know?" Unfortunately, within the context of *Magnolia,* children decidedly know they are likely to be mistreated. Significantly, in the show itself, the child contestants are pitted against adults. Evidently, Anderson comes by his quiz show knowledge honestly, having been a production assistant on the program "Quiz Kids Challenge" (2000, 199).

Heterosexual Relations

> *Sexual sadism actualizes male identity. Women are tortured, whipped, and chained; women are bound and gagged, branded and burned, cut with knives and wires . . . and all of this to establish in the male a viable sense of his own worth.*
>
> —Andrea Dworkin (1996)

If *Magnolia* tempers machismo through certain "feminized" male characters, it counterpoises them to the hyper-masculine figure of Frank T. Mackey (played by movie star/heart-throb Tom Cruise). Frank is a motivational speaker who specializes in instructing men how to aggressively lure and discipline women.

(His phone number is: 1-800-TAME HER.) Deemed "Seduce and Destroy," his course offers a sexist, misogynistic curriculum of which the following tirade is indicative:

> FRANK: Tame it. Take it on, head first—with your skills at work and say, "No. you will not control me. You will not take my soul and you will not win this game." 'cause it is a game, guys, you wanna think it's not—go back to the schoolyard and have a crush on Mary Jane—respect the cock—you are embedding this thought: I'm in charge. I'm the one who says yes, no, now or here. . . . [Women] are universal. They are sheep. They are to be studied and watched—they have their patterns that must be stopped, interrupted and resisted. . . . It's a harsh, hard unfair place, but it's not gonna stop me from getting my fair share of hair pie.

Clearly, with its discourse of "respecting the cock" (and "taming the cunt"), Frank's is an entirely male-oriented view of heterosexual relations. With its impulse toward seduction and destruction his program also participates in rampant hostility and sadism toward the female sex. He complains about what society "does to little boys" who, he claims, are taught by females that they "are shit." Finally, in advising men to "study and watch" their women, we have evidence of theories of the masculine gaze originally formulated by such critics as John Berger and Laura Mulvey.

On a broader level, Frank's antagonism toward the contemporary American woman can be seen as part of what feminists such as Susan Faludi have seen as a post–women's liberation "backlash." As she wrote in 1991:

> The truth is that the last decade has seen a powerful counterassault on women's rights, a backlash, an attempt to retract the handful of small and hard-won victories that the feminist movement did manage to win for women. This counterassault is largely insidious: in a kind of pop-culture version of the Big Lie, it stands the truth boldly on its head and proclaims that the very steps that have elevated women's position have actually led to their downfall. The backlash is at once sophisticated and banal, deceptively "progressive" and proudly backward. (61)

The one female with whom we see Frank interact is the television journalist Gwenovier (April Grace), who attends his seminar at the Holiday Inn in order to videotape an interview with him. At one point, he strips down to his underwear in front of this striking woman and then lasciviously pants at her as he sticks out his tongue. Finally, in a swaggering move, he states that, after completing a seminar, he feels like "a fucking action hero." These seductive moves remind us that his program advises men on scenarios for attracting women (or "hotties"). In the maneuver outlined below, he conceives a game plan for using female friends as decoys for making potential lovers jealous:

FRANK : Listen up 'cause we're gonna learn later on in Chapter 23 that having a couple of chick-friends laying around can come in real handy in setting Jealousy Traps. But we'll get to that. Number One (this is page 18 in your booklets, blue cover—go to it and follow along with me.) . . . Create a crisis—simple and clean, and if done properly can be quite effective in getting some bush. Here we go: Set a date with your so-called "friend."

Despite Frank's display of insistent masculinity, the man doth protest too much. At one point, he talks about how men today need to demonstrate to women that they are not gay, and at another he reveals his view that it is women who seek to obliterate men (rather than the other way around). Shortly, thereafter, he accuses Gwenovier of attacking him because she is skeptical of his version of his past. Finally, in the scene at Earl's deathbed, we learn that he was essentially a "mama's boy," left fatherless at home to tend a dying mother. (Significantly, it is when Gwenovier asks Frank to "talk about [his] mother" that Frank goes silent and terminates the interview.)

Ironically, Anderson calls *Magnolia* "the Mother of All Movies About The San Fernando Valley"; but, in truth, mothers are either absent or powerless within the text itself (2000, vii).[1]

Race and Gender

Class, race, sexuality, gender—and all other categories by which we categorize and dismiss each other—need to be excavated from the inside.
—Dorothy Allison (1996)

Within the context of the film, it is important that Gwenovier is African American, especially since it is she who gets the better of male supremacist Frank Mackey.[2] She does not respond to his sexual innuendoes: when she indicates that she has reserved a suite for their interview, he makes a lewd remark about her having gotten a room for them so quickly. Similarly, she reacts distrustfully to his claim that he can "pick up any fuckin' pootie" on the street in just one second. She tests him in further ways: doubting his official bio, asking whether his mother would approve of his "Seduce and Destroy" program, and questioning whether he ever enrolled at Berkeley or UCLA as he has claimed. When she continues to "tr[y] to figure out who [he is]," Frank becomes defensive, using gender-specific epithets (like "bitch") to put her down:

FRANK : Is this the "attack" portion of the interview, I figured this was coming sooner or later—Is "the girl" coming in for the kill?

Eventually, he storms out of the room, cutting their session short.

There is another powerful black woman in the drama but of a more perverse nature. In a scene involving policeman Jim at work, we see him enter an apartment in North Hollywood where he encounters Marcie (Cleo King)—a large, matronly African American woman who is "ranting and raving" (Anderson 2000, 23). Although Jim has come to the door in response to a disturbance report, she assertively insists that he has no right to enter. When he instructs her to calm down, she screams back, "I am calm!" She denies that there is anyone else in her apartment, but when Jim hears a thump from another room, he handcuffs her to the sofa so that he can investigate the sound. At this point (as the screenplay describes it), she "goes crazy, screaming and yelling the whole time," moving around, dragging the sofa with her, shouting, "What the fuck is this bullshit? What the fuck are you doing, motherfuckers? Mother-god-damn fucker. Where are you goin'? Don't go into my god damn bedroom" (Anderson 2000, 28). Eventually, Jim finds a dead white man in her closet. When he asks her, "What the hell is this, Marcie?" she responds "That's not mine." While Gwenovier is a gorgeous, middle-class, professional black woman (a rare figure in mainstream cinema), Marcie is more typical: a tough, criminal, African American female.

The only other black character of any significance is Dixon, the kid whom Jim encounters outside Marcie's apartment complex. He claims to have information concerning the murder and, attempting to sell it to Jim, offers him clues in the form of rap lyrics:

> DIXON: Check that ego—come off it—
> I'm the prophet—the professor
> Ima teach you 'bout The Worm,
> Who eventually turned to catch wreck
> With the neck of a long time oppressor
> And he's runnin from the devil, but this
> Debt is always gaining
> And if he's worth being hurt, he's worth
> Bringin' pain in
> When the sunshine don't work, the Good Lord bring the rain in.

While most of the rhyme seems nonsensical, some lines reverberate with meaning. The reference to rain links to an earlier title: "Partly Cloudy, 75% chance of rain." The reference to "long time oppressor" has associations to white/black relations—a factor in the murder and its discovery. Dixon reappears two other times in the drama: once, we see him watching the quiz show on television, tying him to the question: What do kids know? His second reemergence occurs when he discovers Linda Partridge unconscious in her car; he steals money from her purse but calls the paramedics. Given that Dixon exists in a world of crime, homicide, and poverty, we would seem to have another example of child abuse—this time of a broad social nature involving institutionalized racism.

The Queer Eye

The queer gaze is immediately recognizable, whether one participates in it or just observes it. As a man who cruised Leicester Square during World War Two said, "The eyes, the eyes, they're a dead giveaway. . . . If someone looks at you with a lingering look, and looks away, and then looks at you again."
                                                                    —Norton Rictor (2002)

In a peripheral fashion, *Magnolia* touches upon issues of sexual preference. We have already mentioned how Frank tells his male "students" about the need to convince women that one is not gay (especially funny, given the rumors that have circulated around Tom Cruise).[3] But the issue is most relevant for former quiz kid Donnie Smith. We are first introduced to him in a dentist's office, where a nurse remarks on how cute he was as a child. In a later sequence, when Donnie gets fired from a store, he tells his boss that he needs money for corrective oral surgery. His employer is puzzled as to why Donnie needs braces, since his teeth seem just fine. (It is this store that Donnie will ultimately burglarize in an act of revenge.)

  Later in the drama, we find Donnie inebriated in a saloon. From the way he looks desirously at Brad (the young, handsome, bartender [Craig Kvinsland])—with the camera powerfully tracing his gaze—it is clear that Donnie is smitten. Later, in fact, he drunkenly confesses to Brad: "I love you and I'm sick." Donnie also shares his thoughts on romance with Thurston Howell (Henry Gibson), another bar customer: "My name is Donnie Smith and I have lots of love to give." In a close-up of Brad laughing, we notice that he has braces (a shot that reminds us that the bar is called The *Smiling* Peanut). Suddenly, in a bizarre fashion, Donnie's otherwise inexplicable quest for an oral appliance makes sense. It is a gesture of doubling that seems almost to parody those theories of same-sex attraction that see it as a form of neurotic mirroring. As Freud wrote in 1914: "isolated features of the narcissistic attitude are found in many people who are characterized by other aberrations—for instance . . . in homosexuals" (1991, 56). Braces are generally acquired in childhood and, therefore, Donnie's belated wish for them seems a regressive act, pointing back to the youth he was denied as a professional quiz show contestant. In light of such implications, it seems unlikely that the film imagines homosexuality in a progressive fashion. While we accept Donnie's amorous yearnings, the film tends to contextualize them as just another sign of "Little" Donnie Smith's malad-justment to adult life—a further indication that he is a case of "arrested devel-opment." Significantly, as Donnie gazes at Brad in the saloon, we hear a male falsetto voice on the soundtrack. Thus, while the film critiques patriarchy from the point of view of male/female relations, it may not do so from the perspec-tive of homosocial (or homoerotic) dynamics.

The Politics of Form

> To me style is just the outside of content, and content the inside of style, like the outside and the inside of the human body—both go together, they can't be sep-arated.
>
> —Jean-Luc Godard (1996)

Aside from its resonant thematics and poignant character studies, *Magnolia* has been cited or praised for its inventive technique and structure. Mark Olsen calls it a work "in thrall to the process of movie-making" (2000, 28); Leslie Dick deems it a film "about narrative" (2000, 56); and Emanuel Levy calls it "oper-atic" (1999, 105). In the quote above, Jean-Luc Godard uses the trope of the human body to indicate how style consists equally of shape and content. As we know, bodies are gendered and, if we extend Godard's metaphor to style, we will see how form can have gendered connotations as well.

Magnolia's narrative is highly fragmented and difficult to follow and it is only retrospectively that we realize it is meant to take place in a single locale in a single day. It begins with three brief and disconnected mini-dramas (described by a male voice-over) that will have no direct relevance to the body of the tale: One about the hanging of three men in 1911, another about a dead scuba diver found hanging from a tree limb in 1983, and another about the death of Sydney Barringer in 1958. For guidance, the only statement that the narrator offers us is: "These strange things happen all the time." Ironically, the story that follows is far from strange, but rather involves what we might deem "the psychopathology of everyday life."

Following the film's title, the drama shuttles between several locations (which we later realize are all in the San Fernando Valley): a suburban home, a bar, Claudia Gator's apartment, Jimmy Gator's office, a hospital, Stanley Spec-tor's home, a dentist's office, Earl Partridge's house, Jim Kurring's place, Mar-cie's apartment—all this in the first segment of the film. Thus, scenes involving myriad characters and places abruptly follow one another without any clear exposition or indication of their relationship. (Kent Jones calls the film "a veritable ecstasy of cross-cutting" [2000, 38]). As the work progresses, we return to each individual as his or her personal plot line unfolds—sometimes in isolation, sometimes entwined with those of others. As a testament to how confusing the narrative truly is, critics cannot seem to agree on how many characters the drama follows. Clearly, there are precedents for *Magnolia's* cinematic construction. Robert Altman pioneered the disjointed, multi-character story with *Nashville* (1975) and extended it in such subsequent films as *A Wedding* (1978) and *Short Cuts* (1993).

Critics have different takes on the multi-character drama. Some have seen it as progressively subverting the bourgeois individualism stylistically identified with the classical Hollywood film (as such titles as *Mr. Smith Goes to Washington, Jezebel* and *Gilda* indicate) (Carmago 2002, 1, 5). Scholars have also seen *Magnolia's* structure as televisual—a fact that seems underscored by its focus on a TV game show and the plethora of television screens that are glimpsed throughout the film at various locales (e.g. apartments, bars, and studio "green rooms"). As Joanne Clarke Dillman states, "*Magnolia* displaces film narrative to television text" (2005, 143). One might also read the work as loaded with citations of specific television programs and genres: *The Partridge Family* (in Earl's surname), *Cops* (in Jim Kurring's urban adventures),[4] celebrity interview shows (in Gwenovier's scenes with Frank), MTV (the song "Wise Up" as the musical "glue" holding several scenes together), and infomercials (in Frank's TV ads), among many other possible references.

In particular, however, writers have identified *Magnolia's* narrative style with that of soap opera as both share stories that begin in medias res and involve complex intersecting plot lines, ensembles of dramatis personae, diffused spectator identification, emotionally charged situations, and family-centered scenarios (Carmago 2002, 2). What is most interesting about this parallel is that it has implications for issues of gender, as soap opera has traditionally been identified with female viewers. In the title of her groundbreaking 1984 article on the topic, Tania Modleski calls it a "feminine narrative form" (1984, 12). Specifically, she sees the typical soap opera viewer as occupying a maternal position:

> The subject/spectator of soaps, it could be said, is constituted as a sort of ideal mother: a person who possesses greater wisdom than all her children, whose sympathy is large enough to encompass all the conflicting claims of her family (she identifies with them all), and who has no demands or claims of her own. (1984, 14)

As Modleski further explains, soap opera never idealizes the family but presents it with all its warts as a composite of saints and sinners. The spectator (like a mother) is, thus, in a position to "forgive all the crimes against the family [for] to know all is to forgive all" (1984, 15). Clearly, this is our only option as view-ers of *Magnolia*, and within the context of the drama, our stance is doubled by the most sympathetic male character, Jim Kurring, who asks repeatedly at one point: "What can we forgive?"

Certainly the notion of generations in turmoil squares with the vision presented in *Magnolia*; and, if Dillman and Modleski are correct, the film's par-allels with soap opera assure that the maternal function is always felt, even if it is displaced outside the narrative onto the viewer. But, *Magnolia*, unlike tra-ditional soap operas, shows no empowered mothers on-screen, casting doubt on the work's strong relation to women: Frank's mother is dead; Stanley's is absent, and Claudia's is ineffective (in both her marital and maternal roles). Modleski also sees the tendency for soap-opera narratives to tolerate continual interrup-tion as part of its challenge to dominant male forms. As she remarks, "Soap opera is . . . antiprogressive . . . Soap opera is opposed to the classic film narra-tive, which, with maximum action and minimal, always pertinent dialogue, speeds its way to the restoration of order" (1984, 19). Others have seen soap opera's fragmentation and recourse to multiple characters and story-lines as more amenable to women than to men, since traditional females (with respon-sibilities of home, extended family, and children) must constantly multi-task and shift between registers (cleaning, cooking, changing diapers, helping with homework) as well as tend to a bevy of ancillary individuals: neighbors, mer-chants, and relatives. Moreover, some have asserted that soap operas (and their fans) provide a sense of community for housewives who are largely isolated from broader networks and support systems (especially in vast suburban land-scapes like the San Fernando Valley). Finally, if soap operas tend to be never—ending (since they come to us in ongoing daily installments), Anderson partially invokes this surplus by making a film that is three hours long.

Dillman also sees the "feminized" structure of *Magnolia* as augmented by its soundtrack, comprised largely of songs by Aimee Mann: "The predomi-nance of a strong female voice working against and at times doubling the text . . . point to *Magnolia*'s challenge to the 'male' textual film system and more traditionally 'masculine' narratives" (2005, 144). Thus, Mann's vocals function as "a commentary on the action, pulling us in to watch the film from a female viewing position" (2005, 44). Significantly (given women's tendency to be medi-ators and bridge-builders), the title of one of the songs she sings is "One," and its verse advises that: "One is the loneliest number that you'll ever do."[5] Ander-son admits that it was a song by Mann that served as an inspiration for *Mag-nolia*—specifically "Deathly" with its line: "Now that I've met you, would you object to never seeing me again?" He speaks of the lyric as encapsulating "the whole notion of people feeling unlovable" (2000, 198, 204). There is also another moment when a female singing voice is prominent in *Magnolia*. When

Jim talks to Claudia in her apartment, a female operatic vocal (from *Carmen*) is heard. Significantly, it intones: "Love is a rebellious bird no one can tame"— a direct assault on Frank Mackey's order to "tame the cunt."

Beyond using Mann's voice and music within the film, Anderson credits her as a major influence on the film, as a kind of joint "auteur." As he notes: "This 'original' screenplay could, for all intents and purposes, be called an adaptation of Aimee Mann songs. I owe her some cash, probably" (2000, viii). On the one hand, this statement seems quite generous; on the other, however, it may betray Anderson's discomfort (as a male auteur) with "owing" Mann anything or with having his "original" work reduced by collaboration. In light of this, it is interesting to find a buried reference to female authorship in the film that comes in the form of a clue given to the panel of kids on the game show: "This female author's most famous work is *O Pioneers*."

But, of course, the musical scene that is most heralded in *Magnolia* is when sequentially (in a montage shots) the drama's prominent characters sing along to Aimee Mann's "Wise Up" and repeat the line is: "It's not going to stop"—signifying their pessimism toward the prevalence of misfortune in the world. Anderson explains the scene's origins:

> I had reached the end of Earl's monologue and was searching for a little vibe—I was lost a bit and on the headphones came Aimee singing "Wise Up." I wrote as I listened—and the most natural course of action was that everyone should sing—sing how they feel. In the good old-fashioned Hollywood Musical Way. (2000, viii)

Elsewhere he confesses: "I've always wanted to do a musical number, [so he asked himself] how about right here?" (2000, 205).

Again, we might argue that the movie musical has tended to be identified with a female audience, with its themes of romance and courtship and its aestheticized mode. When not associated with women, it has been linked to gay culture—placing it, again, at a distance from traditional manhood. So, once more, we can read gendered implications into Anderson's stylistic choices.

Dillman also opines that *Magnolia* challenges traditional cinema by deflecting "the classic masculine gaze and audience address usually associated with film" and by placing the viewer in a "masochistic" as opposed to an empowered stance (2005, 145). Why might she claim this? In terms of the gaze, as we have already noted, one of the only moments of clear sexual attraction in the film (as underscored by the camera's look) is that of Donnie surveying Brad—a homo—rather than heterosexual encounter. Furthermore, the only actor who serves as real "eye candy" in the film is Tom Cruise, who gets to preen and display his body as Frank Mackey. While many of the actresses are attractive and might have been presented as such, their characters all suffer breakdowns (Claudia as a drug addict and Linda as a hysteric), robbing them of their erotic aura. While the female viewer (who is steeped in traditions of melodrama, be it the cinematic "weepie" or televisual "soap") is accustomed to occupying the masochistic stance, the male viewer is not—yet more than anything *Magnolia* is a male melodrama.

The notion of this form dates back to feminist literary criticism when, in 1981, Nina Baym commented on how "the theory of American fiction has boiled down to . . . a melodrama of beset manhood" (139). It was later taken up by such film critics as Joy Fuqua, Janet Staiger, Lucy Fischer, Marcia Landy, and Tania Modleski. In *Magnolia,* male torment is endless: Jimmy and Earl are dying and also regretful about their lives; Phil is bereft at the impending death of his charge; Frank is forced to confront his estranged father; Jim must admit his incompetence as a cop; Stanley is humiliated before a national audience; and Donnie loses his job and faces unrequited love. Perhaps the reduced viewing position the film offers the masculine spectator explains the ferocity with which *Magnolia* was rejected by many mainstream male critics. Mark Olsen calls it "messy" (2000, 26); Kent Jones deems it "maddeningly, deeply pretentious . . . [and] severely miscalculated" (2000, 38) and David Denby labels it a "mad crackup derby" (1999, 102).

Clearly, at one point in the film, quotidian male melodrama takes on biblical proportions as when, in the midst of Donnie's act of burglary, the sky unleashes a storm of frogs. When asked about this bizarre denouement for the film, Anderson mentioned that he had read about such occurrences in the work of Charles Fort, "a turn-of-the-century writer who wrote mainly about odd phenomena" (2000, 206). Anderson also remarked that he had known that, in various cultures, people "judge[d] the health of a society by the health of its frogs" (2000, 206). Finally, in the midst of shooting, *Magnolia,* actor Henry Gibson gave him a copy of the Bible bookmarked to the "appropriate frog passage" (2000, 206).

> And the LORD spake unto Moses, Go unto Pharaoh, and say unto him, Thus saith the LORD, Let my people go, that they may serve me. And if thou refuse to let them go, behold, I will smite all thy borders with frogs: And the river shall bring forth frogs abundantly, which shall go up and come into thine house, and into thy bedchamber, and upon thy bed, and into the house of thy servants, and upon thy people, and into thine ovens, and into thy kneading troughs: And the frogs shall come up both on thee, and upon thy people, and upon all thy servants. And the LORD spake unto Moses, Say unto Aaron, Stretch forth thine hand with thy rod over the streams, over the rivers, and over the ponds, and cause frogs to come up upon the land of Egypt. And Aaron stretched out his hand over the waters of Egypt; and the frogs came up, and covered the land of Egypt. (Exodus 8:1–6)

Significantly, as the frogs fall down on Jim's car, he passes an unlikely illuminated billboard which reads: "Exodus 8."[6]

Certainly, in *Magnolia*, the rain of frogs is a sign that the world portrayed is in dismal condition—dysfunctional versus healthy. (As Bob Dylan once wrote: "You don't need a weatherman to know which way the wind blows.") The frogs are also an indication that some "higher power" (perhaps God the Director—another male patriarch?) wishes his flock to be liberated from oppression (much as Yahweh wanted the Jews freed from Pharaoh). But, beyond the Bible, there is perhaps another text implied by the amphibians, one not noted by *Magnolia*'s critics: Aristophanes' play *The Frogs* (405 BC). It is about how Dionysus, dissatisfied with the current stock of tragedies, travels to Hades to bring back the recently deceased playwright Euripides. (Note that, for Aristophanes, the fate of writers is Hell.) In Hades he finds Euripides engaged in a contest with the older playwright, Aeschylus, and when the more senior writer wins, Dionysus brings him back to earth instead. The point, however, is that *The Frogs* is a comedy—though one about tragedy.

Such a dynamic may help us understand why *Magnolia* undercuts tragedies "of beset manhood" with a heavy dose of farce. As Anderson once noted, in the closing moments of *Magnolia* he tried to create "the saddest happy ending" he possibly could (2000, 208). There are other aspects of the film that lead us to believe that Anderson is invoking tragic form—if only to undermine it. First, the action of the drama takes place in a unified time and space. Second, one of Frank's seminar slides advises men to "Form a Tragedy" as a ploy for seducing women. Finally, one game show clue addressed to the child panelists references the famous tragedian Thomas Kyd. But another clue alludes to Molière, reminding us that Anderson is also interested in comedy. Furthermore, in the intermittent weather forecasts (rendered as print set against shots of the sky), we perhaps see a second reference to Aristophanes, this time to his comedy *The Clouds*.

In destabilizing tragedy (a form that focuses on the male protagonist) with a quasi-ludicrous hail of frogs (and attendant spectator laughter), Anderson blasts open and upends grim masculine Pathos. Furthermore, in closing *Magnolia* on the dual image of Claudia and Jim, he rejects the maudlin, hermetic focus of tragedy on the single, devastated hero in favor of the hopeful heterosexual couple—comedy's favored and heartening dyad. Yes, as the song tells us, "one *is* the loneliest number."

NOTES

1. Frank's and Stanley's mothers are absent; Claudia's is powerless.
2. It seems significant that Gwenovier and certain other black characters in the film (e.g.,

Marcie, Dixon) have no last names indicated in the cast list. Does this mean that their roles are of less significance than those of white characters? Is it yet another example of how gender often trumps race in the discourses of liberalism?

3. See this section of the entry on Tom Cruise in Wikipedia: http://en.wikipedia.org/wiki/Tom_cruise#Trapped_in_the_Closet.

4. Anderson specifically mentions *Cops* in an interview following the shooting script (2000, 202).

5. The song, though sung by Mann, was written by Harry Nilsson and earlier performed by the group Three Dog Night.

6. Signs bearing these words appear at other moments in the film as well.

Gendering Stars

Stars, Gender, and Nation: Marcello Mastroianni and Italian Masculinity

Marcello Mastroianni died on December 19, 1996, of pancreatic cancer. I remember waking up that morning to "Morning Edition" on National Public Radio, where it was the lead story. In listening and later reading about his life, I began to notice a pattern in both American and Italian tributes. Almost all obituaries somehow referenced his star image as the consummate Latin lover, while at the same time introducing some antithetical element, be it "self-deprecation" (*The New York Times*), "imperfection" (*Time Magazine*), or "reluctance" (the UK's *Daily Telegraph*). I began to consider the contradictions in these descriptions: that although Mastroianni, as commodity, was often marketed as the quintessential Italian man, his characters betrayed instead a much more conflicting image of Italian masculinity than the category of the Latin lover allowed.

Scholars of American screen masculinity have shown how cinema, stardom, and gender shape and reflect significant shifts in contemporary culture and society.[1] Italy is no exception and constitutes a unique case study, given the many social and political upheavals of the second half of the twentieth century: its fifty-nine postwar governments (at last count); the transition from the hardships of postwar Reconstruction in the 1940s and the 1950s to the economic boom of the 1960s; the cultural, social, and sexual upheavals of the 1970s, in particular the feminist movement; and the aging of its population. Mastroianni's films provide a revealing window into the image of contemporary Italian masculinity in Italian cinema. They unmask the antihero underneath the supposedly hypermasculine façade, the Italian *inetto*, the inept man at odds with and out of place in a rapidly changing political, social, and sexual environment. In the course of his long career, Mastroianni appeared in such diverse roles as the sexually impotent protagonist of *Il bell'Antonio* (Marco Bellocchio, 1960), the gay anti–Fascist radio announcer in *A Special Day* (Ettore Scola, 1977), and an older man who marries a young dwarf in Maria Luisa Bemberg's *De eso no se habla* (I don't want to talk about it, 1993). Moreover, as antiheroes rather than Latin lovers, his characters collide with important political, social, and economic changes in postwar Italy. In *Big Deal on Madonna Street* (Mario Monicelli, 1958), the rapid growth of the Italian economy in the 1950s and the ensuing division between rich and poor form the backdrop for Mastroianni's unemployed photographer forced to care for his infant son while his wife serves jail time for black marketeering. In the post-1960s malaise depicted in Marco Ferreri's *La Grande Bouffe* (1973), characters eat themselves to death in a last hedonistic frenzy. And Fellini's *City of Women* (1980), the film I analyze in detail, ridicules Mastroianni's middle-aged Don Giovanni within the context of the 1970s feminist movement.

Italian Masculinity Unmasked

What are the cultural and social constructions that constitute Italian masculinity? From the anthropological perspective, David Gilmore, subscribing to the theory that masculinity is not predetermined but rather "culturally and publicly sustained," notes how Mediterranean masculinity is defined publicly rather than privately. Gilmore unifies the geographical unit of the Mediterranean countries (Spain, Italy, Morocco, Greece) in their ecology, settlement patterns, economic adaptations, and most significantly a "sense of cultural homogeneity" in a shared image of manhood. A good Spanish/Italian/Greek man is "good at being a man": in the public space he proves his masculinity first through sexual potency (the spreading of the seed) and then by providing for and protecting the family (Gilmore 1990, 30–36).[2]

This notion of publicly performed masculinity relates specifically to the Italian concept of the *bella figura*, the manifestation of the private self in the public arena (Nardini 1999, 15).[3] The *bella figura* draws on the Renaissance concept of *sprezzatura* as elucidated in Baldassare Castiglione's *The Book of the Courtier*—a naturalness in appearance that conceals the effort of its preparation and projects an aura of grace—as well as Machiavelli's emphasis on the Prince's appearance. For Machiavelli, the public is essentially separate from the private: "Everyone sees what you appear to be, few touch upon what you are" (Castiglione 1959, 26:44; Machiavelli 1979, 59–60). Like the courtier and the prince, the modern *bella figura*, self-conscious and self-consciously aware, is at once both spectacle and spectator. His aim is both to be seen and be recognized as important and full of honor, as well as to see that others recognize this trait in him. Public space, be it the town's main street or piazza, is the site of the *bella figura*'s performance (Pitkin 1993, 95–101). The time of display is more than not the evening *passeggiata*, when Italian citizens traditionally congregate after work and before supper to discuss politics, sports, local gossip, and other events of the day. The architectonics of the *bella figura* thus breaks the typical spectator/spectacle dichotomy—the structure of public space, as opposed to the private stage, allows for the simultaneous situation of looking and being looked at. His aim is to see and be seen.

Furthermore, that public space in Italy has traditionally been coded as masculine to differentiate it from the private, domestic, feminine sphere. This separation between masculine/public and feminine/private is necessary, according to Gilmore, because the greatest threat to masculinity is feminization. Traditional psychoanalytic theory has attributed the formation of masculine identity to castration anxiety. The male child must renounce the pre-Oedipal world of the mother and identify with the authority of the father. In the child's mind, the penalty for refusing to renounce the mother is castration, what the child assumes the father has already inflicted on the mother. Pre-Oedipal desire is either repressed into the unconscious or channeled into socially acceptable heterosexual desire in the post-Oedipal economy.

Gilmore notes, however, that in Mediterranean countries primary pre-Oedipal identification is difficult to overcome due to the primacy of mother/son intimacy and father distance. Although puberty marks the transition period in which the young male leaves the domestic arena for the homosocial public sphere, there is no rite of passage to initiate this transformation, and thus no clear-cut rupture with femininity. As a result, the feminine is a constant menace to the masculine, for the boundaries between them in the construction of masculinity are tenuous at best. In addition, female chastity codes, which make the visceral distinction between the *Madonna* (virgin) and the *puttana* (the whore), constitute a key component of male honor: if a female family member transgresses these boundaries, it destroys the honor and reputation of all the male family members. No longer a real man, he becomes instead the *cornuto* (cuckold).[4]

If the feminine is othered in the Mediterranean world, the homosexual is even more vilified as a threat to traditional masculinity, because he fails to prove his manliness through the most visible means: sexual reproduction. The Mediterranean man who does not publicly manifest the honor of masculinity through "virile performance" is shamed, cuckolded, and feminized. As a result, Mediterranean cults of masculinity are "at the same time powerful and inherently fragile," requiring "constant vigilance and defense" against the threat of feminization, female sexuality, and homosexuality (Gilmore 1987, 10–13).

On screen, Marcello Mastroianni's characters epitomize the unstable nature of Italian masculinity through the cultural configuration of what might be called the *schlemiel*. According to Sanford Pinsker, in Jewish literature and culture the *schlemiel* "handles a situation in the worst possible manner or is dogged by an ill luck that is more or less due to his own ineptness."[5] As opposed to the *schlimazl*, who is more the victim of pure bad luck, the *schlemiel* is usually an agent in his own destruction. Gian Paolo Biasin has isolated the Italian version of the *schlemiel*—the *inetto*—in twentieth-century Italian poetry and prose. He is a failure rather than a success, mired in bourgeois mediocrity rather than stellar achievement (Biasin 1989, 69–107). The *inetto* is passive rather than active, cowardly rather than brave, and physically or emotionally impotent rather than powerful, always in direct opposition to the deeply rooted masculine norms of Italian culture.

If, as Steven Cohan has argued, masculinity in the United States is a performance that must not reveal itself as such, performativity is also essential to Italian masculinity (Cohan 1997). The Italian male is "good at being a man" precisely because he masks the *inetto* through the performative aspects of the *bella figura*. Postwar Italian cinema highlights this performativity, drawing on and departing from the legacy of postwar neorealism, whose aim, according to one of its greatest theorists Cesare Zavattini, was to return to "man" as a being who is *tutto spettacolo*—the show/performance in and of himself: "[the idea is] to plant the camera in the street, in a room, watch with insatiable patience, educate ourselves by contemplating someone like us in his everyday, elementary actions. We will renounce tricks, the transparency, the infinite subterfuges so dear to Méliès. What is fantastic must be in us, but must be expressed without fantasy" (Zavattini 1979, 25–26, translation mine).[6] With "man" at the center of this new Italian postwar cinema, even in the case of some of Italy's non-neorealist-oriented postwar directors (think, for instance, of a Pier Paolo Pasolini or a Bernardo Bertolucci), he could not help but reflect, as Mastroianni's characters do, masculinity's arbitrary nature.

Mastroianni, Stardom, and the Nation

Although the American film industry is often seen as the center of star-obsessed culture, *divismo*, or star-worshipping, actually began in Italy, with the emergence of the silent stars Lyda Borelli and Francesca Bertini in the 1910s. The success of Rudolph Valentino, Italy's home-grown star, furthered the intercultural exchange of celebrity commodities. Many Italian stars who achieved fame, particularly in the 1930s and 1940s, were billed as Italian versions of popular American stars: Chiaretta Gelli was known as the Italian Deanna Durbin, and, although she was not a success in Hollywood, Isa Miranda was marketed as the Italian Marlene Dietrich. After the fall of Fascism, however, the aesthetics of neorealism, with its penchant for non-professional actors as icons of the everyday, failed to produce the new faces to replace the established stars tainted by their associations with the Fascist regime. It was not until Silvana Mangano's magnificent emergence from the rice fields in Giuseppe de Santis's *Bitter Rice* (1948) that a new postwar Italian stardom was born. Mangano's breakthrough role opened the door for other former beauty queens, such as Sophia Loren, Lucia Bosè, and Gina Lollobrigida to make their fortunes in Italian (and later American) cinema, many of them aided by strategic alliances and in some case marriages with important producers (Gundle 1996, 309–326). On the male front in the 1950s, Totò and Amedeo Nazzari maintained popularity, and Alberto Sordi, Vittorio Gassman, and Marcello Mastroianni achieved stardom in national and international film industries (Brunetta 1993, 247–263; Spinazzola 1985, 304–317).

Mastroianni was born on September 28, 1924, in Fontana-Liri, halfway between Rome and Naples. He began his acting career as a film extra during the late 1930s to help support his lower-middle-class family. He appeared on stage for the first time with his church group and then at the University theater in Rome (Mastroianni 1997, 22–23). In his first big theatrical break Mastroianni played Mitch in Luchino Visconti's production of *A Streetcar Named Desire*. Successful in the role, Mastroianni continued to work in the theater for the following ten years in such plays as Arthur Miller's *Death of a Salesman* and Chekhov's *Three Sisters* and *Uncle Vanya*. Throughout his theatrical work during the 1950s, Mastroianni never abandoned the more financially lucrative film industry, including the first of many successful collaborations with Sophia Loren, and Mario Monicelli's *Big Deal on Madonna Street* (1958). He was planning to form a theatrical troupe of his own to stage the works of his favorite playwright Chekhov when Federico Fellini offered him the part of the tortured journalist Marcello Rubini in *La dolce vita* (1959), the film that made him an international star. Throughout his long career, Mastroianni made over 150 films, working with some of the most prominent filmmakers in European and American cinema, including Michelangelo Antonioni, Louis Malle, Robert Altman, and Marco Ferreri.

But Mastroianni might not have achieved stardom had he not successfully embodied some specifically Italian qualities. Stephen Gundle points out that Italy's status as a recently unified nation-state as well as its continued fragmentation on both political and economic levels has contributed to the celebration of sports and actors as "shared national cultural symbols" (Gundle 1996, 312).[7] The fact that most Italian actors who achieved fame on an international level were, like Mastroianni, from the South speaks to the extranational image that international audiences desire. For Richard Dyer, interpretations of any particular star change with respect to cultural context, be it regional, national, or international (Dyer 1986, 18). In the consumption of Italian stars, the dark, voluptuous, sensuous earth mother (a la Anna Magnani), the "mamma mia" (a la Gina Lollobrigida and Loren), or the handsome, dark male (Rossano Brazzi and Mastroianni) echoed American notions of Mediterranean ideals of exotic and erotic femininity and masculinity, as well as class— this dark eroticism has its origins not so much in the industrialized and Europeanized Northern Italy but rather in the more agrarian and impoverished South (Golden 1978, 3–10; Grignafini 1988, 111–123). The ubiquitous image of Italy as a primitive, earthly, and uncomplicated nation continued to proliferate precisely due to the South's persisting economic, social, and political troubles.

Although, for the American public, Mastroianni came to embody the dark, Mediterranean eroticism of the Latin lover, he consistently accepted roles that deliberately played against that image; for instance, the impotent protagonist of *Il bell'Antonio* (Mauro Bolognini, 1960) and the self-fashioned but inept Barone Cefalù of *Divorce Italian Style* (Pietro Germi, 1961). Gian Piero Brunetta notes how in the 1960s, male stars like Mastroianni (as well as Sordi and Gassman) began to eclipse their female counterparts in terms of recognition and star power. He explains their appeal in two ways: (1) that unlike the female stars, who seemed larger than life, the men appeared as regular guys, in both their good and bad qualities; and (2) rather than epitomizing a gender icon, they ridiculed "national mythologies of virility and power" (Brunetta 1993, 3:139–141).[8] This industry's deconstruction of gender mythologies arises from the political and social uncertainty of the postwar era as Italy's transformation from the devastation of war to one of the world's major industrial forces destabilized traditional gender roles. Italian cinema's constant interchange with uncertain historical conditions resulted in films that overtly and covertly addressed changing roles for men in the second half of the twentieth century. Much like Cohan has argued about American cinema, the contradictions in received notions of Italian masculinity were so huge that filmmakers could not avoid revealing them. Yet a director like Federico Fellini, arguably Italy's most self-conscious postwar filmmaker, was able to recognize these fantasies of Italian masculinity and, in *City of Women*, consciously critique them.

Fellini's *City of Women* and Men

Prior to *City of Women*, Fellini made two other feature films with Mastroianni— *La dolce vita* and *8 1/2* (1963)—and the pseudo-documentaries *Fellini: A Director's Notebook* (1970). With Mastroianni as his masculine muse, Fellini

Marcello Mastroianni in City of Women *(1980). Opera Film Produzione/Gaumont International. From the author's collection.*

consistently turned an ironic lens onto Italian masculinity. Through humor, parody, and satire, his films expose the fallacy of its myths and the shortcomings of its reality, in particular, the myth of his sexual prowess and potency.

City of Women addresses head on Fellini's own self-professed fear and bewilderment around women, which he foregrounds in light of Italy's recent feminist movement. Based predominantly in the North, Italian feminism grew out of and went beyond the student and worker protest movements of the late 1960s. Groups such as Lotta femminile and the Movimento della liberazione della donna excoriated women's economic exploitation in the home and advocated a wages for housework campaign; they encouraged women to take control of their bodies, promoting birth control, abortion rights, and "take back the night" protests; they attacked the traditional gender constructions of the *madonna/puttana* dichotomy; and they promoted legal equality for the sexes. Although on the wane, feminist consciousness was still very much present and alive when Fellini both conceived of and executed *City of Women*.[9]

Like other Fellini films, *City of Women* is highly ironic and self-referential. Mastroianni plays a character alternatively referred to as both Marcello and Snàporaz, which was in fact Fellini's private nickname for Mastroianni (Mastroianni called him Callaghan).[10] Snàporaz is asleep in a train compartment as the train enters and then emerges from a dark tunnel.[11] After suggestively staring at the woman in the fur hat seated across from him and perceiving her responsive to his sexual overtures, Snàporaz follows her into the train's bathroom for what he hopes will be a sexual tryst. Their liaison is soon interrupted when the train abruptly stops. It is clear from their initial encounter that Snàporaz fashions himself to be a Don Giovanni, but he is completely out of touch with the women he intends to seduce and remains inept at sexual conquest.[12] His lack of sexual success is due, in part, to the decidedly childlike nature of his sexuality, one that relies on verbal vulgarities and egotistical satisfaction rather than reciprocal passion. Throughout the film, Snàporaz is consistently associated with the pre-Oedipal, be it the made-up exclamations he spouts ("Smick! Smack!" "Sloff!"), or the infant-like nightgown he wears for much of the second half of the film.[13] Moreover, Snàporaz's journey parallels in many ways that of another famous literary child: Lewis Carroll's Alice. Like Alice, Snàporaz is caught between dream and nightmare; and like the women who populate *City of Women*, Alice comes to represent, as Nina Auerbach has observed, "the perversities of the fallen woman and the distortions of the monster," a dichotomy apparent in what is perhaps the film's most notorious, and funniest, episode: the feminist convention (Auerbach 1985, 165).[14] Yet in Fellini's world, no one is spared, as both the feminists and Snàporaz become objects of ridicule.

The mysterious woman descends from the train, and Snàporaz follows her into a forest. As Snàporaz enters a hotel in pursuit, he is thrown into the middle of the most comically opposite of situations—the lone male (except the hotel's employees and journalists covering the event) among hundreds of women from different nationalities at a feminist convention. He passes from room to room, seeing a slide-show acclaiming the beauty of the vagina and condemning phallic power, a vociferous rebuke of fellatio and sexual penetration, and a documentary film about a woman with six husbands. His final humiliation is a public berating by the woman in the fur hat whom he encountered on the train. The feminist convention clearly evokes the realm of the carnival: the world is literally turned upside-down with the women now "on top" in positions of power through patriarchal subversion (O'Healy 1992, 325–329; Milliken 1990, 37–42).

The segment that best illustrates this use of humor is a musically pantomimed skit entitled "The average housewife." A woman, dressed in rags and rag curlers with a baby attached to her breast, frenetically attempts to accomplish all her tasks—ironing, sewing, cooking, washing the stacks of dishes and vats of clothing, bathing and feeding her children, and sexually satisfying her Frankenstein-like monster of a husband. Filmed at a feverish pace with a piano score and choreography designed to evoke pre-sound film comedies, the scene elicits boisterous laughter from the crowd, who shout *"matrimonio-manicomio"* (marriage = insane asylum) at the performance's conclusion. Throughout this and other encounters at the feminist convention, Snàporaz remains the passive, mildly bemused spectator who is at a loss to comprehend his situation, proxemically expressed through his marginal positioning with respect to the action: he is usually shaded, standing by a doorway or in a hallway, literally on the sidelines. Also typical of his attitude is his verbal response to seeing two women who are the only ones to offer smiles amid the angry glares. He inquires: "What have we done? I understand the problems of feminism, but is it necessary to be so angry?" The irony here is that the women do not understand Italian, and thus this exchange becomes a metaphor for man's failure to understand women as well as Snàporaz's, and perhaps Fellini's, ultimate incomprehension of the feminist movement.

Snàporaz's passive marginality reaches its culmination in his encounter with Donatella, who ultimately saves him from a feminist lynching. Donatella is a smiling, squeaky-voiced, extremely large-breasted woman who symbolizes both a feminine sensuality and a maternal nurturing and who reappears throughout the film in key episodes.[15] She leads him to a basement gymnasium, complete with roller-skating rink and a male dummy being pummeled in the testicles by women learning self-defense. Alternately referring to Snàporaz as "Grandpa" and "Daddy," Donatella makes him don roller skates in order to join the others. On skates Snàporaz is a klutzy buffoon, unable to take even the smallest steps on his own while the women energetically and athletically skate circles around him, an aging man out of step with a changing notion of femininity.

Eventually Snàporaz falls down a staircase, where he encounters *la donna della caldaia* (the boiler woman), a menacingly matronly figure who speaks in a hybrid of German and Triestine dialect. She is the first of several characters with Germanic echoes, introducing an element of militaristic and overpowering female sexuality into the film. After a wild ride with a car of drugged-out punk nymphets, he finds himself at the estate of Katzone, a Teutonic Don Giovanni who throws a party to celebrate his 10,000th sexual conquest. Literally meaning "Big Cock" (*cazzone* in a non-Germanicized Italian), the character of Katzone reportedly was based on the author Georges Simenon, who claimed to have seduced precisely that number of women (Chandler 1995, 215).[16] His villa is replete with phallic furniture and sexually suggestive *objets d'art*, including a light with a long tongue that licks Snàporaz's ear and an automatic vibrator with a speed of three thousand rotations per minute. Here Snàporaz reunites with Elena, his estranged wife, who berates Snàporaz's boring, bourgeois existence and the demise of their love. Donatella also appears at the party, where she reveals herself to be the daughter and niece of a famous showgirl duo that Snàporaz had admired in his youth. The party is broken up by the militaristic feminist police, including Francesca, a long lost friend of Elena, and the *donna della caldaia*, who embarrassingly strip-searches Snàporaz for documents, loudly making fun of his flaccid penis.

Despite its phallic iconography, images of impotence abound in Katzone's hyper-masculine villa, as commentary on Snàporaz's own sexual failings and his inability to understand or control female sexuality. After Katzone shows him the amazing vibrator, Snàporaz turns it on in secret after his host leaves the room, but it spins out of control and he is unable to either turn it off or to hide it. The unruly dildo suggests Snàporaz's own unease with phallic expectations as well as the castrating power of female desire. Similarly, in Katzone's hall of conquests, which features audio-visual reminders of all the women with whom Katzone has had sexual relations, Snàporaz finds marvelous wonder in each amusing photograph and accompanying recording of sexual satisfaction, and pushes each button with great physical and verbal fanfare, using the adolescent comic book-like exclamations described above ("Squish!" "Smick, Smack!"). But when these individual images and sounds join together in a cacophony as they spin out of control, they become a collective, menacing, and monstrous force, reducing the man to impotent insignificance. The sequence's establishing shot foreshadows his impotence: Snàporaz enters the darkened hall, shot from a high angle so that he appears small and inconsequential, encased, once again, by a liminal door-frame. In the end, the one who "mans" the controls of the rambunctious dissonance is Elena, and she is ultimately the power that reins them in.

After he leaves Katzone's villa, the film transports Snàporaz through a variety of other dreamlike sequences—a bedtime fantasy turned nightmare, an amusement park-like toboggan ride through the sexual memories of his youth, and a prison run by a gender-bending group of feminists. He awakes to find himself back on the train, sitting across from Elena and soon joined by the first woman from the train, Donatella, and her friend.

This final scene begs further detailed analysis, for it draws together several of the film's key themes as well as the role of humor and jokes in elucidating them. In terms of its communality, the joke is, for Freud, by nature a shared process, necessarily involving three people: the self or the first person (the narrator of the joke), the object of the joke, and the outside person or the listener. In this final scene on the train, Snàporaz and the spectator come to realize that the film, in essence, has been one big joke, with Fellini as narrator; Snàporaz and, by extension, the spectator as the subject; and the women as the "audience" of the joke (Freud 1960, 176, 184). The filmmaker has led us into the world of his own fantasies and fears, tricked us into believing them to be real, until he reveals that Snàporaz's journey through the city of women was in fact all a dream/nightmare. Snàporaz, like the spectator, awakens to find himself as the butt of the joke—pun intended, given Fellini's obsession with the female posterior and its dominant presence in this film—as the women conspiringly and knowingly look at each other with bemused smiles.[17] In *City of Women*, Snàporaz's return to the conscious world is far from comforting. As the classic Italian *inetto*, he chooses the passive way out: sleep.

Italian cinema's postwar orientation toward social and political realism could not help but reflect the many social and political changes of the second half of the twentieth century—reconstruction, the economic boom, and the social and sexual revolutions of the 1960s and 1970s. With respect to gender, films failed to conceal the fallacies inherent in Italian masculinity, producing unsteady and conflicting roles for male characters who, more often than not, were inept in adapting to the transformations of Italian culture and society. The self-reflexive Fellini pierces the façade of performativity that attempts to conceal these conflicts and contradictions. Fellini said: "Through the ages, from the beginning of time, I'm certain man has covered woman's face with masks. They are, however, his masks, not hers. They are the masks of the viewer, not of the woman, and what they hide is not what they seem to cover. The masks come from the man's own subconscious and they represent that unknown part of himself" (Chandler 1995, 212). In *City of Women*, humor functions as a tool that removes the mask, bringing the subconscious fears and anxieties of Italian masculinity to the surface.

NOTES

1. See Bingham 1994, de Cordova 1990, Holmund 2002, Krutnik 1991, Smith 1993, Studlar 1988, and Willis 1997.

2. This is not unique to the Italian situation. There are, in fact, a number of cultures with which Italy shares this phenomenon. Gilmore's work alone reflects fieldwork done in Africa, East and Southeast Asia, and Brazil, among other places. With respect to effeminacy, Gilmore parallels Mediterranean, Jewish, and Indian cultures.

3. While Nardini focuses on women in her analysis of the *bella figura* in Italian American culture, the *bella figura* is a phenomenon that crosses gender lines.

4. See Giovannini 1981, and Gilmore 1990, 11–12, 127–128, 183–184. The work of Brandes (1981, 1985) reveals how male sexual ideology betrays a powerlessness at the root of Spanish masculinity in the face of the feminine.

5. Pinsker relies upon the *Universal Jewish Encyclopedia* for his precise definition of the schlemiel (1991, 2).

6. Here is the original: "Piazzare la macchina in una strada, in una camera, vedere con pazienza insaziabile, educarci all contemplazione del nostro simile nelle sue azioni elementari. Rinunceremo alla 'truca,' al 'trasparente,' agli infiniti sotterfugi cari a Méliès. La meraviglia deve essere in noi, esprimersi senza meraviglia." For more on Zavattini's impact on Italian and world cinema, see *Diviso in due*.

7. Upon his death, Mastroianni's body was placed in state as thousands came from all over Italy to pay their respects, and the waters of the Trevi fountain, the scene of Mastroianni's famous romp with Anita Ekberg in *La dolce vita*, were shut off in tribute.

8. Similarly, Patrizia Carrano takes the position that Mastroianni represents the summa of Italian masculinity's defects (1988, 241). Marcia Landy integrates the idea of performative masculinity into her assessment of Mastroianni's legacy (2000, 331–334).

9. See Basnett 1986, 91–131, Chiavola-Birnbaum 1986, 79–231, Gramaglia 1979, 179–201, Holub 1981–1982, 89–107, and Lumley 1990, 313–336.

10. Fellini often gave nicknames to his friends, and he coined this one when he and Mastroianni first worked together on *La dolce vita*. Its origins are not specific, although most sources cite it as echoing the name of a comic book character. See Lazzerini 1999, 83. Monti notes how all the language in the film echoes the ironic characteristics of Fellini's and Mastroianni's own private conversations (1981, 162).

11. Critics have been quick to note the dream-like structuring of the film, in particular, the repetitive pattern of ascending and falling and much phallic and vaginal symbolism (Lederman 1981, 118; Bondanella 1993, 319–320).

12. Bondanella observes that throughout the film, none of his sexual encounters leads to complete sexual satisfaction (1993, 321).

13. Milliken (1990, 44–45) ties the child-like language to Lacanian prelinguistic jouissance. See also Monti 1981, 164–166.

14. Lederman was the first to establish parallels between *8 1/2* and *Alice in Wonderland* (1981, 115).

15. For Milliken (1990, 41), she is "a conflation of the four traditional female stereotypes of Virgin/Whore/Mother and Muse."

16. Marrone (1993, 243) cites Bernardino Zapponi, Fellini's co-writer, as referring to Katzone as Marcello's "scurril" double—the vulgar part of himself.

17. Bondanella (1993, 324) also observes a "sense of complicity" between the women in this final scene.

Chris Holmlund

Wham! Bam! Pam!:
Pam Grier as Hot Action Babe
and Cool Action Mama

Alive and Kicking: "On the Seventh Day She Didn't Rest"

Now fifty-four, Pam Grier has almost as many films to her credit. One of the most charismatic action goddesses ever, she often works, by choice and by necessity, in TV and theater. As the Norwegian film magazine *Z* puts it: "on the seventh day she didn't rest" (Knutsvik 1998, 11). My goal in reviewing Grier's action—and occasional other—film output is twofold. I want to reconsider how action heroines have been characterized in relation to femininity and masculinity, and I want to emphasize how crucial "playing the race card" is with respect to female action stars.

Most critics who appraise female action stars begin by talking about 1980s white "hard body hardware heroines" like Ripley (Sigourney Weaver) and Sarah Connor (Linda Hamilton).[1] Action ancestresses are bypassed, in part because the action "mode" has been defined, *Jaws*-like, in terms of "high concept" blockbusters, that is, by the big budget films that swallowed up independents as blaxploitation was ending.[2] Unfortunately, this amnesia regarding earlier female figures hampers appraisals of today's action trends: for the most part, white women get all the attention, and they are typically measured in terms of masculinity.

Still kicking after all these years, the voluptuous, 5 8, Grier offers a salutary counter model to the white "hard body hardware heroines" of the 1980s. Even in middle age, she flaunts what she sees as her femininity; when younger, she proclaimed that "Foxy Brown was every woman: able to be assertive, yet feminine, the goal of the women's movement!"[3] Unlike white 1980s action heroines, moreover, wits and wiles usually matter more to Grier's gals than do muscles and guns: the blaxploitation babes in particular excel at invention and seduction. Yet there's been a salient shift: while in the 1970s "melodramas of racial abuse" (to adopt Linda Williams's term) fueled Grier's characters' vengeance, this is much less frequently the case in the early years of the twenty-first century.[4]

Today Grier is a cultural icon. Popular films like *Austin Powers in Goldmember* (Jay Roach, 2002) and *Undercover Brother* (Malcolm D. Lee, 2002) send up her blaxploitation characters; she's won awards;[5] she's even been the subject of an experimental video (Inyan Etang's 1996 *Badass Supermama*). Nor should the box office draw and cross-over appeal of her 1970s films be underestimated. Grier was not only the first—and in the 1970s the biggest—female action star, she was also one of only three female stars (with Liza Minnelli and Barbra Streisand) who could be counted on to open a film, and (with Streisand and Ellen Burstyn) one of the three most bankable female stars.[6]

Several studies of Grier's prison and blaxploitation films have been published, but to my knowledge there have been no academic assessments of her career as a whole.[7] To begin to measure Grier's impact as (then) hot action babe and (now) cool action mama, therefore, I axe my observations around three key contradictions subtending her casting, characters, and performances: (1) kick ass and in control, she is nevertheless frequently positioned as beautiful spectacle; noteworthy exceptions exist, however, from the 1980s onward; (2) articulating black power and proto- or quasi-feminist positions in the 1970s, she simultaneously functions as exotic "other"; this is less frequently true today; (3) connected to the family and often figuring as an "icon of home,"[8] many of the 1970s but none of the 1980s films and few of the 1990s films also reference queer sexualities.

Throughout this essay I invoke a range of industry-connected discourses, from critical appraisals, to the film texts, to studio publicity, to mainstream and alternative reviews, to star and director interviews. I have organized the body of my piece historically, and subdivided it into three sections titled with lines taken from her films. The first, "Blaxploitation Blast-Off: 'She's a whole lotta woman!'" concentrates on two of Grier's biggest 1970s American International Pictures blaxploitation hits, *Coffy* (Jack Hill, 1973) and *Foxy Brown* (Jack Hill, 1974); I mention *Friday Foster* (Arthur Marks, 1975) in passing. In all three, Grier is the heroine. As backdrop I reference her first screen appearances in prison films, also for AIP; in one, she's a villain. The second section, "'Something Wicked This Way Comes': Supporting Role Survival," surveys Grier's work as villain in two 1980s studio films, *Fort Apache, the Bronx* (Daniel Petrie, 1981) and *Something Wicked This Way Comes* (Jack Clayton, 1983). I enlist a third supporting performance, as Steven Seagal's "good guy" sidekick in the 1988 *Above the Law* (Andrew Davis) as conduit to the third section, "'I'm Glad to See You're Still Packing a Gun . . . Between Your Legs': From Cameo to Star, Revival!" This last section studies six 1990s films that variously showcase Grier's now leg-

Pam Grier in the 1970s. Jerry Ohlinger's Movie Materials Store.

endary figure: *Posse* (Mario van Peebles, 1993), *Original Gangstas* (Larry Cohen, 1993), *Jackie Brown* (Quentin Tarantino, 1997), *Escape from L.A.* (John Carpenter, 1996), *Mars Attacks!* (Tim Burton, 1996), and *Holy Smoke* (Jane Campion, 1999). Save for *Jackie Brown*, since 1993 she has always played supporting roles, and in all six she is a likeable character.

In conclusion, weaving my comments around two other lines extracted from press coverage—"the Pam principle" and "not just another body for the camera" (Salvo 1976, 49, 53)—and a final sequence culled from *Original Gangstas*, I survey who now reveres and who still ignores her, why, with an eye to what this might indicate for today's more full-bodied and, arguably, more feminine (occasionally even queer) action heroines. Significantly, several, like Grier, are women of color.[9]

Blaxploitation Blast-Off: "She's a Whole Lotta Woman"

Unlike the (white) action heroines of the 1980s who, Yvonne Tasker and others have argued, were often linked to reproduction and motherhood at the same time as they were deemed "masculine,"[10] Grier began her action career in the 1970s playing swinging singles, lesbians, and/or prostitutes in exploitation prison flicks. In 1973, with the extraordinary success of blaxploitation and *Coffy*, she became a star. The shift from prison to ghetto action films brought significant changes to how her characters were portrayed.

Although Judith Mayne argues that surveillance in prison films "involves women watching other women, . . . women objectifying other women" (2000, 118), Grier's 1970s blaxploitation heroines are primarily the objects of male scrutiny and lust. Compare, for example, an early shower scene in Eddie Romero's cheezy 1972 remake of *The Defiant Ones* (Stanley Kramer, 1958), *Black Mama, White Mama*, with the opening sequence of *Coffy*. In *Black Mama, White Mama*, lesbian prison warden Denamore (Lynn Borden) eagerly watches Lee (Grier), Karen (Margaret Markov), and other inmates through a peephole until another warden, her partner Logan (Laurie Burton), cuts her pleasure short. This scene and the command "meeting" between Denamore and Lee that follows stand apart from the rest of the film, Mayne argues. For her, "the interracial friendship" that develops between Lee and Karen after they escape can only occur "at the price of expunging the lesbianism, of setting up the two pairs of women—Lee and Karen on the one hand, the two prison guards on the other—in strict opposition" (Mayne 2000, 135). In contrast, even in the opening scenes of *Coffy*, Grier's eponymous heroine is ogled by male, not female, characters. After displaying her ample breasts, nurse Coffy rises from a bed, wearing a micro-mini dress, and suddenly hefting a sawed-off shotgun. "This is the end of your rotten life, you mother-f***ing dope pusher!" she tells the fat, black, drug kingpin (Morris Buchanan) who hoped to sleep with her, then blasts him into oblivion. Quickly she picks up a pre-loaded syringe, moves to the bathroom, and treats the junkie pimp (Mwako Cumbuka), who presumably has procured her, to an overdose of his own "medicine."

Here, as in *Foxy Brown* and *Friday Foster*, she's certainly "a whole lotta woman," as her drug-dealing brother (Anthony Fargas) says admiringly in *Foxy Brown* after Foxy has shot up his apartment and shot off his ear. In each blaxploitation film, Grier's "cups runneth over" as black and white men look at, and often paw, the feminine wares presented for their pleasure.[11] Added bonus: when Grier's characters are covered, other women characters aren't. As an advertising tag line for *Coffy* suggestively promised: "Coffy, she'll cream you." The "creaming" occurs on two registers: quite literally via blow jobs and more metaphorically via guns, razors, rocks, a flower pot, a broken bottle, and a carefully honed hairpin. Foxy Brown is equally inviting and inventive, hiding a small pearl pistol in her bra and a razor under her tongue, dousing a rapist with gasoline then setting him ablaze, and so on. Friday Foster is a bit more "traditional": she relies on guns and vehicles; in one scene, however, she hefts a big milk bottle.

Second key change: whereas the prison films are largely white cast and are all situated in unidentified, exotic locales, the blaxploitation films feature black actors and are set in U.S. cities.[12] For Omayra Cruz, *Black Mama, White Mama*'s characterization of Karen (Margaret Markov), not Lee (Grier), as the revolutionary thus "suggests a double displacement": references to the film's Philippine location and to black and Third World liberation movements are similarly silenced (Cruz 2002, 7). In contrast, the blaxploitation films make Grier a "grassroots avenger" (Eimer 1998, 18). Posters billed Foxy Brown as an "action heroine with a social conscience"; as Cedric Robinson notes disapprovingly, both Grier's look and Foxy's actions are modeled on those of Angela Davis (Robinson 1998, 7).[13] Nowhere is this more obvious than in the scene where, framed by posters that read "Free George Jackson!" and "Black Is Beautiful!" sporting an Afro and wearing tight bell bottoms and a blue "African" shirt (with plunging neckline), Foxy asks the muscular male members of the neighborhood "anti-slavery" committee to help her secure justice for the deaths of her brother and her boyfriend. "I'll handle the revenge myself," she says, confidently.

Robinson objects to the way Grier's blaxploitation movies *advertise* black power and link black female sexuality to savagery.[14] In fairness, however—if admittedly in passing—these movies always somehow indict the white power establishment as responsible for the Vietnam War, drugs, and economic misery. In *Foxy Brown*, moreover, Grier is never sexually or verbally abused by black men, only by white men, and her sleazy brother even makes a speech about being a black man that, according to director Jack Hill, was modeled on James Baldwin's *The Fire Next Time*.[15]

Might one therefore argue, as George Lipsitz does of *Blacula* (William Crane, 1972) (Grier appeared in the sequel), that "by addressing the context of inner city life in the 1970s, [Grier's blaxploitation vehicles] also gestur[e] to an even greater horror off-screen, to white racism"? (Lipsitz 1998, 218). Though she would later characterize her blaxploitation films as so many "jerk jobs" (Salvo 1976, 52), Grier herself has consistently insisted that, to create her characters, she drew on "women in my community who were standing up to the world and saying, 'Oh no, you're not going to steal the last five dollars I have to feed my children with. You're not going to rob my house.' . . . I just exemplified [black consciousness], reflecting it back to society" (Grier 1998, 53).

Third key change: in the prison films—not just *Black Mama, White Mama*, but also *The Big Doll House* (Jack Hill, 1971), *Women in Cages* (Jerry de Leon, 1971), and *The Arena* (Steve Carver, 1974)—Grier is paired with a white woman and in two (*The Big Doll House* and *Women in Cages*) herself plays a lesbian. In the blaxploitation films, whites are never her partners, let alone (by choice) her lovers: those privileges are reserved for black men. As Mayne observes, the prison films in contrast rely on "not just the coexistence of discourses of race and discourses of lesbianism, but also on profound connections between them. The lesbian plot requires the racial plot, and the racial plot requires the lesbian plot" (2000, 138).

The blaxploitation films move most relationships between women of different races to the background. When black and white women interact, they usually "perform" for male spectators via cat fights, strip tease acts, and/or modeling events. Lesbians (and the occasional swishy gay man) become secondary or bit characters, though *Foxy Brown* devotes a lengthy sequence to a brawl in a lesbian bar, with Foxy and a black prostitute (Juanita Brown) on one side and white lesbians on the other.[16] Here Grier's characters are always single, in serial relationships with good-looking African American men. At the same time, they take care of family members who are sometimes sympathetic, sometimes just pathetic. Nurse Coffy, for example, used to be involved with a nice cop named Carter (William Elliott); now she's in love with a black (hopeful) congressman (Booker Bradshaw). In between her work shifts and revenge hits, Coffy visits her younger sister, an invalid as a result of drug abuse. But Coffy's lover turns out to be in league with the white Mafia and even tries to kill her; just in time she shoots him—in the balls. In *Foxy Brown*, Foxy comes to the rescue of her ne'er-do-well brother, then makes love to a handsome undercover cop (William Elliott); her brother betrays them both and is finally himself killed by mobsters. *Friday Foster* outfits glamorous fashion photographer Friday (Grier) with two powerful black lovers, one a senator (Paul Benjamin), the other a millionaire (Thalmus Rasulala). Every other adult black male, including Grier's private eye partner and ex-lover (Yaphet Kotto), *wants* to be involved with her. Friday, too, has a little brother, who for once is likeable, if a hustler.

In every blaxploitation film, Grier's vigilante violence—"as American as apple pie," as she says in *Foxy Brown*—is thus multiply motivated: by concern for community, on behalf of "family," and in response to personal abuse by racist whites and the occasional sell-out black. Obviously positioned for consumption (*Coffy*'s theme song guarantees she's "sweet as a chocolate bar"; posters suggested "why not skim a little cream from *Coffy* for yourself"),[17] Grier's blaxploitation vehicles cannot easily be hailed as simply "pro-feminist" or purely "pro-black." By foregrounding femininity and rethinking racism, however, they definitely disrupt conventions common to exploitation action films, whether directed by whites or blacks.[18]

At first phenomenally successful, these films had lost their "oomph" by 1975. Fed up with what she termed AIP head Sam Arkoff's "peanut head" management, post–*Sheba, Baby* (William Girdler, 1975) Grier looked to hone, not another hairpin, but her craft (Salvo 1976, 52). Her success in 1980s studio vehicles is a feat that easily compares with her rise from nowhere to stardom in the 1970s.

"Something Wicked This Way Comes": Supporting Role Survival

As Jesse Rhines points out in *Black Film, White Money* (1996, 82), roles for black performers, in particular women, vanished in the 1980s: even exploitative and stereotypical roles now went to Latinas. Grier herself disappeared from film for four years, but her departure was voluntary: she went back to school, studying directing and producing with Roman Polanski at UCLA (Salvo 1976, 50).[19]

In 1981, she returned to acting, playing a homicidal hooker in *Fort Apache, the Bronx*. The role was written for a Puerto Rican, but Grier snatched it for her own, turning down the chance to play Paul Newman's love interest. Based on a true story, the film tries to target racism, unemployment, drugs, the welfare system, and police corruption, but militant blacks and Latinos are at best sporadically heard, and echoes of her exploitation past obviously underpin Grier's casting, too. Nonetheless, as an actress, Grier makes the most of her part.

As Charlotte, she steals the show in every major scene she has. In the opening sequence, she staggers lasciviously over to a cop car, dressed in gold, eyes glazed, gaunt. "I'm on my jail beat, too," she drawls huskily, then offers the boys in blue a little "something." Then she blows them to kingdom come with a pistol she unpacks from her purse. Later, working the street in the rain, she lures a john out of his limo and into an abandoned building, breathing, "I'm gonna give it up, 'cuz I likes you!" She stoops over him; they kiss; pulling a razor from her mouth, she stabs this man in the throat. In her final big scene, she rouses from a drugged stupor to sinuously slither her way through a snake dance, sighing, "Snake'll sneak up on you ever' time . . . snake's a cold blooded killer, baby." Now she pulls a razor from her bra and slashes her Latino john's face, only to be overpowered and killed by his partner.[20]

Significantly, though still a "whole lotta woman," as Charlotte, Grier is now repulsively "feminine." Few noticed earlier, but she had always been willing to make herself look bad: in several scenes in *Foxy Brown*, for example, her hair is a mess and bruises cover her face and body. In preparation for *Fort Apache*, however, Grier went much further. She hung out in seamy sections of New York, carefully modeling her character on drug-addicted hookers, letting the hair under her arms and on her legs grow, painting her nails and letting the paint chip away, not bathing, losing lots of weight. Her friends told her she looked like death (Hunt 1994, 1).[21] Mixed on the film, Pauline Kael singled out Grier's performance for applause, writing "each time [she] . . . appears, . . . making snaky movements with her tongue, she gives us a feeling of obscene terror. . . . She's a death machine. Yet we understand why nobody pays much attention to her: she's so slowed down she seems harmless—just one more psycho junkie, the kind who look like they couldn't make it across the street on their own power"(Kael 1981, 101).

In her second 1980s role, as the Dust Witch in Disney's 1983 *Something Wicked This Way Comes*, Grier is, in contrast and for the first time, quietly, graciously feminine. This part too, was not originally written for a black actress: director Jack Clayton chose Grier instead of an actress who was white like the character in Ray Bradbury's book because, he said, she was beautiful and strange and "exotic" ("Pam Grier is Sinister" 1983, 5). A figure of indistinct ethnicity (pre-performance, Grier's body was covered with silver- and gold-based mineral oil), the Dust Witch speaks in educated whispers and wears long gowns, lacy gloves, and flowing veils; one enraptured suitor describes her as "more beautiful than Pocahontas or Helen of Troy." The role thus allows Grier to transcend her working-class blaxploitation past. Nonetheless, escorted by dwarves, spiders, and freaks, she is still associated with "otherness," and she is now exclusively—and lethally—paired with white men, whether Mr. Dark (Jonathan Pryce), Charles Halloway (Jason Robards), or Tom Fury (Royal Dano).

Made at the end of the decade, Steven Seagal's first film, *Above the Law*, plays most overtly with Grier's blaxploitation persona. As "Jax," Grier is not associated with glamour or exoticism: her focus is on her career as a cop. As in most contemporary white cast films with the occasional black character, she has no visible family or community ties. Her partner, ex-Vietnam vet and CIA agent Nico (Seagal), gets all the "politically correct" lines, and performs most of the (politically incorrect) actions. About to leave for another job, per 1980s white hero/black sidekick buddy cop film rules "Jax" would seem slated to die. Yet, Tasker comments, *Above the Law* is so over the top that "Jax" miraculously survives: although shot, we assume fatally, mid-way through the film, we learn in conclusion that she was wearing a bullet-proof vest (1993, 23). Desson Howe's *Washington Post* review suggests how seductive Grier remains, even in uniform: "With the cooing assistance of partner Dolores 'Jax' Jackson (Pam Grier), [Nico] wiretaps bad guys' phones illegally . . . , squashes cocaine dealers' faces into their cocaine mirrors ('You wanna get high?'), even shoots an unarmed criminal who gives him backchat" (Howe 1998).

Sadly, so few film roles were available to African American actresses in the 1980s that most of Grier's work during this decade was in TV or theater.[22] In the 1990s, however, black as well as white film makers again capitalized on her charisma, casting her frequently in cameo and supporting parts. Yet Quentin Tarantino's blaxploitation tribute, *Jackie Brown*, is the only 1990s film that provides Grier with the chance to strut her acting stuff as a star.

"I'm Glad to See You're Still Packing a Gun . . . Between Your Legs": From Cameo to Star, Revival!

Most of Pam Grier's 1990s roles are in some variant of action film: of sixteen movies, only two are purely comedies.[23] The only non-action feature among the six discussed here is Jane Campion's oddball drama/romance, *Holy Smoke*: its baroque plot focuses on the tempestuous love affair between Ruth (Kate Winslet) and P. J. (Harvey Keitel), with Ruth's desire at the core and P. J.'s partner/wife, Carol (Grier), in the background.[24]

In this sense, then, Grier is still type cast. But there are changes as well as continuities. Even in the many 1990s action variants where she has supporting roles—whether in over the top pastiches like *Mars Attacks!* and *Escape from L.A.* or in nostalgic revisions like *Posse* and *Original Gangstas*—her characters always stand out thanks to their intelligence, and they always know more than the male characters do. As the gun-toting Phoebe in *Posse,* for example, Grier teaches soldier/cowboy/freedom fighter Jesse Lee (Mario van Peebles) about the "grandfather clause" that prevented African Americans whose grandfathers were slaves from voting. As the male-to-female gang leader Hershe Las Palmas in *Escape from L.A.*, she informs Snake Plissken (Kurt Russell) that the "Plutoxin" virus he's been told will kill him is just so much government b.s.

Unlike her 1970s prison and blaxploitation movies, Grier's 1990s action films rarely turn her into a "spectacle": that "privilege" is reserved for younger female characters or, indeed, for the male stars themselves.[25] *Escape* is one of the rare exceptions: although her voice is electronically altered to sound like a man's, as Hershe Grier still looks glamorous. In one scene she is poured into a low-cut gold gown, tattoos on her shapely arms; in the next, she is encased in leopard skin and leather. *Mars Attacks!* and *Original Gangstas* are more typical of her 1990s work: in the former, she wears a bus driver's uniform and sensible shoes; in the latter, she dons rather matronly dresses, work out clothes, and sneakers.

Even in her starring role as down-on-her-luck airline stewardess Jackie Brown, Grier sometimes looks disheveled and haggard. After a night spent in jail on charges of ferrying money illegally across the border, she looks understandably "rough" when bail bondsman co-star Max Cherry (Robert Forster) first sees her. But the song "Natural High" (Bloodstone) that accompanies her as she walks, slowly, in long shot, head bowed, hair a mess, feet slightly splayed, out of jail toward him (intercut in close-up reverse shot, reverently watching), signals his (Tarantino's? our?) interest. The lyrics leave little room for doubt: "Why do I keep my mind on you all the time, when I don't even know you? Why do I feel this way, thinking about you everyday, when I don't even know you?"

The next day, wearing a bathrobe and no makeup, Jackie/Grier opens the door of her apartment to find Max, come to see if she's okay. She invites him in, fixes coffee, then rummages through her record collection. After selecting a Delfonics' hit with the haunting refrain, "I gave my heart and soul to you, babe," the two move to the kitchen and banter about getting older. He says he has a hairpiece, but feels good, then assures her, "I bet you look the same as you did twenty years ago." She laughs, dryly: "Well, my ass ain't the same." "Bigger?" he replies, appreciatively, "Ain't nothing wrong with that!"

He's right. When push comes to shove, as "Jackie" Grier still looks *good*, though she's never on display to the extent she was in her blaxploitation films. Replacing the repetitive shots on tits and ass in those earlier flicks, in *Jackie Brown* the "chemistry" between Grier and Robert Forster is, to quote Roger Ebert, "at the heart of the movie."[26] Intent on evoking—while applauding and updating—Grier's blaxploitation personae, Tarantino rewrote the role (in the Elmore Leonard novel, a white woman) specifically for her. When Jackie engineers an ingenious heist with Max's help, double-crossing both the drug-dealing Ordell (Samuel L. Jackson), his bumbling associates (Robert de Niro and Bridget Fonda), and two special task force cops (Michael Keaton and Michael Bowen) *while* buying a designer pants suit, therefore, this speaks volumes about both Grier-the-blaxploitation-star *and* Grier-the 1990s-survivor's grit, smarts, poise, and panache.

Also unlike the blaxploitation heroines, many of Grier's 1990s characters are either married or monogamously partnered. In *Holy Smoke* as well as *Jackie Brown*, Grier's characters are happily involved with white men (though in *Jackie Brown*, Jackie does end up driving off alone). In *Posse,* Phoebe is usually seen at Papa Joe (Melvin Van Peebles)'s side. In *Mars Attacks!* and *Original Gangstas*, Louise Williams and Laurie Thompson are first estranged from, then reunited with their husbands (both roles are played by former football player turned blaxploitation star, Jim Brown).

Grier's 1990s gals rarely brandish "everyday" weapons. Instead, influenced undoubtedly by the white action heroes and heroines of the 1980s, probably also by hip hop gangsta films like *Set It Off* (Gary Gray, 1996) and *New Jack City* (Mario van Peebles, 1991), her 1990s warriors now wave little (lady-like) or big (manly) GUNS.[27] Some films justify her characters' violence in light of political, social, and economic discrimination, but few indict whites directly: to do so would alienate cross-over audiences. *Posse* most resembles Grier's blaxploitation work. Starring and directed by Mario Van Peebles, assembling two generations of African American cultural figures (the cast includes filmmakers, actors, musicians, sports stars, and more), in *Variety*'s words, *Posse* "evinces film buff and socially relevant awareness in roughly equal measures" (McCarthy 1993, 40). The worst villains here are the greedy whites who rob, sexually threaten, and kill Native Americans, African Americans, and Asians with impunity.[28] In contrast, though set in a mid-1990s Gary, Indiana, "full of abandoned houses, vacant lots, old movie theaters, and forsaken businesses," and reuniting Grier with four male blaxploitation stars, *Original Gangstas* says little about the white power structures responsible for Gary's economic decline (Boyd 1996, 50).

In the biggest change from the earlier movies and common to five of these six films, Grier's 1990s characters are now "normal," not exotic or "other." Not coincidentally, they are often also mothers. In *Original Gangstas*, Grier fights for her community and on behalf of her son, killed by young gang members. In *Mars Attacks!*, playing a character "so realistic and plausible" that, Roger Ebert charges, "apparently Burton forgot to tell her she was in a comedy" (R. Ebert 1996), she fights like a demon to protect her kids. Reunited with her husband by movie's end, theirs is the *only* family left intact. In *Holy Smoke*, however, Grier' Carol is once again—per the prison films—the sole African American with a semi-major part. But by comparison with P. J., Ruth, and Ruth's bizarre family, she is now the epitome of normalcy. In a surprise coda she appears behind her husband holding twin babies, unwittingly embodying what *Séquences* calls the "symbolisme excessif" of the film as a whole (Pellerin 2000, 46). Actually, only as the post-male-to-female-"op" Hershe in *Escape from L.A.* is Grier still "odd." Snake teases her as he runs his hand up her leg to remove a hidden pistol: "The more things change, the more things stay the same. I see you're still packing a gun . . . between your legs."[29]

In her post-2000 film appearances, Grier continues to be associated with lusciously full-figured avenging or protecting "angels." As in the blaxploitation films—but as in only three of her sixteen 1990s films (*Posse, Original Gangstas,* and *In Too Deep* [Michael Rhymer, 1999])—Grier again plays opposite African American actors in much of her recent work. In 2001, for example, she joined Ice Cube in *Ghosts of Mars* (John Carpenter), Snoop Doggy Dogg in *Bones* (Ernest R. Dickerson), and Danny Glover and Michelle Rodriguez in *3 A.M.* (Lee Davis); in 2002 she supported Eddie Murphy in *Adventures of Pluto Nash* (Ron Underwood).[30]

For three decades, Grier's voluptuous "look" and bad-ass "attitude" have thus made her a model, whether as "hot action babe" or "cool action mama," for younger actresses working in action movies. Like Grier, many of today's action "babes" are not particularly "buff" or "cut" or "masculine"; many are women of color; several boast queer fans. Count, variously, among them Angelina Jolie, Jennifer Lopez, Cameron Diaz, Nia Long, Halle Berry, Michelle Rodriguez, Famke Janssen, Salma Hayek, and Rosario Dawson.

Nonetheless, when asked in 1997 whether opportunities had improved for women who wanted to play (in Grier's words) "tough, smart, assertive characters who were still feminine, soft and caring," Grier tellingly mentioned only white actresses (including some whom academics have deemed "masculine"): "Well, there's Sigourney Weaver in the *Alien* films. There's *La Femme Nikita.* And look at *G. I. Jane.* . . . But you have to have the actresses who can take it and still open a movie and still be dynamic and still be pretty and be all the fantasies. That's a lot of work" (Major 1997, 28).

So what might it mean that more women of color are now popping up in action? Several factors are doubtless in play. As with Grier's 1970s heroines, carnality, violence, and color are, unfortunately, still connected: witness the emphasis on J Lo's butt and breasts in her films.[31] Simultaneously, as was the case with Grier's 1970s blaxploitation heroines, the casting of women of color in key if not always starring roles is clearly meant to please growing niche markets: Grier is right to emphasize how few women can really "open" a film.

But why is Grier's influence on action films and their audiences still undervalued by so many critics and contested by certain organizations, too?

The "Pam Principle" or "Not Just Another Body for the Camera"?

As Donald Bogle, Mark Reid, and Ed Guerrero have observed, Pam Grier's full-bodied, "feminine" action figure clearly appeals to men. I would add that she maintains this appeal even though—indeed because!—her "bad black mamas" so frequently attack male genitalia.[32] As one "super-intellectual publication" commented regarding what it called "the Pam principle," "the celebrated assault on the groin is not a humiliation but a confirmation of male potency" (Salvo 1976, 49). Translated to everyday "speak": Grier's characters' shots, slashes, hand jobs and blow jobs make the darn "tool" "cool."

Of course, not everyone liked or likes these films. Individual African American intellectuals as well as organizations like the NAACP have condemned the blaxploitation films as unrealistic, demoralizing, and incapacitating. More recently, Jacquie Jones has charged that *Jackie Brown* "exists as a modification of sensationalist Hollywood formulae," "co-opt[ing] a ghetto aesthetic and displaying it across the bodies and screens of middle-class whites" (Smith-Shomade 2003, 29) while Spike Lee and others have condemned the film's use and abuse of the "n-" word.

But aren't dismissals of blaxploitation and action films as simply abusive or merely manipulative overly general? After all, as Tommy Lott maintains, lumping all blaxploitation films together "overlook[s] their many differences in style, audience orientation, and political context" (Lott 1997, 86). It also assumes that audiences are monolithic. Surely it is significant that, although black and Latino community groups demonstrated against *Fort Apache, the Bronx*,[33] *Jackie Brown* did extremely well in black theaters in L.A. and elsewhere.[34]

I would argue, with Lott, that "some weight at least must be given to the viewpoint of black audiences, inasmuch as it is imprudent at best continually to posit a black aesthetic [based on independent and experimental films] that very few black audiences share"—or see (1997, 90). And of course, those who object most vehemently to blaxploitation and contemporary action films typically articulate middle-class values.[35] Grier's retort to Spike Lee strikes me as pertinent: "Do you want fantasy or realism? The characters are based on realism. . . . I don't use the ["—"] word, but I know people who use it all day long as an endearment—that's how they talk. If people are offended by this word, they don't live in Compton" ("Term of Endearment" 1998, 138). At the root of middle-class resentment may well be the fact that, as Valerie Smith notes, "blaxploitation films . . . responded to the bourgeois propriety of early black independent films and of mainstream race problem movies with their focus on black and white criminality and the urban black working poor, [by] constructing these subjects and types *as more racially authentic* than members of the black middle class" (1998, 127, emphasis mine).[36]

Undoubtedly, some working-class *and* middle-class blacks "were [and are] weary of" what Donald Bogle has called "the whole sexy-vulgar-slut image" (1980, 95). Nonetheless, there's evidence that many black women valued and value Grier for her spunky, take-charge attitude, not just for her sexy body.[37] Her blaxploitation films appealed to many white women as well because, as a *Ms.* cover story trumpeted in 1975, "*Coffy, Foxy Brown* and *Sheba, Baby* . . . are the only films . . . in a long time to show us a woman who is independent, resourceful, self-confident, strong and courageous. Above all, they are the only films to show us a woman who triumphs" (Kincaid 1975, 52). Looking back on her career, Grier herself comments, "That was the underlying message of those movies; that women can be self-sufficient, and don't have to fold like a house of cards in adversity" (Johnson and Fantle 1997, 64).

Now on video, Grier's blaxploitation work has outlasted that of most of the male stars, earning her the fond appreciation of critics like Judith Mayne, rappers like Foxy Brown,[38] and makers like Cheryl Dunye and Inyang Etang. Grier has also found devotees and friends abroad, foremost among them Federico Fellini, who became a friend and a fan when the black stallion she was riding in *The Arena* ran onto the set where he was filming. Grier was wearing a skimpy leopard print dress. As Grier tells it, Fellini just "threw up his hands, started laughing and said, 'Now my fantasy has come true! Bella! Bella! Bella!'" (Beck and Smith 2001, n.p.).[39] Her 1980s, 1990s, and 2000s characters' survival and successes distinguish them, also, from the legions of black male and female sidekicks who dedicate themselves to the causes of white heroes, then often die in their place.[40]

Grier may thus have only partially attained the goals she set herself in 1975—"no mindless women, no dumb situations"—but she has certainly proven that "this girl is just not another body for the camera" (Salvo 1976, 53). As she told *Essence* in 1979, "I created a new kind of screen woman. Physically strong and active, she was able to look after herself and others. If you think about it, you'll see she was the prototype" (A. Ebert 1979, 107).[41]

Bottom line, Grier's popularity is probably best evaluated in view of what bell hooks has termed an "oppositional gaze." For hooks, this gaze is practiced by black female spectators exercising their "power in looking" through the "contestation and confrontation" of dominant images (hooks 1992, 115–117). Yet I'd like to think that others, too, find joy in Grier's ingenuity and pluck. When, for example, as ex-Rebel gang member Laurie Thompson she becomes a middle-aged model of *mojo*, teaching overweight and older African American women to fight back in *Original Gangstas*, I imagine both hooks and myself among the dozens of women and handful of men, most black, a few white, who look on and love Grier's lesson. The scene starts when Laurie strides up to the "plate," grunting as she smashes a male dummy with a baseball bat. "I want you to hit somethin' that breaks," she yells. "Like the face or the ribs or the knee caps! This is just like a gun! Don't pull it unless you're gonna use it, all right? Got that?" At her urging, an elderly woman (Idella Haywood) reluctantly steps up. "Now Mrs. Haywood," Laurie prompts encouragingly, "the Reverend told me that God said it's okay to be prepared, didn't he? Well, all right then. Now

I'm gonna prepare you!" Reassured, her pupil grasps her weapon, then slams the dummy, first in the chest, then—repeatedly—in the groin. Pleased as punch, she high fives Grier as her friends and neighbors yelp approval.

To paraphrase George Lipsitz, "by using race [and, I'd add, gender and age] as a way of disrupting and restructuring genre conventions," doesn't "a new spin on an old story" briefly flicker into view? (Lipsitz 1998, 210, 215). Surely scenes like this one make it easier to see, if only for an instant, how *gender-bounded*, white-dominated, and youth-oriented critical considerations of strong women have been!

Grier's three decades of roles challenge generalities. First a hot action babe, now a cool action mama, a role model for generations past, present, and surely future, she deserves credit for her acting skill, longevity, and intelligence. Not for nothing does Roger Ebert compare her to Sean Connery, saying, "she knows how to keep her action in character, make it believable. She remained likable in those roles while doing some truly horrible things to her enemies."

That he snidely concludes, "she should have done them to her directors," nonetheless indicates how stark the differences are for black female and white male stars in action (Ebert, cited in Farber 1983, 4). Given her devotion to her craft, it's easy to understand why Grier says she would love to work with Meryl Streep and Jackie Chan.[42] Sadly, she's never been given the chance to do so, and she has never been offered anywhere near the quality, size, or range of roles that Connery has.

In the final analysis, then, hers is a damning example of "the primary place that race has in all of Hollywood's considerations of gender" (Green 1998, 239, note 32).

NOTES

Thanks to the participants of the Columbia Film Seminar and to audience members at a 2003 SCMS panel on "Action Heroes/Heroines and the Mojo of Race" for their comments. Paula Massood and Raiford Guins provided valuable bibliographic and film tips. Thanks especially to Omayra Cruz and Marie Caudie Beltrán for sharing their work on Pam Grier and Latina actresses, respectively, and to Krin Gabbard for sharing his work on gender and race in 1990s films. Last but not least, warm thanks to Yvonne Tasker for her work on related issues and for her illuminating observations as respondent at the Columbia Film Seminar.

1. While Brown draws extensively on Tasker (1993), the phrase "hard body hardware heroines" is his, and is obviously meant to recall the earlier work of Jeffords (1984) on 1980s male action stars. See Brown 1996, 52–71. See also Tasker 1993 and Jeffords 1993.

2. Because so much work concentrates on female stars from the 1980s on, Singer's work on serial queens, Johnston's discussion of 1940s pirate molls, Taves's mention of women in adventure films, and Neale's survey of action antecedents are eminently useful. See Singer 1990, 91–129, Johnston 1975, 36–44, Taves 1993, and Neale 2000, especially 52–60.

3. Grier, quoted on an MTV special on the DVD version of *Jackie Brown*. Academic critics split over how they define Grier, but even those who emphasize her macho attributes also somehow acknowledge her femininity. Reid (1993, 87), for example, finds Grier "a physically

threatening but sexually appealing Amazon." Guerrero (1993, 97) says she is a "black female superheroin[e] configured along the *macho* lines of the black action-fantasy heroes." Tasker (1993, 21) refers to the "hybridity" of masculine/feminine attributes in her personae.

4. As Williams (2001, 5) observes: "The [race] card has been in play whenever racial abuse is invoked to cast one racially constituted group as the victim of another. It would seem, then, that there is no single race card; rather, there is a history of mutually informing, perpetually trumping, race cards animating a long tradition of black and white racial melodrama."

5. Grier is one of very few black actresses to be nominated for a Golden Globe as best actress (for *Jackie Brown*). She won the Phoenix Award from the Black Cinema Society for career achievement.

6. See Salvo 1976, 48–54, Kincaid 1975, 49–53, Eimer 1998, 18, and Rickey 1981, 42.

7. See Guerrero 1993, especially 97–100, and Reid 1993, especially 86–88. See also Robinson 1998, 1–12, Mayne 2000, 115–145, and Cruz 2002. Mask (2001, 97–167) is working on a book that includes Grier, based on her dissertation.

8. Williams cites Brooks (1995, 29). For Williams (2001, 7), as for Brooks, the "icon of home" is a not a person but a place which "helps establish the 'space of innocence' of its virtuous victims."

9. Studio publicity for *Coffy* ("Synopsis" 1973, 2) described Grier as "part Afro, part Mexican, part Indian . . . part Filipino [and] yet all vengeance." See also Kincaid 1975, 50. Arguably, as someone of "mixed blood" (listing African, Asian, Caucasian, and American Indian ancestors), Grier also serves as model for younger male stars with multi-ethnic appeal, among them Keanu Reeves and Vin Diesel.

10. The studies of Ripley and Sarah Connor as mothers are too numerous to list. See, for example, Tasker 1993, 65–88.

11. There is somewhat less nudity in *Foxy Brown* and *Friday Foster*, but both offer glimpses of Grier, completely naked.

12. The only exception is Grier's girl gladiator film, *The Arena* (Steve Carver, 1974).

13. Robinson argues that Grier impersonated Angela Davis in all her prison and blaxploitation work.

14. According to Robinson (1998, 5), "Only Black women possessed the savage, primordial instinct of self-survival to resist sexual degradation and their male predators." Tasker (1993, 21) notes that "it is in part Grier's blackness . . . that opens up, through notions of black animality, the production of an aggressive female heroine within existing traditions of representation."

15. See Jack Hill's commentary on the DVD version of *Foxy Brown*.

16. According to Hill's DVD commentary, this scene was the first time that women stunt artists appeared, and they relished getting the chance to "fight." For an insightful and detailed commentary on the sequence and Inyang Etang's appropriation of it in *Badass Supermama*, see Hankin 2002, 81–113.

17. Tag lines for *Foxy Brown* and *Friday Foster* followed suit: "She's MURDER 'Foxy' style"; "She's smoother 'n satin and sexier 'n sin. . . . A pinch of sugar and a kiss of spice and, for an ace she keeps a cold steel .38 in a nice warm place."

18. For a similar argument regarding gender and Stephanie Rothman's work for AIP and, especially, New World Productions, see Cook (1976, 122–127). For a similar argument regarding race, see Lipsitz 1998.

19. See also Jacobson 1975, 44.

20. That Charlotte attacks men with less rhyme or reason than Coffy, Foxy, or Friday did makes her seem truly crazy. Perhaps she's a lesbian? In the book the film is based on, Charlotte lives with a rough-looking older woman who is described as bisexual. See Stacy and Hale 1986, 55.

21. See also Rickey 1981, 42.

22. For her stage roles, Grier altered her body more drastically still, in 1990 gaining eighty pounds to play Frankie in *Frankie and Johnny in the Clair de Lune* because, she said, "I

wanted to improve my acting and expand my repertoire . . . When you're thin and glamorous all you get is the shallow roles, the pretty 'F me' parts" (Schubert 1998, 53).

23. The comedies are *Bill and Ted's Bogus Journey* (Peter Hewitt, 1991) and *Fakin' Da Funk* (Timothy Chey, 1997).

24. See McHugh 2001, 193–218.

25. Watching Mario Van Peebles parade and preen in *Posse*, Hoberman ("New Jack Prairie," n.p.) derisively remarked: "The director-star keeps sneaking up on his stylish self in fractured 360-degree pans (a reminder that the anagram of Posse is Poses)."

26. See Ebert's commentary on the Collector's Edition DVD version of *Jackie Brown*. *Jackie Brown*'s emphasis on romance is especially apparent by comparison with Grier's blaxploitation movies: Tarantino's film contains very little graphic violence. See further Andrew 1999, 334–340.

27. On gangsta films, see Smith-Shomade 2003, 25–40.

28. See further Holmlund 2002, 51–67, 182–184.

29. Queer characters appear in none of the other films, save in *Holy Smoke*. There, to make P. J. Jealous, Ruth briefly flirts with a lesbian in a bar. Of course, P. J.'s cross-dressing near film's end is certainly queer, if also all about heterosexual power relations.

30. That Grier is so frequently associated with singers is no coincidence: many 1990s and 2000 films rely on world and hip hop music connections. In the 1980s, moreover, Grier often provided vocals for commercial jingles and for artists like Quincy Jones. In 1996 she appeared with Snoop Doggy Dogg in the music video "It's a Doggy Dogg World." The performance netted her 7,000 pieces of mail (Schubert 1998, 53). See also Braxton 1995, 4, 31–32.

31. On Jennifer Lopez, see further Holmlund 2002, 117–122, 194–198 and Negrón-Muntaner 1997, 189–194.

32. Bogle (1980, 190) suggests that the blaxploitation Grier was a favorite pin-up of black college boys. Guerrero maintains that audiences for these movies were predominantly comprised of black, inner-city, adolescent males (1993, 98). Reid (1993, 87) argues the films were made to engage male fantasies.

33. See Freydberg 1995, 236.

34. See Quentin Tarantino's commentary on the Collector's Edition DVD version of *Jackie Brown*.

35. See, for example, Leab 1976, 258, Lott 1997, 86, and Reid 1993, 90.

36. Similarly, Mims charges that the NAACP preferred "films like *Sounder* which portrayed blacks as 'servile and defeatist'" ("1970–1975," 128, translation mine).

37. See, for example, Sims 2000, especially 160–167, and Dunye 1998, 145–148. My students, too, often tell me how much their moms, not just their dads, loved Coffy, Foxy, and Friday.

38. See Diones 1997, 253: "Grier's toughness, her confidence, her raw sexuality announced a new direction for African-American women. . . . You can still detect her influence in the wise-ass bravado of Salt-N-Pepe, Lil'Kim, and any number of other rap divas."

39. See also Singleton 1996, 40.

40. See Gabbard 2004, 143–176.

41. Grier remarked similarly in *Jet*: "I really believe that I did open a door at the time and other women weren't ready to be as physical. . . . There was still a mindset of not being as independent . . . it was okay to be tough, okay to be smart, okay to be assertive and still be feminine and soft and caring" (Grier, cited in Sims 2000, 155). See also Grier 1998, 53.

42. See Braxton 1995, 31.

Patricia Mellencamp

Crisis and Fear at the Movies and in Life, or On Being as Old as My Grandmother

In life, women over sixty are everywhere, in the sequined majority on cruise ships and in drab tatters at homeless shelters. We live longer than men, and we have less money. Although the joke is that we talk too much, we must become rather quiet with age—for not only are we not seen, we are not heard. So it is not surprising that in places of power like the upper echelons of business, law, and politics, older women are the exception; the older we are, the more exceptional we become. In representation, particularly electronic media, sixty-year old women are even rarer: on TV, they make irregular appearances; at the movies, they are largely absent onscreen, yet they're in the audience.

Who are these older women sitting in the dark, in the movie theater?[1] They are missing, almost discarded, persons, at least in the media. Maybe they are dancing on cruise ships with paid escorts or pushing stolen carts through city streets or looking out of drab windows in retirement homes. Or just maybe they are living intelligent, exciting lives, free at last to make their own choices and pursue their own talents. These sixty-year-olds have no desire whatsoever to be thirty or forty, with all the insecurity and duty of those decades. But they do want to be smart, interesting, healthy, in shape, and stylish. They wish that someone had told them that this would be the finest decade—intellectually, spiritually, and sexually a triple whammy.

At least this has been my experience as a white, educated woman living in the United States during an unsettling time. The last thing I expected was to be enjoying this decade so much—despite its disquieting politics. Why did I dread my sixtieth birthday? The following scattered thoughts attempt to explain the way media culture, my field of expertise, worked me over. Despite my having written about women and aging, I simultaneously incorporated the media's negative representations into my perception of myself. Feminism was right—it is not easy to bring unconscious thoughts and patterns into awareness, and hence to dispel their power. But this is what women must do for themselves.

degeneration of the heart muscle. There was no explanation and no cure other than an eventual heart transplant. While Rob's life had been an ongoing series of medical crises, with forty-one broken bones and several surgeries (due to osteogenesis imperfecta), this was primordial. God had upped the ante to live or die (or so I thought). I can still recall the pounding, constricting terror I felt each day when I walked down the hospital corridor to his room. I tried to pretend I wasn't literally "panic stricken." But I was. At night I would sit bolt upright in bed, awakened by fear.

My anxiety was exacerbated by the lack of diagnosis and prognosis. This was a story without origin, without linear progress (improvement or cure), without cause-effect logic, without closure, and without a future. This long-term catastrophe had no time frame—it could be weeks, years, even decades. It was a continuous, indeterminate crisis, a contradiction in terms, at least for Western rational logic. Paralyzed by fear, I counted on my mind, ironically enough, to get me through.[2] I turned my frantic thoughts to intellectual sources for consolation.

I read Sigmund Freud, then Walter Benjamin, the German cultural critic, and René Thom, the French mathematical theorist, on catastrophe, shock, and anxiety. It all made perfect sense. My life had resembled Thom's words: "Our everyday may be a tissue of ordinary catastrophes, but our death is a generalized catastrophe" (Thom 1975, 251). My reaction to Rob's initial diagnosis was textbook Freud. As the doctor spoke, I began to feel panic. Anxiety is *very* physical. I remember visually receding, down a long, narrow wind tunnel. Sound became barely audible, only a reverberation. My body was separated from reality as if encased in thick glass. A shield, like a cellophane membrane, distanced me from both the world and my own senses. Then it blanketed me in exhaustion. I slept for two days, afraid to wake up. If I didn't open my eyes, this trauma would go away. (The relations among perception, knowledge, and pain were unstable, fluctuating. If I don't see it, I won't know it, and if I don't know it, it won't hurt. The regression back to early childhood confusion between presence, absence, and perception—kids hiding by covering their eyes—was a momentary escape.)

As Freud put it, I had "two reactions to real [as distinguished from neurotic] danger"; the first was "an affective reaction, an outbreak of anxiety," the other was "a protective action" (Freud 1969, 20:165). Or as Samuel Weber said, the shield is porous. It has a "double function" that protects us "against excess excitation . . . and also transmits excitation from the outside to the inside of the organism" (1982, 143).

One solace for my helplessness was to seek further information—doing research on heart transplants and talking with medical specialists. But science offered no hope or solution. Because I couldn't escape or quiet my thoughts, I sublimated, displaced, avoided, whatever: I wrote a book, *High Anxiety: Catastrophe, Scandal, Age, and Comedy*, about catastrophic, obsessive logic, with an analysis of television, electronic culture, as both shock and shield.[3] Although I included a cancer scare, a medical misdiagnosis, in the first pages, the book ignores the true catastrophe that is at its core. To be honest, I don't think I saw the connection until the manuscript was finished two years later, in 1990, when I realized that the shield that protected me was also my problem—an outer crust where all my fear, attachments, identifications, addictions, and obsessions had accumulated. It bombarded me with danger; it could not protect me from my own mind.

In "Inhibitions, Symptoms and Anxiety" (1926), a late Freudian text long overlooked by contemporary cultural theory, anxiety was a physical response to a danger situation, real or remembered, fictive or factual. The amount of stimulation rises to an unpleasurable level without being mastered or discharged (1969, 20:137). Anxiety is a situation of helplessness, predicated on "missing someone who is loved and longed for." "Longing turns into anxiety" (Freud 1969, 20:136). Thoughts of Rob, memories really, would trigger my original panic. In essence, emotion was inseparable from memory. As Freud had said, every affect was a reminiscence (Freud 1969, 20:133).

In retrospect, what intrigues me is this denial, even repudiation, of the personal experience of a crisis—the thread through this essay. These small thoughts are what Weber calls an "aftereffect," which repeats and alters events, rendering them "psychically real" (Weber 1982, 147). This process of disfiguration is stoppable for Freud only by myth and Eros or thanatos, or by what Weber calls "the death drive as another name for a story" (Weber 1982, 145). For now, I agree that the death drive is inspirational, and that love can turn life into legend. But I am getting ahead of myself.

For the longer span of my life, intimately and intellectually, crises made life more exciting. I created drama, even chaos, in personal affairs. Like so many visual culture critics whose aesthetic came from events that rocked universities in the 1960s, an era of social causes and political movements forged in crises, I had taken my academic cue from Walter Benjamin, the German cultural critic whose translated writings, situated in Europe in the 1930s, were published in translation in the United States in 1968, when I was in graduate school. Like Benjamin, I wanted history to change—particularly for women. And shock and discontinuity were central to his determination of *changing* history. In fact, crisis in the form of battles and wars is the primary story of history itself—starring and primarily written by men. Why should women's history be any different? I can only answer my blockheadedness with "?!"

When Benjamin wrote about technological culture, or modernity, in the 1920s and 1930s, he looked to the editing theory of conflict advanced by the

Russian film director Sergei Eisenstein around the same time. And he looked to the recent writings of his Austrian neighbor, Sigmund Freud, particularly "Inhibitions, Symptoms and Anxiety" (Benjamin 1969). Freud described a thought process of fear and anxiety, while Benjamin provided the social context that fueled this mental logic. For both theorists of crisis (Eisenstein being the third), the danger situation came from the modern world, from war (particularly World War I), crowds, new communication technologies, and industrial, assembly line production. Technological, social change was the key for Benjamin, who examined public spaces and city dramas. For Freud, looking at private, familial dramas, along with victims of World War I (and shell shock), the personal experience of loss was central. For both, crisis was in the act of perception—where "I see" is linked to "I understand." Cultural studies from the 1970s through the 1990s embraced Benjamin with rarely a mention of (his debt to) Freud. But Freud's treatise on anxiety is (or should be) attracting renewed interest in the social sphere and the current War on Terror, just as intimate experiences are beginning to count as useful knowledge, even evidence.[4]

Like other early boomers born to Cold War logic and nuclear fear, which held out a Soviet attack as imminent danger to 1950s U.S. suburbia, I had been taught to think catastrophically—globally, historically, and personally. Later, as a good consumer, I had also learned obsessive thought, a logic of more; the same was never good enough. The logic inevitably turns against the self—"I" can never be good enough.

The similarity between the military, corporate, and psychoanalytic logics of obsession, all driven by fear, is truly uncanny. Although events in the world can trigger them, our thoughts perpetuate, exaggerate, and even create fear. The United States attacked another country, Iraq, based on fear—that the country had nuclear capabilities and "weapons of mass destruction." The stock market, presumed to be rational like the military, is continually roiled by fear, which spreads among Wall Street brokers like a virus.

Fear, Aging, Death

Gradually I realized that anxiety production had imploded even further. The logic of crisis has been applied to virtually anything. The same structure of thought can apply to a war, an earthquake, a faculty meeting, being late, being overweight, being forty or sixty, and growing old. We have been trained to think obsessively, compulsively—as the norm, not the exception. At least this was true for me, and it dovetailed with my addiction. I think it is the way many women in our culture view the process of aging, dealing with it only by denial—which can take many forms, particularly cosmetic surgery and various injection procedures like Botox or Restylane. This ritual of pain can become obsessive, a costly compulsion, and hence endless (except for death). The ritual is paradoxical—to handle the psychic and social trauma of aging, one inflicts physical trauma on the body, especially the face, our own face, and then compares it to other images. The trauma becomes real; yet we are in control, it is self-inflicted; we do it for and to ourselves. It is deeply masochistic. Ironically, the best cosmetic surgery or treatment will remain invisible, a secret of aging.

Fear of death is, of course, a great explanation for negative representations and personal anxieties, although Freud denied that death was the general fear beneath specific fears (Freud 1969, 19:57–58). One way of dealing with fear is avoidance or denial, what Freud calls "negation." A thought reveals itself by the act of denial. Ironically, denial is one way Freud, like Western culture, deals with death. For Freud, the moment of death remained a mystery. He repeatedly asserts that "nothing resembling death can ever have been experienced; or if it has, as in fainting, it has left no observable traces behind" (1969, 20:130). "No human being really grasps it, and our unconscious has as little use now as it ever had for the idea of its own mortality." The "unconscious seems to contain nothing" that could imagine its own annihilation (1969, 20:129).

Although for Freud we cannot foresee our own death, the "primitive fear of the dead" (distinguished from fear of *death*) is "strong within us" (1969, 17:242). He encapsulates this fear in the experience of the "uncanny," which often occurs in relation to "death, dead bodies, and to the return of the dead" (1969, 17:241). The "uncanny," an experience where the boundaries between self and other, alive or dead, real or not are blurred, what Freud called doubling, is as close as Freud comes to imagining death—and it is inextricable from fear, or horror, Freud's perennial and constant fear of castration and the loss of vision. The uncanny is an experience where duality, difference, and separation—young or old, man or woman, you or me—become unclear, and frightening.

The concept of the double—a lack of certainty between dualities, an inability to distinguish between subject and object, between self and other—as the ultimate source of fear, an "uncanny experience," is instructive. Freud's thought, and Western logic in general, depends on dualities, difference, and separation. In the "uncanny," the perception, or status, of these qualities is uncertain, and fear is the result for Freud.

In *Beyond the Pleasure Principle*, Freud distinguishes "'fright,' 'fear' and 'anxiety,'" which are "not synonymous." "'Anxiety' describes a particular state of expecting the danger or preparing for it, even though it may be unknown. 'Fear' requires a definite object of which to be afraid." "Fright" is the "state of being surprised when danger is unexpected" (1961, 12). All three responses are defined in terms of knowledge, temporality, and expectation. In anxiety, we have some knowledge, although no object; in fear, we have knowledge and an object for it; in fright, we have neither knowledge nor an object.

Anxiety concerns expectation and the future, fear remembers the past, and fright exists in the present.

Hollywood capitalizes on these fears—particularly fear of the dark and of loud noises. The sound track increases modulation to create "scary" moments in even the most benign children's films. Horror movies are predicated on re-creating raw fear. Thrillers play on Freud's distinctions. The films of Alfred Hitchcock are portraits of techniques for eliciting fear, fright, and anxiety, almost textbook Freud. In fact, I suspect that the British film scholar Peter Wollen's intriguing taxonomy of mystery, suspense, and surprise or shock, derived from an analysis of Hitchcock's films, is indebted to Freud's distinction, although he makes no note of it. Wollen's analysis involves an emotional relay between the film viewer and the film protagonist based on narrative time and knowledge. In suspense, the "spectator knows the secret but the character does not"; in mystery, while the spectator and the character know a secret exists, they don't know what it is; and in shock, the spectator (and most likely the character) does not know there is a secret (Wollen 1982, 40–49; 47). Suspense equates with fear, mystery with anxiety, and shock with fright. All three involve knowledge and perception, primarily sight but also sound.

Regarding anxiety and the status of the object, Freud makes a further distinction in an addendum to "Inhibitions, Symptoms, Anxiety" (1969, 20:169). Pain is the "actual reaction to loss of object," while anxiety is the "reaction to the danger which that loss entails . . . and to the danger of the loss of that object" (20:170). Regarding Rob's heart, I felt anxiety most of the time; but when I worried, when I imagined losing him, I felt pain. I kept crossing the borders between real and remembered, fact and fiction, projecting into the future. Freud wonders, "When does separation from an object produce anxiety, when does it produce mourning, and when does it produce . . . only pain?" In my thoughts, I experienced all of these emotions—until I could no longer bear their stultifying weight. Freud's words were prescient: "Every affect is a reminiscence." Emotions and past memory are linked. If I could reinterpret the memory, perhaps I could change the emotions.

In "The 'Uncanny,'" Freud distinguishes between "the uncanny that we actually experience and the uncanny that we merely picture or read about" (1969, 17:247). The *experience* is infinitely rarer than its representation. In addition, things that are not uncanny in fiction will be "in real life" (17:249). This distinction between representation and experience, real life, is, for me, critical. The theoretical models we derived from Freud (who argued from personal insights) were applied to movies and books more than to our lives. With aging, however, our experience is inextricable from the representation of aging, on screen or in the mirror. We measure our mirror image against the magazine cover models, the movie star's close-up, the television celebrity interview—air-brushed, soft-focused, high-lighted, surgically altered. This mirror image, often magnified, is our reality. But our aging face (our primary emblem of time) is *only* a reflection (from a mirror or a pair of eyes), a representation. In a telling footnote, Freud describes his experience of seeing himself unexpectedly in a mirror—he is shabby, old, and for a minute, an unfamiliar stranger (1969, 17:248, note 1). His aging is an uncanny experience of misrecognition between self and other. It is real, it is a representation, and it frightens him.

For Freud, anxiety, like fear and fright, was related to perception. "The first determinant of anxiety . . . is loss of perception of the object (which is equated with loss of the object itself)" (1969, 20:170). Youth can be imagined or represented as a lost object, even a loss of perception, rather than as a subjective process or a passage through time. Our face in the mirror can become unfamiliar, causing anxiety and even fear. The magnifying mirrors necessary for makeup as vision blurs with age turn the face into a ruined landscape, a distorted image. Or we look at old photographs, which we may not have previously liked, with fondness. We imagine that we "looked" better then. But we were only younger, not better. As Freud tells us in "Mourning and Melancholia," we displace libido from an object (our reminiscences of the past, or our youthful selves) and withdraw it into the ego, resulting in "an identification of the ego with the abandoned object. Thus the shadow of the object fell upon the ego . . . judged . . . as an object, the forsaken object . . . An object-loss was transformed into an ego loss" (Freud 1969, 14:249).[5]

The modeling of ego or self as an object rather than a subject, an object defined by the physical body, especially the face, which applies to the history of women in cinema, with age portrayed as a series of losses rather than achievements for women, says much about the logic of enduring multiple plastic surgeries and tells us about the fears of aging, which can be a trauma. We imagine that we have or will become the "forsaken object." *This* anxiety, or fear, is supported by life as children grow up and leave home, and by social reality, as older men replace their initial women with younger versions.

Aging can be a "situation of non-satisfaction," predicated on missing someone, the youthful self (associated with one's children or nuclear family, or even the family of childhood). For Freud writes: "It is precisely in women that the danger-situation of loss of object seems to have remained the most effective" (1969, 20:143). Women's "loss" of youth as if it were a tangible object, not a productive time, measured by our faces and bodies, is a manufactured fear that verges on a national obsession-compulsion. Obsession, based on reproaches, guilt, and shame, is applicable to the aging body. Physical changes linked to sexual attractiveness become the anxieties and fears that drive the marketing of age remedies. This nexus of personal fears locates our identity in our bodily image, in our appearance, and in our relation to the material world. Marketing turns obsession into normality by concealing the cultural as the natural. That our standard comes from the movies, that it is historical and therefore changes, is forgotten. If all the female stars of movies suddenly had lines and wrinkles, which has never been true of Hollywood, the ideal would change. The ideal that is projected on women, by the look of others and by their own look into the mirror, could and would change. Despite all the historical bodily changes over time, from tiny rosebud lips to wide, protruding lips, from short and round to tall and thin, from Lillian Gish and Mary Pickford, cast in their early teens because they had no wrinkles, the female face has been smooth, high-lighted, and air-brushed, vastly different from male faces, wherein lines and sags can and do represent character. Think Al Pacino, with sunken eyes, or Jack Nicholson, with jowls and balding. And then try and imagine a female counterpart. Furthermore, there is desirability, or being dumped for and replaced by a younger woman.

At the Movies

This is the premise of the 1996 film, *The First Wives' Club*. Goldie Hawn, Diane Keaton, and Bette Midler, "acting their age" (mid-forties), reunite at the funeral of a college friend who committed suicide. Her husband left her for a younger woman. The same fate has befallen her three college friends. Hawn's movie producer husband has left her for a young actress; Midler's electronics entrepreneur for his young secretary; and Keaton's advertising executive for their mutual therapist. These women unite and uncover information to extract "justice" from their former husbands. They take Ivana Trump literally: they don't get mad, or even, they get everything! And they are very funny along the way, all three being/acting comic personae they perfected in previous films.

The delight of the film is watching these three powerful women, who have become producers and directors with real influence in Hollywood, talking about the double standards of age. I found it deeply moving to watch them project positive energy together as friends. Along with women over thirty, female friendship has been a rarity for Hollywood cinema, obsessed with the youthful couple and romance or male buddies as its narrative has been for over one hundred years.

Eight years later, Diane Keaton, in her fifties, returned in a romantic comedy for older folks, *Something's Gotta Give*—this time with a comic nude scene. She plays a famous, wealthy, stylish, yet unpretentious Broadway playwright, living happily alone in a gorgeous summer house in the Hamptons. The woman and the house are elegant yet comfortable. Two men fall in love with her—a sixty something Jack Nicholson, paunchy, balding, cigar-smoking music/mogul womanizer, currently dating her daughter, Amanda Peet, and a late thirties Keanu Reeves, one-woman, slim, tight-bodied medical doctor who loves her work and takes her to Paris. In Paris, Keaton picks Nicholson (while rudely dumping Reeves)—a choice that baffled many older women in the audience. The film's last scene is a family one—a dinner with her husband (presumably), daughter, son-in-law, and grandchild. She has become a grandmother, Nicholson a step-grandfather. This is progress for cinema.

Keaton's choice of men aside, a fifty-year-old woman is not only the star, but she is also the lead in a romantic comedy, a rare sighting indeed. Her love scenes with Reeves are presented as "normal," not aberrant. Another radical element of the film is its revelation of lines and wrinkles on Keaton's face—although minimal, there in the close-ups, they are not air-brushed or high-lighted or surgically removed. She is in her fifties and it shows, quite beautifully. Granted, she is not your ordinary fifty-year-old woman—she has no gray hairs and is pencil thin. But compare this portrait to Norma Desmond and the distance is remarkable. We have come a long way, baby. This woman is not only living and working and *writing* productively alone, with loving relationships with her sister and her daughter, she is attractive and desirable to men, due to her achievements as well as her appearance. Okay, granted that seeing her fifty-year-old naked body is the film's shock (not!), but unlike Jack Nicholson's saggy butt, her body looks great!

Sunset Boulevard is the classic film portrayal of aging as trauma (and scandal) for women. It focuses on a silent cinema star, Norma Desmond, who has enclosed herself in her dark mansion, watching her old films. Fantasizing a comeback, she is writing a screenplay about Salome. Billy Wilder and Charles Brackett won an Academy Award for this original screenplay, which was first offered to Mae West. Then Mary Pickford decided that the seduction of a younger man was not appropriate for her image. The part finally went to Gloria Swanson. Like Pickford, Swanson performed most of her highly stylized performances in silent cinema, including the films she produced under the aegis of Joseph Kennedy during their affair. Swanson retired from films in 1934, when she was thirty-seven. She was fifty-two (although looking forty) when she made *Sunset Boulevard*, ancient for a female star by cinema's double standard. In cameo appearances, Cecil B. DeMille and Erich Von Stroheim, both directors of silent films, look light years older than Swanson—particularly the bald, paunchy DeMille, who appears as himself. These old men are productive and working, while her desire to make another movie is represented as pathetic. No one takes it seriously. Like a female starring in a film at fifty-two, her screenplay is also a joke and a delusion.

In order to entrap a young, handsome screenwriter (William Holden as Joe Gillis, who wandered into her lair while fleeing creditors), she hires him to rewrite her screenplay, moves him into her mansion, bribes him with expensive gifts, and attempts suicide to seal her need for him. Later, he will be rescued by a younger woman, Susan, a reader for a studio who wants to work with him on a script. Susan and Norma both fall in love with this passive, whining failure. Two women fighting over the same man is a familiar scenario for cinema, as in, for example, *Singin' in the Rain*. Usually the star ends up with the guy. However, this film presents the older woman/younger man scenario as grotesque, improper, almost incestuous. But just reverse the scene to the older man with the much younger woman, say in two subsequent Wilder films, where *Sabrina* casts Humphrey Bogart and *Love in the Afternoon* casts Gary Cooper, both with a teenaged-looking Audrey Hepburn, and the double standard of age applied to women in cinema becomes apparent. As women age, they become grotesque and pathetic; men become powerful and attractive.

The older woman is also measured against the younger woman, the proper partner for Holden. While Swanson is all masquerade, makeup, and melodramatic affectation, the younger woman is natural, pure, and, hence, real.

Rather than this old scenario of two women desiring and fighting over the same man, I can see another possibility—that they work together rather than compete for the man. Rather than killing the young screenwriter in a fit of jealousy, Swanson hires the young woman to work on *Salome* with her. They co-produce a successful film about women pioneers in the silent cinema days, causing a flood of women to become interested in filmmaking. There were role models in history—they just didn't make it to the history books until recently. They write great ensemble and starring roles for women over forty—amazing. Rather than star in her film, Swanson plays the director. She hires her old friend, Pickford, for the lead. The story is no longer so seamy. Mae West makes a pivotal cameo appearance as Pickford's close friend. Von Stroheim has retired, along with DeMille. The screenplay tells great stories about their idiosyncrasies and affectations, mentioning the fact that DeMille had a female co-writer on most of his films. Hmmmmm. The male screenwriter, the William Holden character, vanishes into obscurity. Although he is technically dead, shot in the opening scene, floating face down in the swimming pool, the old *Sunset Boulevard* is told from his point of view. In the new film, the director's voice tells the tale. The whining, judgmental male voice-over that tells the story of women's aging as a tale of decline, is silenced, and is replaced by an older woman's voice, seasoned, witty, and very wise.

Rather than the close-up of Swanson as a deranged murderer, the film concludes with a close-up of Pickford, looking out at the audience, smiling, then laughing, the soft lines on her face testifying to the wisdom and character of her age, another stage of beauty. This is the role that Annette Benning almost plays in *Being Julia*. This film reverses the equation, making the younger woman the foolish one, without the beauty and seasoned talent of the older stage (and movie) star, Benning. She controls the plot, and indeed, the entire film. It is a brilliant portrayal of a powerful and clever woman—yet one woman still undoes another. Unlike the courage of Bette Davis in *All About Eve*, playing the older actress against a more beautiful younger actress, Ann Baxter, Benning plays against a horsey looking actress—her beauty suggested but not really there, just enough off.

In Life . . .

In 2005, I was struck with the comeback role of Jane Fonda, after a fifteen-year absence, in *Monster-in-Law*, as well as her visibility as author of her best-selling autobiography. In the movie, although cast against the much-younger Jennifer Lopez, she very much holds her own as a stylish actress adept at comedy. I became intrigued with the photograph of her face on the cover of her book, showing few marks of age, and compared it with mine. Even after so many years of feminism, I was fixated upon her actual appearance, especially the skin around her eyes and lips. During the following month, I had a number of treatments upon my own face. To be honest, I was not aware of this coincidence until just now when I realized that I was emulating Fonda as I used to do with clothing.

The face (distinct from the head), its contours and masquerade, is another way of thinking Freud's protective shield. Makeup and cosmetic surgery can be protection from the negative social representations that our eyes and ears register as responses (our own and others) to our aging faces. As Freud said, anxiety is a matter of perception. I will never know whether my personal anxiety triggered my earlier fear of aging or vice versa. But as I worried about Rob's heart, I began to focus on the bags under my eyes, which I would compare to the eyes of others. I had reduced my identity to a small area of skin, which was ridiculous until I calculated the astronomical profits made on this square inch by the cosmetics and plastic surgery industries. The compulsive workings of my mind and the obsessive logics of culture coalesced into a logic of contradiction, eat/diet, spend/save, be old/look young. Obsession, derived from thought and the fear of catastrophe, and how it was culturally constructed, became intellectually clear.

Everything from the stock market and the *Wall Street Journal* to plastic surgery, from the funeral, cosmetic, makeup, lingerie, drug, gossip, and fashion industries fit my model. In fact, there was *nothing* in popular culture my model of obsession could not explain. All went into my book, *High Anxiety: Catastrophe, Scandal, Age, and Comedy*, which I still consider a helpful analysis of the way television, or media culture, produces fear and anxiety. It is not just terrorist acts that are making us fearful. It is also the way television and media culture are re-presenting those acts to us. Media create events for us that demand more media time to explain them. But explanations rarely come, usually repetitions of the same, made by a variety of talking heads, speaking banalities with authority. On the news shows, the female talking heads are increasingly glamorous, becoming more so the longer they are on the show. Several women who began their stints on CNBC as plain to unattractive Janes have emerged in 2005 as glamour girls. The female reporters on the Fox news channel reminded me of Dallas Cowboy cheerleaders, cheering on "the boys" in the War in Iraq.

Good for me, thought I. I've mastered fear, and *all* the cultural world, through intellect. While my analysis of television's logic still stands, and is pertinent to contemporary political rhetoric that is also producing fear, I failed to see how my thoughts, now in overdrive, were still my problem. Furthermore, reading the book produced anxiety! I had mimicked TV's logic too well. Although I had *analyzed* my emotional state, nothing had changed. My anxiety level was high. Likewise, while Freud always plots an intriguing situation, his conclusions can be crashing letdowns, as Gilles Deleuze and Felix Guattari, the French cultural theorists, often said. Other than blaming the past (especially family members and childhood), Freud's causal interpretations (infantile sexuality, particularly fear of castration) are of little help in changing anything in the present. How could I live with any tranquility, or happiness? I longed for equanimity, for serenity (experiences *and* qualities), but saw them beyond my life's reach.

Then I had a startling and simple insight. I realized that Rob's heart condition was not my biggest problem. My *fear* for his heart was my greatest problem, and my anxiety magnified his worry, creating pain for both of us. Despite my reassuring words, he could feel my fear. On top of this, my desire for a cure or a miracle made acceptance impossible. Stasis was not good enough. This was my turning point, the pivotal moment when my life began to change. My thoughts were determining my reality, not the other away around.

I imagined myself on a journey through fear that began with facing death. But my fear was so deep and archaic that the mind couldn't touch it. Besides, my noisy, restless mind was part, if not most, of the problem. In 1990, out of desperation, I went to India, to a small, poor village outside Bombay, called Ganeshpuri (after the elephant-god Ganesh, the remover of obstacles), where I had the darshan, a personal meeting, a sharing of a glance, a word, an acknowledgment, of a brilliant woman, Gurumayi Chidvilasananda, who became my teacher. I stayed in the ashram for two weeks, sleeping on a cot on an outdoor balcony with many other women. Fortified with ancient texts and the practice of meditation, I began to recover from fear, and eventually from logics of duality, difference, and separation. Like Germaine Greer in her book, *The Change*, I was learning to shift my attention away from my body ego toward the soul. But Greer couldn't find any role models, "no signposts to show the way" (12). I found wisdom everywhere, especially in Gurumayi Chidvilasananda who taught me that the senses, abetted by the mind, ever restless with desire, move outwardly, seeking gratification and pleasure in the world, never finding anything that lasts, while the soul, cherishing tranquility and silence, turns inward, and at last finds happiness. I have experienced the beauty of stillness, the magnificence of silence, and the profound joy of contentment through meditation. It was bliss itself. But that's another story . . .

According to the Tao te Ching: "If you realize that all things change, there is nothing you will try and hold on to. If you aren't afraid of dying, there is nothing you cannot achieve."

NOTES

1. To children, women in their forties are older women. To men in their sixties and seventies, these are younger women. Take Jack Welch, the former CEO of General Electric, and Suzy Wetlaufer (the name alone a good reason for marriage), the sanctioned older man and younger woman coupling. Demi Moore, in her forties (and younger than Wetlaufer-Welch), is the older woman to her younger man, Ashton Kutcher (who should consider taking Moore's last name). After being fodder for the tabloids, recently the latter have been glamorously proclaimed in *Harper's Bazaar*. The Wetlaufer/Welches are a book-writing power couple interviewed with solemnity by a very old Dan Rather on *60 Minutes*, holding on to his job into his seventies unlike Barbara Walters.

2. I had just returned from the Betty Ford Center in Palm Springs and treatment for a grudgingly admitted addiction to valium. Seventeen years earlier, my gynecologist had prescribed this tranquilizer for my difficulty sleeping. I was a single parent, with little money, two children, one chronically ill with osteogenesis imperfecta, a full-time job, and no daycare. No wonder I had trouble sleeping! Over time, valium became a problem, not a solution, resulting in blackouts, suicidal thoughts of death. Then came the recovery years of skin-crawling anxiety.

3. It included an analysis of women's aging, and a long section on gossip, along with a brief history of *The National Enquirer* and defamation law.

4. Homi Bhabha is using anxiety as a basis for postcolonial theory, for example.

5. This is in Freud's comparison of the melancholic (a good description of an addict) and mourning, with the melancholic inflicting self-hatred as the result of low self-esteem: "The patient represents his ego to us as worthless, incapable of any achievement . . . He reproaches himself, vilifies himself" ("Mourning," 14: 246). This is developed further in Mellencamp 1992, 281.

Gay, Straight,
Queer, and Beyond

David Lugowski

Ginger Rogers and Gay Men?
Queer Film Studies, Richard Dyer,
and Diva Worship

Establishing "Lesbian and Gay" Film Studies

A central contribution to film analysis in recent decades has come from lesbian-gay-bisexual-transgendered (LGBT) and queer film studies as inflected by queer theory. The study of "gender" became that of "gender and sexuality." In a society that reads sexuality in terms of gender, masculinity and heterosexuality are linked in hegemonic discourses; masculinity-in-film is "ideally" white, male, bourgeois, Christian, and not physically challenged. Queer theory paralleled developments within critical race theory, cultural studies, postcolonial and film theory, and these discourses have informed each other compellingly. Analyses of film returned the favor, influencing these theories within their disciplines (literature, women's studies, area studies). I want to survey LGBT and queer film studies in dialogue with queer theory, and then segue into a case study illustrating the interplay of various strategies.

While one might open with Vito Russo's seminal *The Celluloid Closet*, queer theory aspires to both interdisciplinarity and an anti-foundationalist stance (as much as that is possible). Let's begin instead with historical absences, such as auteurism that disregarded sexuality or gender performance. Or ideological analysis that neglected the heterosexist oppression embodied in "boy meets girl" narratives, and studies that bypassed sexuality in avant-garde films. Theories of perception and realism ignored gender diversity and sexuality in the organization of image and sound, and the psychic needs film purported to fulfill. Psychoanalytic apparatus theory did not address qualities that might adhere to spectators removed from history and agency. Indeed, the ahistorical, universalizing, and Eurocentric master narratives of psychoanalysis—Western culture might have Greek myths and *Hamlet*, but did every African or Asian culture have similar stories?—relied heavily on *analogies* in speculating on film.

Ginger Rogers in her element, from her stage show in the 1970s. Photofest Film Archive.

Early feminism, eager to claim Dorothy Arzner as an auteur, neglected her lesbianism. Psychoanalytic feminism was similarly heterocentric in its sexual binaries: in Mulvey's thesis, the "male" gaze, presumed to be heterosexual, was a point of identification and a means of mastery over the "to-be-looked-at" female, also presumed to be heterosexual. But where did this leave lesbian or gay representation, queer artists, or bisexual spectators enjoying many "objects"? Even heterosexual women's pleasures were pigeonholed into a psychic transvestism.[1] In such theories and in others that flirted with how spectators bond with characters of the same sex, transvestism suggested queerness as a structuring absence within film studies until the 1990s.

Although other works had addressed the many-gendered thing that is spectatorship, *The Celluloid Closet* was a landmark, one well-situated to inspire scholars and activists fighting AIDS and Reagan-era homophobia. Russo did not pull any punches, denouncing what he called "the big lie" that lesbians and gays "do not exist." The book was an overtly political "coming out" as no previous book had been. And Russo did not let up, remarking in his 1987 revision that homophobia "may be more prevalent now than at any other time in our history" (Russo 1987, xii, 250). Effeminacy, however, occupied an ambiguous place in his work, and lesbian representation was far less considered than gay male imagery. Nonetheless, Russo had done graduate work in cinema studies at NYU, and his writing is consonant with what apparatus theory and feminism were producing. The appendix where he catalogues a necrology of gay characters' deaths, often by murder or suicide, signaled the thrust of his intervention, one still worth savoring for its anger toward homophobia.

Contemporaneous work was in dialogue with Russo's analysis of stereotypes. Essays collected by Richard Dyer for *Gays and Film* examined how "types" function iconographically, narratively, and socially (1984). Their place in propping up conservative terrains of understanding received attention, as did the challenges confronting lesbian artists and audiences. Dyer's volume, and Russo's, compiled filmographies of "lesbian and gay film." The question of what constitutes such cinema would need further thought, but seeing filmmakers using every format and venue possible helped. Amy Villarejo and Matthew Tinkcom summarize the goals of early gay and lesbian film studies: to point out how the media demonized images of homosexuals, to find moments when gay and lesbian desire appears, and to promote a lesbian and gay film culture (2001, 16). Harry Benshoff and Sean Griffin conceptualized such a culture in terms of textuality, readership, and authorship (2005). Does a story about homosexuality make a film queer? Do gay, lesbian, or otherwise queer characters do it? Both fiction films and documentaries, especially but not exclusively about AIDS, engaged with early critical discourse. But were films using mainstream techniques queer "enough," and was an overt subject matter required? This elusive yet omnipresent queerness could reside in the spectacle; cinema studies has emphasized how mise-en-scène, sound, and editing complicate films rather than always support storylines and characterizations. Whether intentional or not, a film having trouble maintaining "straight and narrow" ideologies might somehow be queer(ed).

Once queerness appeared via style, other boundaries were questioned. Queer cinema could exist in what Patricia White calls "retrospectatorship," a consideration of the very possibilities of representability, and a rereading of the traces, absences, and intertexts of cinema (1999). Camp, for example, drawn to things theatrical and excessive, both mocking and appropriating the culturally outmoded, was evaluated as a form of oppositional reading (Babuscio in Dyer 1984, 40–57). That said, was camp ultimately accepting of the status quo, was it misogynistic, or could it be progressive?

With these political strategies came a need to reconsider authorship. Where queers are concerned, tension exists between a need to (re)discover auteurs to add to the canon as part of a prideful history, and a poststructuralist "death of the author" gesture, knocking the (heterosexual) author off his (and it usually was "his") throne. Negotiating tensions has not been easy, but following auteur-structuralism and later theories, seeing authors as historical subjects, "brand names," and pleasurable textual effects has helped.

For Judith Mayne, "Dorothy Arzner" was not only a talented director who happened to be lesbian, but also a text that in a male-dominated field was negotiated in publicity, studio dealings, *and* her films. Discourses of lesbianism interact among aspects of her style, her collaborations with actresses and female writers, the presentation of her persona, and negotiations between her biography and work (Mayne 1994). It is not a matter of "intentions" either; Arzner was very cagey late in life in discussing lesbian-feminist angles to her work. After years of quiet living, who were these people coming at her, eager to claim her work in (re)writing women's history?

Critics have revisited Hollywood's LGB auteurs (James Whale, George Cukor), those from international art cinema (Chantal Akerman, Luchino Visconti), and the avant-garde (Kenneth Anger, Barbara Hammer). (Hollywood had no known transgendered directors, although cross-dressing Ed Wood makes a fascinating case at the fringes of popular culture.) Other queer readings (e.g., of Ford and Hawks) could no longer be negated by asserting a director's "straightness." It was never easy to reconcile critiques of homophobic institutions with our pleasures in films—Russo worshipped divas, but you might not know that from his book—but a "lesbian and gay" film culture was taking shape . . . perhaps too much.

Gay versus Queer

The slippages among paradigms suggested more than an oppressed minority claiming its stake in academia, activism, and art. Even in my terminology, *gay* becomes *lesbian and gay*, but is this link ill-considered? We surely do not want the medical-sounding *homosexual*. *Bisexuality* and *transgenderism* seem tacked on amid attempts at inclusion rather than the challenges they present. And, even as I use it, I know that *LGBT* is too inclusive and not inclusive enough. Sexual diversity should be embraced by queers, though that does not always happen.

I have also used *queer* as a verb, noun, and adjective. Queer theory, channeled through Foucault and other fields of in(queer)y, challenged boundaries throughout the academy. Before long, Eve Sedgwick targeted the anti-homophobic goal of elucidating knowledge engineered by "the closet"; Judith Butler posed questions about the "drag act" of identity; and Diana Fuss explored essentialism versus constructionism.[2] Soon Alexander Doty critiqued the "closet of connotation" constructed by those burying queerness within "subtexts," and asserted the equality of his pleasures as a "scholar-fan" (1993, 2000).

Some, however, wondered if *queer*, aiming to be more inclusive than *gay*, was simply a chic response to "political correctness." Other fields fighting to maintain their edge (Africana studies, Latino/a studies) did not adopt names based on pejoratives. Was queer theory angrier? Maybe it just borrowed a more ambiguous word; *queer* could suggest everything from hateful exclusion to profound strangeness, whereas slurs against other minorities lacked this vagueness. In film studies queerness developed alongside the New Queer Cinema of the 1990s and documentaries, especially those dealing with AIDS. Queerness aimed to include that which straight (!) gay and lesbian studies neglected, such as transgenderism and intersexedness, even including non-normative straightnesses (Doty 1998, 146–150).

Many embraced the term, while others did not or did so ambiguously. Doty's influential *Making Things Perfectly Queer* came out in 1993, while Dyer's well-known *Now You See It* was subtitled "Studies on Lesbian and Gay Film" in both its 1990 and 2003 editions. Some worried that *queer* would displace lesbian and gay concerns in examining even the mildest deviations. If a heterosexual couple chooses not to have children, how might this (non-)act of separating sex from breeding benefit LGBTQ people or relate to their issues? Queer studies, of course, worked to turn such openness to effective political ends. A gay man might take "gay" pleasure in a gay film but "queer" pleasure in lesbian cinema. Even Jerry Falwell hypocritically relied upon queerness in reading TV's Tinky Winky, with its lavender color, purse, and triangle atop its head, as a subversive influence upon children.

Such concerns led scholars to reconsider many concepts, for example, camp. Susan Sontag famously argued that the heart of mainstream entertainment is a mixture of gay male aestheticism and camp, and Jewish moral seriousness (1967). What does it mean when this is done for predominantly Christian heterosexual audiences? Is camp necessarily satirical, or limited to gay men? We have recently heard much about lesbian and feminist camp, not simply as appropriations of gay camp, but rather as performance strategies extending back to burlesque, and reading positions with their own history (Robertson 1996). Given how camp has been argued as central to a "gay sensibility," one might be surprised by talk of "straight" camp, even to defining postmodernism as straight people catching up with camp. If so, we need to rethink camp—the camp that performers do, camp readings that audiences make, and camp that artists use as a strategy. Yet camp clearly is not enough. Since, for gay men at least, camp often deals with *identification*, both sincerely devotional and mockingly ironical, with divas, there must be more to *desire* than camp, as Michael DeAngelis argues when it comes to gay men's feelings about male stars (2001).

Early responses to queer work on stars emerged within the (sub)field of masculinity-in-film studies. Scholars, gay and non-gay alike, felt what queer studies, following feminism, added to star studies. (It helped that the landmark *Stars* was written by Dyer.) Examples span Dennis Bingham calling James Stewart "your average bisexual," to Robert Lang exploring links between masculinity and homoeroticism.[3] The spectacle of male bodies, the problems with lumping gay porn in with other kinds (or ignoring it), and male bonding in Westerns became fair game. As a dancer, Gene Kelly's strength might be more actual than John Wayne's, with his determined but oddly sexy walk. Yet Kelly, wiggling his tightly clad ass as the black figure of Chocolat in *An American in Paris* (1951), in a dream sequence filled with intertextuality, heterosexual desire, and camp, embodies queer masculinity (Cohan 2005, 149–199).

Queer film studies has also examined female masculinity and the construction of heterosexuality (Halberstam 1998). Unmooring the body from a priori connections to gender, "'queer' indicates a failure to fit not only categories of sexual identity but also categories of gender identity" (Turner 2000, 11). Queer theory and film studies are due for ongoing historiographic expansion and critique. Transgenderism and more globalized considerations (Indian hijras, the two-spirited) are among the field's more recent and exciting challenges. Queer theory needs to answer "How did that little Mormon boy from Oklahoma I used to be grow up to be a transsexual leatherdyke in San Francisco with a Berkeley Ph.D.?" (Stryker 2006, 244–257). Studies of transgenderism began with those who made an "M to F" or "F to M" transition. That said, transgender theory argues that bodies cannot conform within binaries. Film practices expand our theories, representing cases like Brandon Teena, a young man with a "woman's" body who was killed trying to live as he felt, represented through both docudrama (*Boys Don't Cry*, 1999) and documentary (*The Brandon Teena Story*, 1998), and a transgendered man who developed cancer in one of his only "female" body parts, his ovaries (*Southern Comfort*, 2001). "Transgender rage" critiques categorizing people as "male/female, gay/straight" or even "transsexual." Indeed, transgender studies includes cross-dressing, intersexuality and other performativities, and legalities pertaining to gender identity. Queer film analysis, then, must respond to technologies of the body and other material factors, rereading our histories in their pleasures and contradictions.

Toward Historiography

The gay versus queer debate, the complexity of spectatorship, and the "turn to history" should lead to some healthy backtracking. For example, in casting a queer eye on the historiography of theory, Chris Straayer (1996) characterized a queer genre, the "temporary transvestite film," and "reoriented" the gaze to consider the lesbian desire instantiated through editing between the looks women direct at each other in cinema.

In reading Ginger Rogers, I want to consider spectatorship, star studies, iconography, and camp, and even touches of psychoanalysis and authorship. The essay I engage, Richard Dyer's "Judy Garland and Gay Men," is the most influential case study from his 1986 book *Heavenly Bodies: Film Stars and Society*. Others were working on gay fandom too, but Dyer's essay inspired Janet Staiger to use gay-themed novels of the post–World War Two era to debate with his findings; more recently, Steve Cohan invoked Dyer in considering Garland fans on the Internet (Staiger 1992; Cohan 2001, 119–136).

Dyer's essay combines approaches that became vital to queer media studies. The interviews with gay men, if never analyzed in conventional statistical fashion, nonetheless showed the influence of sociological approaches and impacted later studies of fandom. It was a key work in moving theory away from "the spectator" and toward actual spectators. Its vivid contextualization charts changes, pre- and post-Gay Lib, in responses to Garland, even if Dyer does not distinguish between U.S. and British fans. Keen readings of Garland's films show the influence of literary study, and the analysis is not confined to films, either: concert performances, publicity, costuming, her biography and "legend," even greeting cards, are scrutinized, in a model of what extratextual studies can yield. The current surge in extratextual research is already in Dyer, as is the emphasis upon popular culture rather than high artistic practice. His essay interpreted performance when analysis was focused much more upon camerawork, editing, and mise-en-scene; indeed performativity takes center stage, in both Garland's style and in how gays performed their adoration vis-à-vis their own pride and their often painful closetedness.

Diva worship seems hotter than ever, both within our culture and in academia.[4] Camp is part of this worship, and receives thoughtful consideration in Dyer, yet I also perceive a slight camp tone to the essay itself (indeed, I wish it were stronger), as when Dyer is amused how a radical 1970s newsletter had no problems including a fan-oriented story about Garland.[5] He was thus self-aware that studying the legitimacy of Garland's fandom continued the traditions of ideological film criticism and the activism that motivated Russo. Since reading Ginger Rogers has been so central to my life, I will argue for continuing to apply and debate Dyer's essay.

Ginger Rogers and Gay Men? And Lesbians?

Dyer never mentions Rogers in his essay; indeed, he seems almost too decided about which performers have substantial gay followings (Joan Crawford, Bette Davis) and which do not (Ella Fitzgerald, Peggy Lee, Deanna Durbin). I would disagree with these evaluations, from both my own experience and research (Fitzgerald, Durbin, and especially Lee *do* have gay cults, if not as large as Crawford and Davis); I would add that changes have taken place since Dyer wrote his essay. It is also a matter of degree. I concede that "La Ginge" (as I call her) has not had quite the place in gay culture as Davis. But rather than write off certain stars, I think it productive to explore *why* Rogers has been less prominent in gay culture as well as how she *is* part of it.

Some reasons for a lesser prominence seem obvious, though I will argue that queerness still resides in many of these (flawed) factors. Hard work and many triumphs mark Rogers's life, not scandal and tragedy. Insofar as Dyer and others have perhaps over-emphasized diva worship as a response to gays' marginalization and suffering, there was not much public pain to identify with; insofar as there is an undeniable streak of misogyny within diva readings, her success was hard to attack. Neither she nor her five husbands were known to be gay (though that head count, and her numerous paramours, including queer Cary Grant, question a stable heterosexuality and link her with playfully queer promiscuity). Also, Rogers was politically and religiously conservative; queers can be too, and many adopt, if only as a protective gesture, an apolitical stance.

Still, diva worship is secular, and gay culture has tended to be liberal. Worshipping Rogers requires a stronger feminist reading of her life and image and a more willfully campy take on her politics. Finally, Davis and Crawford onscreen devoured their leading men, and Garland desperately wanted acceptance from hers. Gays could fantasize about, or empathize with, both scenarios, but Rogers was almost too good a screen partner, seemingly "natural" in performing heterosexuality. Her style, often read as subtle, and her happy-diva status, *appears* to lack the over-the-top emotionalism of Davis, Crawford, and Garland.

Rogers, however, offers many talents queers could admire, emulate, or read as campy. The "Never Gonna Dance" number from *Swing Time* (1936) moves me far more than most melodramas. Her best vocals—including "We're in the Money" from *Golddiggers of 1933*, "I'll Be Hard to Handle" from *Roberta* (1935), and stage work from *Hello Dolly!* and *Mame*—have gay followings. When Bernadette Peters sang "We're in the Money" for a 1997 Gay Men's Health Crisis benefit, she performed it in pig Latin à la Rogers. Rogers's musicals (if not her melodramas) have received some queer scholarship, but she—and other divas who are dancers or athletes—has been short-shrifted with relation to the attention given to melodramatic singers and actors.

Rogers may still, however, have such a following. A friend belonged to The Friends of Ginger Rogers Society (as did I), while it existed. She went to a convention and was later asked by a fellow academic, who referred to the religion Rogers shared with Crawford: "So who was there, Christian Scientists and gay men?" Among her films, the musicals with Astaire are important to Rogers's queer appeal, but so are Busby Berkeley films like *42nd Street* (1933). Other films with queer fans include *Kitty Foyle* (1940), *The Major and the Minor* (1942), *Tender Comrade* (1944), *Weekend at the Waldorf* (1945), *Monkey Business* (1952), *Forever Female* (1953), *Black Widow* (1954), and, in more recent years, *Primrose Path* (1940) and *Roxie Hart* (1942, precursor of the stage and film success *Chicago*). Her most prominent cult film is *Lady in the Dark* (1944), and her most important film for both gays and lesbians, *Stage Door* (1937).[6] Indeed, one queer scholar informally asserted to me that *Stage Door* and *Dolores Claiborne* (1995) were the only two truly feminist films Hollywood ever made ("They don't cop out at the end").

Storm Warning (1950), about a woman who witnesses a murder by the KKK and learns that her brother-in-law is involved, even has a gay nickname. With its protagonist visiting her pregnant sister (played by diva Doris Day), only to have her brutish in-law try to rape her, *Storm Warning* has been dubbed "A Streetcar Named Ginger." Gays, knowledgeable about pop culture, create coded slang around a diva's vehicles, referencing a queer play by a gay playwright in a campy, intertextual manner. Queers use such language in astonishing ways. When I chatted with a colleague in a gay bar, unaware that he was being cruised,

Katharine Hepburn with Ginger Rogers in Stage Door *(1937). RKO Radio Pictures. Photofest Film Archive.*

he wittily stopped me by quoting one of Ginger's best *Stage Door* lines: "Please, you're interfering with my art." A drag queen, consoling himself over a diva's death, referred to stories about a famous Hollywood attorney who bedded many female stars, stating that Lana Turner "had to die" so she could "go to heaven to break up Joan and Ginger's feud over Greg Bautzer." Another interviewee, told this "explanation," said it was "the gayest thing I've ever heard in my life."

Evidence from interviews I have conducted suggests that Rogers, in an era when gender-inversion models dominated queerness, was imitated by drag queens in the Depression and World War Two years. Costuming is central to Rogers's queerness, and queens could fashion knock-offs of the feathered dress from *Top Hat* (1935), the beaded gown from *Follow the Fleet* (1936), and the *Lady in the Dark* dress, designed by gay Mitchell Leisen, that was likely the most expensive dress in Hollywood history to that time, with a mink skirt hiding sequins underneath, hyperbolizing sexual difference when Rogers splits open the fur to "expose" herself. Even Rogers's working-girl outfits from her Oscar-winning *Kitty Foyle*, with their huge buttons, were imitated. Recently, the queer appeal of Rogers's costumes was evoked on *Queer as Folk* as a blonde queen in a feathered gown sang "Cheek to Cheek."

Dyer argues that Garland's concerts created a temporary public sphere, but she was not alone in that respect. Interviewees saw Rogers in groups in *Hello Dolly!* and *Mame*, and remarked on her performativity: "Wonderful. Loved performing in front of an audience," "Made everything look easy." Divas need adoration, and queer responses feed their legends, as fans feel empowered by the love they grant to divas. When Rogers made her Broadway entrance in *Dolly*, she received a five-minute standing ovation before uttering a sound, and eyewitnesses said that the mutual love affair continued all night. Not every public sphere, however, requires the diva's actual presence. A gay beach in Will Rogers State Park in California had the nickname "*Ginger* Rogers Beach" decades before Stonewall. Public spheres can be virtual, too: EZboard posters call her "La Ginger," discuss her 1945 salary topping Garland's, and rate her *Stage Door* performance as better than Hepburn's.

Gay artists have also invoked Ginger, an angle Dyer does not consider but one with implications for readership *and* authorship. I like to think that a gay TV writer penned a character named Ginger into the "Tap Dancing Her Way Right Back to Your Heart" episode of the 1970s homosocial action series *Starsky and Hutch*. Andy Warhol's drawing of Rogers was one of the works that constituted his 1962 breakthrough. He later sought her out for *Interview* magazine, and also donned drag often, with at least one writer feeling that he was trying to invoke either Rogers or Betty Grable in so doing.[7] Appropriations have continued over the years, spanning from the pre-Stonewall era to Gay Lib to contemporary queerness. Alexis Arquette plays a queen named Ginger in *Killer Drag Queens on Dope* (2003). Drag artiste Charles Busch has a particular affinity for Rogers. He appeared in a gown on the cover of *HX* ("Homo Xtra") magazine striking a pose with a partner. The title "Shall We Dance" evokes the "Ginger'n'Fred" film, as does a fountain, like the one in the film that Rogers pushes an unwanted suitor into (*HX* #720, June 24, 2005). (Divas require ferocity, a quality Rogers had in spades.) At a nightclub reading ("Viva las Divas!")

of celebrity autobiographies, Busch brought down the house by simply intoning, with seething hauteur, her memoir's title, "Ginger: My Story," before reading about Rogers's wig problems in *Dolly*. Postmodernism has queerly evolved when Madonna includes Rogers in the rap of her song "Vogue" ("Gene Kelly, Fred Astaire/Ginger Rogers, dance on air") and then Boy George parodies Madonna in Broadway's *Taboo* ("Ginger Rogers, Fred Astaire/That Madonna dyes her hair.")

Dyer locates three qualities in Garland's image and performance style that enabled gay identification: first, Garland as an example of "ordinariness" that turns out to be fake; second, Garland as androgynous, relating to an "inbetween" status often applied to gays while also questioning the naturalness of gender; and third, Garland as a campy figure who also performs camp. Possibly Garland combines these attributes in greater proportions than any other diva, such that her cult is the largest of them all. Yet Rogers fills the bill too, possessing these qualities that I would argue are essential to all diva readings, as divas problematize gender and the distance between an "ordinary" self and the performativity of an image.

Often a proletariat-next-door, Rogers represented the ordinary in typically Hollywoodian fashion. *Having Wonderful Time* (1938) illustrates how camerawork and performance construct Rogers as both ordinary and extraordinary. Arlene Croce notes, "Many of her RKO films, and some later ones too, open with a long shot of a crowded place . . . and slowly close in, picking out the one in a million we've come to see" (1995, 71). In *Tom, Dick and Harry* (1941) she is singled out as her Janie watches a film not unlike *Kitty Foyle* the previous year. More reflexivity marks *In Person* (1935), with Rogers as a film star visiting a small town and falling for an ordinary guy, yet both mocking and enjoying her status ("I like being a myth!"). *I'll Be Seeing You* (1944) has her temporarily joining a stereotypical family, yet as a prison inmate on leave, her secret makes her an outsider. *42nd Street*, by contrast, introduces her performing as an "aristocratic dyke" (monocle, tweeds, bowtie), only to reveal her as another chorine hoping for work. Her ultimate example of failed ordinariness, *The Major and the Minor*, with Rogers disguised as a twelve-year-old and coping with the pedophilia she inspires, highlights Rogers as the star most prone to masquerade. Croce writes, "She needs guises the way other actresses need close-ups" (1972, 142).

Given how sexuality is often subsumed under gender performance rather than object choice, divas who dress or act butch appeal to queers. Reading them as queer, we enjoy their pursuit of romantic pleasure and transgressive attacks upon traditional sexuality. In *Top Hat* Rogers runs the gamut from ultra-femme ("Cheek to Cheek") to butch-chic ("Isn't This a Lovely Day?") with her tweeds, slouch hat, and the ultimate daytime lesbian wear, jodhpurs (which she also sported in *Finishing School* [1934], an Americanization of the lesbian classic *Mädchen in Uniform* [1931]). Thrusting her hands into her pockets, imitating Astaire's masculine gestures, she surprises him when she takes the initiative in their dance. Far more than his later co-stars, Rogers fights with Astaire, chasing him with a gun in *Carefree* (1938), challenging his ballet with her tap in *Shall We Dance*, picking fights in *Follow the Fleet*. She forces him to grow up, to be less of a gay young blade, exposing the construction of heterosexuality in the musical. Together they reveal the queerness of gender equality during the Depression, offering that it is best for men and women to work together. And she ended the partnership as the more successful solo item through the World War Two years.

Rogers's ability to carry off glamour, seemingly without the awkwardness of Garland (as per Dyer), suggests an untroubled femininity, yet her resistance to glamour in many roles and her toughness while being glamorous in others make her a complex site of gender struggle. As another prisoner in *Tight Spot* (1955), the juxtaposition of a Jean-Louis polka-dot dress and a fabulous lesbian ducktail hairdo renders her a one-woman butch-femme aesthetic. At work in overalls (*Tender Comrade*) or in a nightclub in a modified tuxedo with top hat and cane (*Stage Door*), Rogers offers famous androgynous moments. Tomboy drag, and throwing rocks, protects her from the unwanted teasing of local boys in *Primrose Path*, even though she must later become a prostitute. In a gown in *Vivacious Lady* (1938), Rogers still can be butch, mocking boxing gestures before she knocks out the local patriarch. As the star who most often plays children—in flashbacks, in masquerades, or in *Monkey Business* because of a youth potion—Rogers sheds her socially acquired femininity. She can self-consciously play in a state of "arrested development," a psychoanalytic idea long used to describe and oppress gays. Dressed as a tomboy, she attacks the more objectified femininity of Marilyn Monroe. Since dishy readings are part of diva worship, can we also see this as an over-forty star attacking the newer generation?

Rogers's constant playing of performers connects her with the camp theatricality Dyer sees as central to queer culture. She, too, can "pass" for what she is not. One African American interviewee enjoyed the Jazz-age aspects of her persona, camping with black maids onscreen, thus complicating readings of Rogers and race. She can camp as a "dumb brunette" (*Roxie Hart*), a star (*Dreamboat* 1952), and in mock-languages (the famous Swedish bit in *Bachelor Mother* 1939). Her superbly effortless dancing, full of skirt-twirling and florid gestures, is both dramatically valid *and* a campy take on courtship rituals. Her scene-stealing countess in *Roberta* is a campy homage to the Broadway originator of the role, Lyda Roberti. Understanding Rogers' camping makes her aging character in *Forever Female* more daringly obnoxious at first and more sympathetic at the end, and it redeems her unjustly maligned but hilarious work as the *grande dame* in *Black Widow*. She can be read as camp too: as Dolley Madison, rolling up the Declaration of Independence in *Magnificent Doll* (1946), in *Weekend at the Waldorf*'s innumerable costumes and hairstyles, and, famously, reciting "La Marseillaise" in *The Barkleys of Broadway* (1949). Camp readings help queers maintain their edge, whether it is George Eells noting that Rogers jammed 118 pieces of pink luggage with "necessities" like tennis balls and sundae syrup, or my catching a slip during the documentary *Hollywood: The Golden Years*, as she gushes, "I think we all like to wear pretty dresses . . . at least the ladies, I mean" (1976, 76).

Given that Rogers was part of a trailblazing generation who "wore the pants" on and offscreen but also looked great in dresses, we can understand her appeal to gay men. But what about lesbians? Of course, the risk of collapsing gay and lesbian concerns in film studies is considerable. As Patricia Juliana Smith states, "It is perhaps too broad a generalization to claim without reservation that while lesbian diva worship is based on desire, gay male diva worship is based on identification," yet divas "inevitably raise 'that quintessentially queer question: do you want to be her or have her'?" (2002). Queer theory questions easy oppositions of identification and desire, as queer culture blurs them. With its complex range of affects and effects, diva worship lets lesbians and gays admire the diva's strength and relate to her struggles on and offscreen, while also identifying with her bisexual or bisexed nature. Brett Farmer posits a "reparative" maintenance of the self in diva worship, as opposed to emphasizing the nursing of psychic pain, while Kelly Hankin argues that femme lesbians have formed cults around baby-butch *divos* like James Dean.[8]

I did find lesbian fans of Rogers; still, one was the first person to suggest that "being Republican" was a strike against her. Yet when I noted Barbara Stanwyck's conservatism, she could only reply, "But *Stella Dallas* is so marvelous." Clearly, neither lesbians nor gays monopolize "political" or "apolitical" readings. One of the richest lesbian responses came from gossip columnist Liz Smith. When co-hosting four films of her choice on Turner Classic Movies, Smith chose two Rogers movies (*Kitty Foyle* and *The Barkleys of Broadway*). She disregarded Rogers's politics, shared her camp reading of Rogers delightedly signing autographs in green ink, and hinted at her attraction ("She was very muscular and athletic, a great tennis player"). Most centrally, though, the working-class Smith, who grew up in Texas like Rogers, was inspired by *Kitty Foyle* to become a professional in New York.

Lesbian readings foreground Rogers as crypto-lesbian, a friend to other women in homosocial settings (*42nd Street, Finishing School, Tender Comrade, Tight Spot*), or a sisterly type (*The Major and the Minor, Tom, Dick and Harry*, where her sister is named Butch!). Gay male readings, meanwhile, might emphasize Rogers as Hollywood's preeminent "fag hag," having worked more times with "sissy" comics (Franklin Pangborn, Grady Sutton, Edward Everett Horton, Eric Blore, Erik Rhodes) and queer directors (Leisen, Arzner, Edmund Goulding, Irving Rapper, Charles Walters, Arthur Lubin, briefly with Cukor on *I'll Be Seeing You*) than any other diva, in addition to queer leads Grant, Clifton Webb, Dan Dailey, and Randolph Scott. Queer authorship should not neglect Rogers's iron-willed manager-mother Lela (who played Rogers's mother in *The Major and the Minor*) shaping her career. Readings blur, however. While gays idolize *Stage Door* for collecting so many divas (Lucille Ball, Ann Miller, Eve Arden) in one film, lesbians enjoy the bonding among them, especially after Rogers and Hepburn reject the same man. That said, an early queer reading came from a male contemporary reviewer in 1937, who found it a "love story" between the two leads (Lugowski 2007). Rogers's feminist angles were cited more by women I interviewed, but I share the feminism of the famous "She did everything Astaire did, except backwards in high heels." Yet I also campily interpret doing something "backwards" in heels as evoking a drag queen enjoying anal sex. Astaire "mounting" Rogers three times near the end of "Waltz in Swing Time," the last jump done with her back to him, is cinema's most sublime evocation of anal sex.

Unlike the tremulous, vulnerable Garland, Rogers is a mistress of the wisecrack. Her greatest? A *Stage Door* riposte when an enemy enters: "Hold on, gangrene just set in." One need only see a queen in *Paris Is Burning* (1990) zapping a group teasing her to know that verbal acuity has been vital in queer cultures. Rogers is also Hollywood's most frequent daydreamer and analysand (*In Person, Carefree, Tom, Dick and Harry, Tender Comrade, Lady in the Dark, It Had to Be You* [1947], *Oh Men! Oh Women!* [1957]). While I share Dyer's reservations about psychoanalysis as methodology, its selective, historicized deployment is relevant to Ginger. Krin and Glen O. Gabbard correctly argue that placing the diva Croce called "the fabulous Miss Average" on the couch spoofed psychiatry, but fantasy theory could diagnose the "average woman" as a patriarchal illusion.[9] And readings and appropriations keep flowing amid global circulation: Tokyo has a Rogers-themed gay bar!

Dyer beautifully writes, "Audiences cannot make media images mean anything they want to, but they can select from the complexity of the image the meanings and feelings, the variations, inflections and contradictions, that work for them" (1986, 5). His work is part of the impressive range of issues LGBTQ film studies addresses in a progressive intervention. Seeing readings of Rogers move from gender-inversion drag to community formation to an informed feminism and queer diversity leads me to rethink my own investment in La Ginge. I think of *being* her leading men while also being *drawn* to them. I see how much Croce's assessment—"In her continually wounded sense of self-worth and her spirited defense of it lies the drama of Ginger Rogers" (1995, 70)—applies to me. If Rogers was rarely a suffering figure for me, perhaps I used her differently from Garland fans. For me, no star is more versatile or talented, or expresses joy as well. At one of her last performances I took for myself a lesson I needed. I watched the 1992 Kennedy Center Honors with my mother, who had introduced me to old films, encouraged me to watch Rogers, and cried during *Kitty Foyle*. Ginger was having a ball, blowing kisses (requisite diva behavior) to every performer who honored her. When I saw her, I gasped; Mom asked what was wrong. I covered by noting that Rogers's infirmity was saddening, given how vibrant her body had been. But what I really noticed was her triangular pink stole atop a black gown. Seeing her as a giant pink triangle prompted the reading "Silence = Death." I had lost people to AIDS and was out in New York, but not to my own family. Here was this diva—the one who performed "Pick Yourself Up," a dance I have watched a million times and never found boring—extravagantly dressed, artificially blonde, blowing campy kisses, accompanied by her female companion. How appropriate that in her obituary tribute, gossip columnist Cindy Adams shared that this "clothes-aholic" owned "the world's largest closet" (1995, 16). Via my queer reading that night, I realized that I would have to pick myself up and come out of my own closet.

NOTES

1. See "Visual Pleasure and Narrative Cinema" and "Afterthoughts on 'Visual Pleasure and Narrative Cinema' Inspired by *Duel in the Sun*" in Mulvey 1989.
2. See Sedgwick 1992; Butler 1990; Fuss 1990.
3. See Dyer 1979; Bingham 1994; Lang 2002.
4. See issue of *Camera Obscura* Fall 2007; Leonardi and Pope 1996; Koestenbaum 1993.
5. For Dyer as diva worshipper see Dyer 1992, 65: "Because I like her." On Margot Fonteyn, see Dyer 1992, 41.
6. *The Advocate*, August 20, 1996, 102, gave pride of place to *Stage Door* as a gay video store chain listed its "canon" of thirty most popular-ever rentals.
7. See www.davidsoul.com; "A Ball in Mascara," www.calamusbooks.com/newsletters/v2_44/.
8. See Bone 2003; Farmer 2005, 165–194; Hankin 1998, 3–18.
9. See Gabbard and Gabbard 1987; Croce 1995, 71; Farmer 2005.

Robert T. Eberwein

"As a Mother Cuddles a Child": Sexuality and Masculinity in World War II Combat Films

Commenting on *The Deer Hunter* (Michael Cimino, 1978), Anthony Easthope observes: "In the dominant versions of men at war, men are permitted to behave towards each other in ways that would not be allowed elsewhere, caressing and holding each other, comforting and weeping together, admitting their love. The pain of war is the price paid for the way it expresses the male bond. War's suffering is a kind of punishment for the release of homosexual desire and male femininity that only the war allows. In this special form the male bond is fully legitimated" (Easthope 1990, 66). Mark Simpson expands on Easthope's argument, calling "the war film . . . perhaps the richest of all texts of masculinity" (Simpson 1994, 212). In *Memphis Belle* (Michael Caton-Jones, 1990) and *A Midnight Clear* (Keith Gordon, 1992), "the war film not only offers a text on masculinity and how to take one's place in patriarchy, it also offers a vision of a world in which the privileges of heterosexual manhood can be combined with boyish homoeroticism—a purely masculine world awash with femininity. . . . The lesson that the buddy film has to teach boys (and remind men) is that 'war' is a place where queer love can not only be expressed but *endorsed*—but only when married to death. Death justifies and romanticizes the signs but not the practice of queer love" (Simpson 1994, 214–215).

Easthope and Simpson offer a totalizing reading of displays of the feminine and of affection in the war film. In effect, they see representations of behavior readable as feminine and/or homosexual as validated by suffering and death. But examination of the combat films made during World War II suggests it would be helpful to qualify their position because their readings do not address the complexities of the earlier films' signifying practices and relation to their sociocultural-historical framework.

If we look at a variety of discourses—training, documentary, and Hollywood films; academic and popular writing; advertisements—we find that two issues pertaining to male sexuality were discussed: venereal disease and homosexuality. Neither could be addressed in commercial Hollywood films because of the restrictions of the Production Code Administration. Venereal disease was treated with varying degrees of specificity in training and documentary films and in professional, academic journals, as well as in popular magazines. Although homosexuality received much less attention, two topics in particular got attention: the effectiveness of the pre-induction physical to screen recruits and the possible effects of military life on sexuality.

Examinations of the discourses mentioned above reveal the extent to which concerns about homosexuality are present as a kind of structuring absence in representations of male sexuality. One of the most complex signifying practices that occurs during World War II involves showing males in ways that connect them to the feminine or that present scenes of non-aggressive close physical contact. When this happens at the level of the mise-en-scène or the image, the implications are negotiated by the narrative or by dialogue and commentary.

As I have indicated elsewhere, training films made for soldiers displayed graphically the results of male sexuality by showing enactments of interactions with prostitutes and contagious women and by revealing the effects of venereal disease on genitals. Such films were part of a larger campaign involving public service documentaries as well as professional and popular literature dealing with the threats posed by venereal disease (Eberwein 1999, 63–101).

The campaign against venereal disease was one part of the government's efforts to protect servicemen while acknowledging their sexual needs. In 1941, Joel T. Boone, the captain of the Naval Medical Corps, spoke at a conference on hygiene. Rather than deny the sexual needs of men, he urged his auditors to recognize "armies and navies use *men*. Men of the very essence of masculinity. Men in the prime of life. . . . [Soldiers'] education befits nature, induces sexual aggression, and makes them the stern dynamic type we associate with men of an armed force. The sexual aggressiveness cannot be stifled" (Boone 1941, 116). Writing in *The American Mercury* in 1941, Irwin Ross voiced his concern about the effects of "enforced abstention" on the mental health of soldiers and the possibility that this "may encourage homosexuality" (668).

Guidelines for detecting homosexuality appear in commentary by C. L. Wittson, a naval psychiatrist. Describing "The Neuropsychiatric Selection of Recruits," he explains that after the physical, the recruit is in "an ideal condition in which to be examined from a naval psychiatric viewpoint. He is naked and stripped of his individuality" (1943, 639). "The recruit who mincingly enters the office immediately arouses a suspicion of homosexuality, either overt or sublimated" (Wittson et. al. 1943, 643).

In addition, *Psychology for the Fighting Man* (1943), a book published in the *Infantry Journal* and circulated among soldiers, openly acknowledged the possibility of encountering homosexual behavior. The collective authors, a committee of the National Research Council, included such notable figures as G. W. Allport of Harvard and S. A. Stouffer of the Special Services Division of the War Department. The authors note that the pre-induction screening mentioned above may fail: "Although medical officers at the induction centers try to keep them out of the Army, a sexually abnormal man who finds satisfaction only with other men may get in." They discuss the possibility of what would later be called situational homosexuality and advance a position that seems to anticipate the current argument of "don't ask, don't tell" (National Research Council 1943, 340). But homosexuality is clearly raised as a negative dimension of sexual behavior.[1]

To see how those in the period negotiated their concerns about male sexuality, let me begin with a film, an essay, and a photograph. In *Thirty Seconds Over Tokyo* (Mervyn LeRoy, 1944), after Ted Lawson (Van Johnson) and his crew participate in the surprise bombing of the Japanese capital, they try but fail to return to their base. Nearly out of fuel, Lawson attempts to land the plane but crashes into the water. The survivors drag themselves to the shore. Hugging and supporting each other, the men cry out in pain and anguish as they are pelted by rain. The dazed Lawson is at the center of a triangular formation including Thatcher (Robert Walker), McClure (Don DeFore), who rests his head on Lawson's shoulder, and Davenport (Tim Murdock), whose head is cradled on Lawson's thigh. The camera dollies in to Lawson's face and the image dissolves to his memory of a scene we saw earlier as his pregnant wife Ellen (Phyllis Thaxter) reassured him: "Ted, Look at me. The baby and I won't ever need anything. The baby is why I know you're coming home." Lawson rises, apparently coming out of his daze, and stumbles away from the men as one of them calls out his name.

The face of Captain Eddie Rickenbacker appears on the cover of the January 25, 1943 issue of *Life* magazine, the first of three issues containing installments of his "Pacific Mission" in which he recounts a remarkable story of heroism and survival. Rickenbacker was at that time the most decorated and successful pilot in American history. When his plane ran out of fuel in October 1942, he and the seven other men of the crew ditched in the Pacific Ocean and, in two rafts, drifted for twenty-one days until being rescued. After exhausting their meager food supply—four oranges, which they divided among themselves in the first few days—they lived on raw fish, a gull, and rain water collected during squalls. One of the men, Sergeant Alexander Kacmarczyk, already weakened before the flight, became ill and did not survive the ordeal. Here is Rickenbacker describing how he tried to help: "I asked . . . to change rafts with Sergeant Alex, thinking that Alex might rest better. It took the combined strength of Bartek, DeAngelis and myself to move him. I stretched him on the lee side of the bottom of the boat and put my arm around him, as a mother cuddles a child, hoping in that way to transfer the heat of my body to him during the night. In an hour or so his shivering stopped and sleep came—a shallow sleep in which Alex mumbled intermittently in Polish—phrases about his mother and his girl 'Snooks.' I kept Alex there all night, the next day and night, and the twelfth day. . . . I knew he couldn't last many hours longer. . . . We had to lift him like a baby" (Rickenbacker 1943, 99–100). The essay includes a drawing of Rickenbacker cuddling the doomed Sergeant.

In the same year as Rickenbacker's report was published, Edward Steichen, the famous photographer who had headed the army photographic unit in World War I and who now had a commission in the navy (even though, at sixty-two, he was well over the age limit), became chief of Naval Photography. In November he was assigned to the USS *Lexington*, an aircraft carrier in the Pacific where he was exposed to various dangers. One of the pictures he took within his first few weeks on board is of sleeping sailors. Three men are intertwined: one lies face down on the deck; a second rests his head on the former's back; a third rests his head on the second's stomach. A fourth man, awake, sits a few feet away, looking off to his left.

In *The Blue Ghost* Steichen comments on this and other photographs of sailors at rest: "There are not many methods of taking things easy on a carrier, but we try all of them. Reading, studying, sleeping, poker, and in secluded corners maybe a nice little crap game" (1947, 54). "The men, in small groups, are sprawled around the deck; some choose the hot sun on the open deck, others park themselves in the shade of a plane's wing; they pillow up for each other in a fine earthly fellowship, reminiscent of colts resting under a tree or alongside the fence of a pasture, the head of one colt is draped over the neck of another, or again, something in the manner of a litter of puppies, are curled up over, under, and about each other" (58). Steichen's caption is: "Here we sprawl like pups in a kennel—pillow up together" (59).

The film, the account, and the commentary share the negotiating tendency I see manifested in representations of sexuality during World War II. *Thirty Seconds* establishes a mise-en-scène consisting of a grouping of intertwined, weeping men and then counteracts any possible sexual implications of the bond by cutting to the leader's memory of his wife whose comment on their unborn baby is followed by his breaking away from the men. Rickenbacker's account of the cuddling with the doomed sergeant qualifies the description of maternal intimacy not only by virtue of the exigencies of survival but also by recounting how the man called out for his girlfriend. Steichen's description of the men in his photograph explains the bonding figuratively in terms of the men's similarity to animals. The various kinds of qualifications illustrate a phenomenon found throughout films and other kinds of wartime discourses in which the heterosexuality of the men is reaffirmed.

Sailors sleeping on the flight deck of the U.S.S. Lexington. *Courtesy National Archives and Records Administration.*

All three are expressions of people in the period responding to manifestations of behavior that foreground the potentialities of male sexuality outside its traditional heterosexual framework. In fact, there seems almost to be a curious compulsion to show something in the mise-en-scène and images that *requires* its own containment and inoculation through negotiation.[2]

Extensive examples of the kinds of qualifications of representations of feminine and maternal behavior and of affectionate and supportive physical contact appear in the combat film and in other manifestations of contemporary culture, such as magazine advertisements. First, in films we find men shown positively or sympathetically enacting behavior associated with the feminine, as occurs in *Bataan* (Tay Garnett, 1943). As the malaria-delirious Ramirez (Desi

Arnaz) succumbs, his medic stands watch over him, offering him water. Ramirez calls out for his mother. In addition, when Purckett (Robert Walker) is unable to bind his own wounds, he is assisted by Todd (Lloyd Nolan). As Todd applies a tourniquet, Purckett looks at him like a child lovingly admiring his mother, and Todd responds negatively by tightening the cloth roughly. The second scene in particular plays it both ways: showing a male acting in a maternal function and then rejecting the appreciative response this evokes in the soldier he helps.

In *Destination Tokyo* (Delmer Daves, 1943), Cary Grant as Captain Cassidy is tough and assured. When one of the sailors (Robert Hutton) on the submarine needs an emergency appendectomy, Cassidy participates in the operation by administering ether to the young boy who, as he would at home, says his prayers before going to "sleep" under the anesthetic. Framed with his hands clasped around a towel over the face of the boy, Cassidy displays maternal tenderness. As the kid comes out of the anesthetic after the successful surgery, Cassidy's head is practically resting on the boy's in order to hear what he is saying: the continuation of his prayers. Earlier, though, before news of the emergency reaches him, Cassidy has been seen tenderly recounting a story about taking his young son to the barbershop. The highlight of his year, he claims, was hearing his son declare that Cassidy was his dad. Thus Cassidy's maternal capacities are complemented by a monologue about his paternal role.

An advertisement sponsored by Nash Kelvinator that is reminiscent of the scene I mentioned in *Bataan* appeared in *Time*. It shows a wounded and apparently dying soldier being ministered to by a medic. The top caption "MOM . . ." is followed by the supposed commentary of the medic: "It was damned hard to just lie there . . . and grind our teeth together and tighten our guts because each time he cried 'Mom' . . . it tore out our insides. . . . I put a syrette into his arm and then another, and he relaxed and his head fell back and his eyes were still wide but I could tell he thought his mother was there by his side" (Nash Kelvinator 1944). Here the medic who is perceived as a mother accedes to the role assigned him by the wounded man in a manner that reinforces his masculinity, underscored by the language ("damned hard," "grind our teeth," "tighten our guts").

Any discussion of sexuality has to deal with behavior associated with the feminine that is not medically related. This is manifested most overtly in musical scenes in which men dance with one another. Although not a combat film as such, *This Is the Army* (Michael Curtiz, 1943) with its numerous drag numbers is relevant. Significantly, the film was Warner Brothers' most successful film of the decade and the highest grossing film made during the war. *This Is the Army* negotiates the problematic of men in drag by using a number of strategies such as overstated disavowals of femininity by one character who objects to dressing up like a woman or by having the men's hairy chests very much in evidence.[3]

Equally relevant here are numerous scenes in films showing men who are not in drag dancing together. One such moment occurs in *The Story of a Transport*, which documents how the *Wakefield*, a Coast Guard ship, is used as a transport vehicle for the army (1944). One sequence displays how the Coast Guard personnel entertain the troops by playing music for them. As a small band plays, two soldiers dance to the lively music ("One O'clock Jump"). They are joined shortly by two Coast Guard sailors. This activity is presented as perfectly routine, and is followed by shots indicating the dancing is one among many common elements of shipboard life, such as boxing and exercising.

In *V.D. Control: The Story of D.E. 733*, a training film on venereal disease made by Paramount for the Navy (1945), the depiction of shipboard life includes one scene in which two sailors dance to "Bell Bottom Trousers." The ship's pharmacist sees them and asks: "What's the matter with you guys? Can't you wait?" One of the dancers responds: "Just practicing."

The most interesting example of male dancing occurs in *Guadalcanal Diary* (Lewis Seiler, 1943). In one scene on board ship, two Marines (one shirtless) dance to "Chattanooga Choo-Choo," which is being played on a harmonica. They are clearly presented as entertaining their fellow troops, who are watching appreciatively. Taxi Potts (William Bendix) enters (holding the group's mascot dog) and talks about a conversation he had with a woman who was rejecting his advances. The dance continues, off camera, and then is seen again as Malone (Lloyd Nolan) announces lights out and "quit your skylarking." The dance concludes as the shirtless man jumps into the arms of his partner. Shortly after, another scene below deck begins as we see Taxi dressed in semi-drag as an Hawaiian "woman" dancing a hula. The ship's chaplain Father Donnelly (Preston Foster) enters and watches Taxi, who, in mild embarrassment takes off some of his make-shift costume. The music changes from the Hawaiian melody to an Irish tune, and Taxi and Father Donnelly dance a jig, concluded with an arm-in-arm spin.

The dancing in these examples is qualified in a way that assuages and negotiates any problematic issues of sexuality. In *Transport*, it is entertainment and part of the usual physical exercise routine; in *D.E. 733*, it is in preparation for a later date; in *Diary*, it is entertainment presented in a context in which heterosexuality is confirmed through conversation and inoculated by the folk dancing.

A similar kind of qualification appears in numerous scenes of close physical bonding in the combat films. For example, in *Wake Island* (John Farrow, 1942), as Smacksie (William Bendix) and Joe (Robert Preston) prepare for a final and deadly assault by their Japanese attackers, the former puts his hand briefly and tenderly on Joe's thigh. In the same scene, the doomed Smacksie and Joe joke about what they're going to miss because of their imminent deaths: "How many blonds are there that we didn't get to?" Thus, the sign of affection is qualified by the testimonial to heterosexuality.

The sharing and exchange of cigarettes serves as a significant way of demonstrating bonding among men in combat films. For example, *Immortal Sergeant* (John Stahl, 1943) contains one of the most remarkable smoking scenes in film. Out of supplies, four men led by Colin Spence (Henry Fonda) share a final cigarette. Spence begins with a couple of drags and then passes it around to the men who silently puff and observe the others, until the camera pans down to show it being extinguished. The prolonged scene suggests the intense intimacy that binds the men together, even though there has been personal friction among them earlier.

Guadalcanal Diary contains two striking scenes demonstrating male affection. The film opens with a shipboard service led by Father Donnelly and then shows the men relaxing. Most are shirtless and closely linked physically. Taxi Potts forms the apex of an extended triangular group of figures. He cradles the head of a shirtless Sosse (Anthony Quinn), on whose arm another Marine's head rests; the head of a shirtless Chicken Anderson (Richard Jaeckel) rests on Taxi's stomach, close to the groin, and Taxi's hand is on Chicken's bare chest. In the second scene, shortly afterward, as the men hear their orders, Sosse rests his head on Chicken's chest.

The physical intimacy displayed in the mise-en-scène is qualified by the conversations that occur. In the first Sosse contemplates which of his two girlfriends he would be dating were he home and opts for both; Taxi talks about baseball. In the second, the bonding between Chicken and Sosse takes place as they hear orders that will send them into dangerous circumstances.

Some scenes in which male sexuality is affirmed and inoculated occur in war films which refer humorously to homosexuality. For example, in *Gung Ho!* (Ray Enright, 1944), one of the soldiers on a troop ship asks Transport (Sam Levene): "Got any pictures of pin-ups?" After Transport comments that he doesn't have pin-up pictures, he says "I got a picture of me in a bathing suit. Want me to autograph it?" A voice (unidentified) asks: "Where is it?" and produces a comic double-take from Levene.

In *Wing and a Prayer* (Henry Hathaway, 1944), one husky character lying on his bunk who is swatted on the behind by another walking through the cabin says: "Do it again! I love it." But that moment is qualified by a major scene in the film in which a large group of men watch *Tin Pan Alley*, with Betty Grable and Alice Faye. They hoot appreciatively at the display of the dancers' bodies and the stars, and become irate when the film breaks.[4]

In some cases, potentially problematic behavior is so exaggerated that it needs only humor to qualify it. For example, in *Immortal Sergeant*, one soldier rips off a towel from another man, leaving him naked (but unseen by the camera), producing a brief comic moment. In *Objective, Burma!* (Raoul Walsh, 1945), we see Gabby (George Tobias) washing out his socks in a pond. Ordered to get moving, he responds in a purposely inflected feminine tone: "I'm washing out my last pair of nylons." Another character asks for a hand with his gear: "Give me a hand with my bustle," and is told: "very fine, sweetheart. If it doesn't work, you can bring it back."

Commenting not on these films but on various defensive strategies used by servicemen in general to deal with their sexual drives and potential homosexual impulses, Bérubé and D'Emilio both draw on the work of psychiatrist William C. Menninger (Bérubé 1991, 37; D'Emilio 1983, 25). He suggests that, among the ways servicemen found to accommodate the absence of women, "physical substitutes were varied. . . . There were numerous psychological substitutes used: possession of 'pin-up girl' photographs; an increased interest in 'dirty' stories, in profanity, and in homosexual buffoonery" (Menninger 1948, 224).

But such buffoonery needs to be understood in the larger context of representations of sexuality and masculinity within American culture during the war. Bérubé in particular cites popular magazine advertisements and articles that can be read as having a potential homosexual appeal (1991, 298, 341). But he does not indicate that the very presence of such representations in the widely read magazines demonstrates the extent to which films and advertisements were constantly reassuring their audiences that there was nothing about which they should be concerned. The heterosexuality of males was validated by emphasizing masculinity, even in the presence of the problematic.

For example, three advertisements worth noting that Bérubé does not mention involve a play on masculinity apparently being undermined by femininity. First, one for Monsanto Chemicals shows the drawing of a shirtless soldier holding a slip in one hand and a lady's undergarment in another, with the caption: "Hey! What goes on here? *Yes, we know—this couldn't actually happen! You'll never encounter any lady whatcha-ma-callits in Army laundry."* The ad copy goes on to argue that the detergent will work for the troops, no matter the quality of the water they have to use; hence it will be fine for "Mrs. Housewife" as well.[5]

An advertisement for the Bead Chain Manufacturing Company shows a drawing of a tough-looking soldier with the caption: "Yeah, I wear a necklace—but brother, I ain't no sissy. Every mother's son of us . . . and daughter, too . . . in the Army, Navy, Marine Corps and Coast Guard wears identification tags around his neck" (*Newsweek*, August 9, 1943, 2).

B. F. Goodrich touts its newest contribution to protecting sailors on ship decks, a helmet with special rubber lining, by displaying a sailor in uniform standing before a mirror. He adjusts his helmet in a pose that suggests a woman before a mirror. The caption reads, "Latest fashion for ocean cruises," and the copy explains: "Because of dive bombers, it's healthier for exposed gunners on ship decks to wear steel helmets. But for real protection a helmet has to fit"—hence the advantages of their new process (*Time*, July 27, 1942, 1).

In different ways all three ads confirm not only that the servicemen are still clearly male but also that their toughness and masculinity are in no way compromised by being linked to the feminine. The representations of the feminine are of the same order as Gabby's "washing out [his] last pair of nylons"—something understood as strictly performative. Displays of overtly and stereotypical feminine behavior or images of apparent confusion about gender identity are instantly qualified in the ads by the valorization of masculinity (the tough soldier, the guy who's not a sissy, the sailor on his way to battle), hence reassuring readers about the males' heterosexuality.

I want to conclude by talking about something that viewers never saw in commercial combat films. The PCA's restrictions precluded any display of the naked male body. Such controls obviously did not apply to training films, in which numerous graphic shots of genitals were presented to show men the physical effects of venereal disease, and in which naked servicemen were not uncommonly shown in showers. But the American public did occasionally see photographs of naked soldiers in *Life* and drawings of them in certain advertisements.[6] I'm interested in the extent to which the display of naked, bathing men is accompanied by qualifying material similar to what we have already seen. *Life* showed the naked male body in a state of sexual innocence, a theme that was constantly inflected in war films, mainly through the raw recruit or kid.[7]

Life's extended coverage of the assault on Guadalcanal included two full-page photographs of naked and semi-naked troops. The "Picture of the Week" for February 8, 1943, shows over two dozen men bathing and relaxing in a river; frontal nudity is shadowed out, but not that from behind. The explanatory caption is: "The gray American transports steamed in near to the beaches of Guadalcanal. Over the sides into landing boats went thousands of American troops, hot and bearded and dirty from weeks at sea with no fresh water to wash in. As soon as their boats crunched up on the sand and their tents were pitched and their foxholes dug, the troops wandered over to a nearby river, gratefully pulled off their clothes, plunged into the cool fresh water" (24). The caption on the photograph itself repeats the notion of their gratitude for the relief afforded by the refreshing water. Three weeks later, *Life* ran a photograph of naked and partially clothed soldiers washing their clothes, again with dorsal but not frontal nudity ("Guadalcanal" 1943, 68).

This display of naked males relaxing and washing themselves or their clothing in *Life* anticipated a remarkable series of six ads that would be run by the Cannon towel company on the inside covers of the same magazine from August 1943 to June 1944 in which naked or partially clothed servicemen were shown bathing in comic scenes. These "true towel tales" were credited to various sources such as "a doctor in the medical corps" or "a sergeant in the tank corps" (*Life*, August 16, 1943, and January 3, 1944). Some reveal the kind of "homosexual buffoonery" referred to earlier. In one of them, a flier throws a bucket of water on a man emerging from a galvanized washing tub, thus sending his towel flying (*Life*, October 4, 1943). This is reminiscent of the scene mentioned in *Immortal Sergeant* when a soldier rips off a man's towel. The "Buna Bathtub" ad, the last in the series, shows a naked soldier posed seductively with a palm frond over his genitals (*Life*, June 26, 1944). In its coverage of Buna Village, *Life* had run another photograph of naked soldiers bathing ("Battle of Buna" 1943, 21). Each of the ads contains a small inserted drawing of a different woman discreetly covered by a towel with the same accompanying caption alerting readers that they may encounter less of a selection in towels because "Millions of Cannon Towels are now going to the Armed Forces." The presence of the women not only evokes the typical Cannon Towel ads which, prior to and after the true towel campaign, featured typical cheesecake illustrations in which women were the objects of visual pleasure.[8] It also inserts an image that negotiates the problematic of male sexuality by reminding viewers that women, not men, are the traditional objects of sexual desire for these tough men.[9]

The significance of this display of nakedness to a mass audience needs comment. According to George H. Roeder Jr.: "By late 1942 *Life* was claiming that tens of millions of civilians and two out of three Americans in the military read the magazine" (Roeder Jr. 1993, 4–5). Such a public display should be understood in the larger context of how sexuality was negotiated in war films. Photographs of naked soldiers washing and at play in *Life* provide testimony that affirms these men *can* be observed; that is, the very act of representing their nakedness serves as an assurance that their sexuality is *representable*. The naked men shown to the American public must be heterosexual. If nakedness can be shown in airbrushed photographs, then the sexuality of those shown in the photographs is not in question.

Although combat films could not show a naked male body, they could and did show males performing feminine roles, a hand resting casually on another man's bare chest, men performing in drag and dancing together, a young man looking lovingly at an older man who has just performed a maternal function, a man joking about a pin-up of himself, and horseplay that constantly evoked the potential range of male sexuality. But these were consistently qualified in a way demonstrating that what was potentially signified at one level needed to be understood at another. The very fact that any of these scenes were shown signified at some level that they *could* be presented—that males' sexuality was contained and inoculated by their masculinity.

The Easthope-Simpson argument that explains such displays as signifiers of homoeroticism sanctioned by the inevitability of death does not take into account the complex logic of representation discussed in this essay. Combat films and other discourses produced during World War II can be seen to have provided some indication of an as yet unarticulated conception of sexuality and masculinity developing in the American consciousness.

NOTES

1. See Bérubé 1991, 49, 51, for commentary on the work. He sees a level of tolerance in the authors' position (51). Cohan (1997, 86) suggests: "The manual's cautious advice about the likelihood of homosexual encounters in the army's all-male environment is . . . quite striking, given the homophobia which erupted in periodic purges of effeminate men during the war and which, more perniciously, came to dominate military policy after the war ended." For additional valuable historical treatments of gays in the military during World War II, see also Costello 1985 and D'Emilio 1983.

2. In this regard I am grateful to Krin Gabbard for suggesting the relevance of Roland Barthes (1977, 40–41), who introduced the concept of "anchorage" in captions. The caption delimits the potential range of meanings in the photograph it explains: "the anchorage may be ideological and indeed this is its principal function; the text directs the reader through the signifieds of the image, causing him to avoid some and receive others; by means of an often subtle dispatching, it remote-controls him towards a meaning chosen in advance . . . Anchorage is the most frequent function of the linguistic message and is commonly found in press photographs and advertisements."

3. In fact the *Time* reviewer spoke of "the horsing and singing of the wool-bearing *Ladies of the Chorus*, who have taken almost excruciating care to be mistaken neither for transvestite chorusmen nor for the quite convincing young ladies they dared to be on Broadway" ("New Picture" 1943, 93–94).

4. As Doherty (1999, 75–78) has explained, servicemen overseas were regularly afforded opportunities to watch Hollywood films. An article in *Time* on domestic camp movie theaters indicated that the most popular films among soldiers were "musicals with girls" ("Second Chain" 1943, 96).

5. This ad was found on the last page of *Newsweek*, December 7, 1942, or the inside cover of December 14, 1942.

6. Doherty (1999, 56) notes: "In the combat reports, GI backsides were exposed during scenes of jungle bathing."

7. For important arguments about showing males naked, see Lehman 1995, 1–36, 147–168.

8. See, for example, the ad in the October 2, 1944 issue.

9. The drawing of naked soldiers bathing in the first True towel ad was repeated in a much smaller ad for Strathmore Letterhead Papers (owned by Cannon). This ad did not have the insert of the woman although it offers the qualifying commentary that stresses the need for the refreshment offered by the water (*Time*, April 17, 1944, 93). The caption reads: "Cannon towels get a mighty hand from the boys at the front. A cooling dip . . . a brisk rubdown with a sturdy, durable Cannon towel . . . that's tops after grilling marches or hours of combat under blazing skies and in steaming jungles." I disagree with Costello (1985, 119), who thinks: "An indication that public attitudes to the taboo of homosexuality were also shifting came with the appearance of homoerotic advertisements in American magazines, which began featuring male 'pinup' such as those for Munsingwear underwear and Cannon bath towels." In fact, as I argue throughout, the opposite is the case.

Chris Straayer

Transgender Mirrors: Queering Sexual Difference

Since the invention of homosexuality more than a century ago, professional and lay "audiences" alike have situated gender as its primary marker—as both what marks it and what it marks. From Weimar Germany's "third sex" to second-wave feminism's "lesbian-woman," gay men and lesbians have been measured in terms of their femininity and masculinity, which then have laid claims on their femaleness and maleness. Although gender displaced sexual orientation in these crude schemes, it also provided a primary visual semiotics through which queers communicated their sexualities. The present essay also reverses the signifying chain: rather than an engendering look at queerness, I take a queering look at gender.[1]

While they are often characterized as distinct traits, gender and sexual orientation are not entities that can be plucked from or implanted in a person. Outside the social event known as "self," they do not exist. Neither are they uniform from self to self. Gender and sexual orientation come into "being" within individual-cultural complexes that variably form and incorporate them. (The concepts of transgender and homosexual identities, born from oppression as well as resistance, always remain most suitable to the oppressors' dehumanizing mode of thought.) Transgendered people and gays and lesbians are fighting and delighting on multiple fronts simultaneously.

In this essay, I discuss two independent video documentaries: *Juggling Gender* (Tami Gold, 1992), which profiles Jennifer Miller, a bearded lesbian; and *OUTLAW* (Alisa Lebow, 1994), which profiles Leslie Feinberg, a transgendered lesbian. These works dispute binary sex and the sex-gender matrix. Because feminism has enacted the most intensive investigation of gender, it offers an appropriate starting point for discussion. While I understand that feminism is not a static and impermeably bounded discipline, I nevertheless find its paradigm of sexual difference inadequate to certain questions about identity raised by *Juggling Gender* and *OUTLAW*.

In writing about independent documentary, I am less concerned with the distinction between representation and reality (the issue of document) than with the competition between different representations to define "reality" (the issue of independence). I take as a given that the documentaries I discuss are instances of discourse rather than windows on reality. Nevertheless, I also assume that the producers and subjects enacting such discourse are communicating with real purpose. Although both mainstream and independent documentaries are mediated, they are differently mediated at the institutional level. Independent productions avoid much of the gate-keeping and censorship of corporate financing entities and exhibition venues.

As I see it, the problem of mistaking representation for reality is now most salient not at the level of the viewership, but in the claim made by dominant ideology on representation itself. I focus on *independent* media production because it dearticulates the "insider" perspective that too often imbues mainstream media as well as contemporary theory. These video profiles in particular represent "outsider" experiences by foregrounding otherwise marginalized voices. Acknowledging the existence of such voices exposes the self-serving conflation of center with all, mainstream with society. I am not suggesting that independent media's sanctioned charge should be to accurately represent reality or even potential reality. Rather, I am looking at these specific videos as counterdominant discourses that produce countermeanings. I value them not only for their difference from mainstream representations but also for the important contributions they offer to theorizations of subjectivity. Again and again, "outsider" representations reveal the inadequacy of dominant ideology—sometimes through wrenching testimony.

Juggling Gender is a portrait of Jennifer Miller, a woman in her early thirties who began to develop a beard in late adolescence. Although beards do not uniformly occupy a sex-defining position across different races and cultures, they do in Miller's family and culture.[2] As her beard thickened, Miller became increasingly estranged from her family. Her grandmother urged her to undergo electrolysis, but Miller experienced the process as an extremely painful mutilation; further, having come out in the lesbian-feminist era and then undergoing electrolysis made Miller feel like a traitor to herself and her cause. If lesbian feminism's aesthetic of natural womanness encouraged letting one's leg and underarm hair grow, why not facial hair too? In lesbian bars and other women-only spaces, however, many women have resented the confusion Miller's appearance can cause. They never expected to mistake a "natural" woman for a man. Ironically, it was cultural feminism's endorsement of essential womanhood that enabled Miller to challenge the codification of sexual difference.

Miller describes how having a full beard has altered her gender, which is formed not only from who she is and how she behaves but also by her inter-

Jennifer Miller in Juggling Gender *(1992)*

actions with society. She would like the term *woman* to include her; however, after years of also being treated like a man, she thinks of herself as not just woman. Her experiences on the street have widened her construction to incorporate sometimes being man.[3]

Against earlier plans for college and professional life, Miller helped create a feminist circus where her "freak" status is acceptable. In the circus, she juggles, bearded and bare-breasted, foregrounding her sexual discontinuity. She eats fire, lies on a bed of nails, and performs other circus acts to make explicit society's ostracizing gaze at her. Performing as a Coney Island sideshow, she reminds the audience that many women have beards, that non-bearded femininity is constructed via shaving and electrolysis. "Women have the potential to have beards," she challenges them, "if only they would reach out." Unlike the women in the audience, however, Miller is the bearded lady, constructed as such by their look *at* her, which, by attributing deviance to her willful gender nonconformance, contributes to her subsequent downward class mobility.

At the end of *Juggling Gender,* Miller is shown at a lesbian and gay pride march performing "faggot" drag. As she notes, there are as yet no codes for performing a bearded lesbian gender. Faggot behavior, she explains, is a response to being looked at, a situation to which she relates. Suddenly the camera pans back and forth between Miller and a drag queen sticking out their tongues to mime each other.

Miller's life as a bearded lesbian combines two discourses that elsewhere have produced altercation—cultural feminism and gay male drag. Many feminists, including many lesbian feminists, have read gay male drag as misogynous, even as they criticize the trappings of femininity for women. The fact that gay drag was read as a criticism of women themselves (rather than a parody of the masquerade)[4] illustrates the lasting power of reactionary codes even as they are deconstructed. In the present semiotic system, it *is* difficult to undo the collapse of woman with feminine masquerade. But Jennifer Miller's decision to let her beard grow exposes the *complicity* of many women in *maintaining* a system in which a beard is an essential definer of sex. Although under severe ideological pressure that would naturalize and thus strongly determine it, most women *consciously* choose electrolysis. If women are essentially different from men, this difference is certainly not attributable to a lack of facial hair. An essentialist position that also claims the accoutrements of masquerade or relies on the reconstruction of bodies is questionable. On the other hand, if one is constructed in the meaning that one's signs have to others, is not the presence or absence of accoutrements and facial hair an important producer of gender?

Miller's performance demonstrates how essentialist and constructionist discourses can lead into each other. Allowing her beard to grow is a direct extension of her cultural feminist training; but in so doing Miller belies the essentialism on which cultural feminism is based. In taking cultural feminism's tenet of "naturalness" to its logical conclusion, Miller risks exclusion from that very community, because to that community, as to mainstream society, she risks appearing to "be" a man.

Jennifer Miller is not the only character in *Juggling Gender,* for video-making is also a means of performing. Offscreen but verbally present, the video-maker Tami Gold narrates her experience of making the tape. Gold initially explores her identity as a feminist, but her contact with Miller causes her to question gender itself. "What is a woman?" she asks. By including herself in the video as a thinking and learning presence, Gold suggests a responsible viewing mode for us. Our similarity to and difference from Coney Island audiences become clearer as Gold situates us to hear and consider what Miller is saying. Like Gold herself, we stare at Miller's image, but the tape infuses this voyeurism with a keen awareness of Jennifer Miller's subjectivity. Rather than hiding Miller's body and shying away from her "freakish" self-presentations, Gold contextualizes such images with Miller's testimony. Gold not only constructs Miller's image but also constructs herself as our surrogate. As such, she encourages self-critical, intellectually engaged, and informed looking.

Endocrinology, psychoanalysis, and object relations are among the dominant discourses that define gender identity. Although many factors distinguish these theories, they all understand gender as basically fixed. Recent endocrinology research looks to the fetal environment for the determination of a core gender identity; psychoanalysis looks to the oedipal stage up to approximately age five and only secondarily to adolescence; object relations theory looks to the preoedipal mother-child relation in very early childhood. Many feminist theorists who assert the construction of gender follow object relations to understand sex attribution as the primary determinant of gender. I agree that sex attribution is influential, but, taking Jennifer Miller's gender juggling as a case in point, I neither locate it exclusively in early childhood nor understand it as fixed. Gender formation is constantly in process; rather than being a root of oneself, it continues throughout life via interactions with others. Not only is one's mother a gender mirror, but also everyone else one meets in life. The process of sex attribution (that is, gendering) does not stop at birth. For most people, complicity with binary gender semiotics (sex role stereotypes, conventional clothing, and so on) allows social interaction to reinforce birthtime sex attribution and thus gender. For others, voluntary or involuntary nonconformity causes radical disruptions and contradictions.

Wearing a beard, Jennifer Miller crosses the semiotic boundary between female and male and thus alters the basis upon which others construct her gender. This circular, interactive formation raises complex issues about "self." Obviously, had Miller concealed her beard, as other women have, her gender

identity today would be different than it is—not because gender resides in biology (which can be controlled), but because of (a different) cultural production.
A person, then, is simultaneously the producer of a persona and the product of
the way(s) others read (and project into) that persona (and its failings).

Although Jennifer Miller is "out" as a lesbian in *Juggling Gender*, the
tape produces meaning for the most part via its feminist voice.[5] Gold underlines the tape's feminist parameters by replacing the disembodied male authority of voice-of-God documentaries with cinema verité segments, performance,
interviews, and attributable, subjective voice-overs by Miller and herself. She
identifies herself as a continuing feminist even as her (particular) feminist perspective and assumptions are challenged by Miller. Miller also identifies as a
feminist even though some feminists reject her. More important, Miller is portrayed as neither hero nor outlaw, for both positions would support an all-or-
nothing mode of thinking. Instead she is cast as a noncomplicit survivor, which
is why she impresses many audiences as a role model.[6] As such, she variously
identifies as a woman and passes as a man.

Miller expresses "contradictory" positions throughout *Juggling Gender*; at times she asserts that she is still a woman (despite mistaken interpretations by strangers), but she also clearly insists that her gender is no longer
reducible to *woman*. In my analysis here, I do not claim direct access to Jennifer Miller, Tami Gold, or *Juggling Gender*. Instead, I am elaborating on *my
reading* of the tape. My own theorization of gender dismisses any prediscursive
nature/body that would fix gender. I understand both gender and sex as "know-
able" and negotiable only through convention. Like Gold and Miller, who are
feminists challenging feminism, *Juggling Gender* pressures feminism rather
than attacks it.

In 1970, at the Second Congress to Unite Women, the "lavender menace" disrupted scheduled events with a staged coming out that confronted
straight feminists with their heterosexism and homophobia. Ironically, while
denaturalizing the gathering's assumed unity, the action ultimately functioned
to unite heterosexual women and lesbians via a circulated position paper from
the Radicalesbians entitled "The Woman Identified Woman." In this short
paper, the authors concisely argued that straight feminists should, like lesbians,
channel their nurturance toward other women. In this way, they posited lesbianism as a feminist practice and feminism as the defining characteristic of
lesbianism. The paper began, "What is a lesbian? A lesbian is the rage of all
women condensed to the point of explosion." The Radicalesbians suggested
that the straight versus lesbian split in the women's movement was attributable to patriarchal oppression on two counts: first, lesbianism, as distinct from
heterosexuality, was the result of women's struggle for self-growth; and second,
accusations of lesbianism were used by men to keep straight women in sub-

servient roles. The paper called for straight women to lose their defensiveness by refusing to consider lesbianism as negative and to replace their internalized sexism with a commitment to women:

> It must be understood that what is crucial is that women begin disengaging from male-defined response patterns. In the privacy of our own psyches, we must cut those cords to the core. For irrespective of where our love and sexual energies flow, if we are male identified in our heads, we cannot realize our autonomy as human beings. . . .
>
> Only women can give each other a new sense of self. That identity we have to develop with reference to ourselves and not in relation to men. This consciousness is the revolutionary force from which all else will follow, for ours is an organic revolution. For this we must be available and supportive to one another, give our commitment and our love, give the emotional support necessary to sustain this movement. Our energies must flow toward our sisters, not backward toward our oppressors. (Radicalesbians 1973, 166)

Terralee Bensinger has argued that this document sacrificed lesbian sexuality to the politics of sexual difference (1992, 74). One can readily see its contribution to a lesbian continuum where feminist mutuality (a.k.a. sisterhood) rather than sexuality defines the term *lesbian.* From a different perspective, Eve Kosofsky Sedgwick has described the document as "a stunningly efficacious coup of feminist redefinition" that provided a rare shift in the understanding of lesbianism, from a model of gender inversion to one of gender separatism (1990, 84, 88). I would like to briefly highlight what I see to be a related and equally important negotiation in the document, between two modes of identity.

Cultural feminism seems an essentialist discourse par excellence. Inverting the sexual hierarchy without disturbing sexual binarism, it valorizes female over male characteristics. Cultural feminism appropriates men's association of women with nature as the model for a better world. Extrapolated from women's birthing capacity, nurturance becomes a gender-defining principle.[7] In "The Woman Identified Woman," the Radicalesbians were able to turn the accusation of male-identification (previously directed at lesbians, who, because of their attraction to women, were assumed to be like men—that is, not real women) back on straight feminists by asserting the source of identity to be relational rather than integral. Directed at lesbians, the accusation of male identification posits a condition of self (virilization); directed at straight women, it posits a condition of (nonfeminist) allegiance. Viewed through this lesbian-feminist lens that understands identity through relations, personal relations with men jeopardize straight women's gender identity, while lesbians' female gender is secured by their romantic relationships. In this sense, sexual practice is not totally absent from the document's scene. In fact, object choice now determines gender via a schematic directly opposed to the assumption of heterogender that previously cast lesbians as "wannabe" men. Rather than basing *feminist* identity on what one is, the privileged ethic of nurturance was deployed to relocate such identity in how and toward whom one directs one's energy. This is a significant shift in terms. Unlike the gender essentialism on which female identity is based, feminist identity (the woman identified woman) is based on relational behavior. Further, such behavior ironically is attributed to natural womanness.

Although situated somewhat differently, Jennifer Miller's gender identity is also relations-based. Treated like a man, she becomes manlike. It is not her beard but rather people's reactions to its mark that have altered her gender. Those who see her as a man (as well as those who see her as a woman, or as a bearded woman) help mold her gender. Their gaze is her gender mirror. Like their gaze, her gender is both multifaceted and culturally specific; thus it disrupts unified concepts of gender. Unlike both cultural feminists and the Radicalesbians, Miller wants the category of women to expand to include her "virilization."

Elizabeth Grosz's book *Volatile* describes the body as a socio-historical product that functions interactively, and implants corporeality in the theorization of subjectivity (1994, x, xi). The material textures of bodies, rather than being blank pages waiting for cultural inscription, participate in and affect such inscriptions. This would seem to support Jennifer Miller's account of her gender formation.

In her final chapter, "Sexed Bodies," Grosz uses the work of Mary Douglas, Julia Kristeva, Luce Irigaray, and Iris Young to scrutinize how, in Western culture, bodily fluids that "attest to the permeability of the body" (1994, 193) are assigned to the feminine. Orifices and leakage threaten a masculine order that relies on a notion of self as closed entity. A production of otherness thus underlies man's projection of the body itself onto woman, which seeks to eliminate his own pervious status and claim for him alone the supposedly more neutral, less situated mind. "Women, insofar as they are human, have the same degree of solidity, occupy the same genus, as men, yet insofar as they are women, they are represented and live themselves as seepage, liquidity" (1994, 203). Patriarchal discourse does not describe subject formation as relational but rather as the ascension to a bounded, phallic self. Grosz challenges the mind-body dualism and presses that challenge against the "mechanics of solids" that inscribes and supports male subjectivity (1994, 204).

The strength of Grosz's work is that it asserts that the experience of one's body (including one's relation to cultural meanings of one's sex) contributes to the formation of subjectivity. From this she rightly concludes that one's previously sexed life experience and subjectivity do not simply drop away with a sex change. However, does the influence of bodily and relational experiences suddenly halt with a sex change? What might Grosz's investigation of corporeal experience throughout her book offer to understanding how subject formation continues as bodily changes occur, whether via sex change or menopause? My pointing to an interplay of representation, perception, and experience with regard to subject formation allows that the (changing) body can influence subjectivity without discounting contrary gender identifications.

Jennifer Miller's beard arrived on her with discursive valence. After all, it is a secondary sex characteristic. As such, it was supposed to (but did not) support an already sexed subjectivity, a sexual identity. A beard is supposed to be a reward at the end of horrifying *male* adolescence, a solidification after that messy stage of bodily transformations. Secondary sex characteristics are conceptualized as the final confirmations, not complications, of one's sex. They are *supposed* to offer relief after prolonged worries about whether our childish bodies will deliver the "appropriate" sexes or ultimately expose our "freakishness."

We patrol gender expressly because our claim to normality (that is, conventional humanness) has been made to rely on it. Not to be one's true sex is a crime against the law of pure difference. Mary Douglas's definition of dirt as that which is (culturally determined to be) out of place describes Jennifer Miller's beard. Hair is a waste product of our bodies, like urine, menstrual blood, and toenails. A man's beard, evidence of "masculine" flow, is best kept shaved or trimmed into a sculpture. A bearded woman, evidence of flow across sexual difference, is cultural feminism's abject.

In *Bodies That Matter*, Judith Butler analyzes how "properly" gendered bodies are materialized through heterosexual norms and how such formation of heterosexual subjects relies on foreclosures that produce homosexuality and gender inversion as abject: "The abject designates here precisely those 'unlivable' and 'uninhabitable' zones of social life which are nevertheless densely populated by those who do not enjoy the status of subject, but whose living under the sign of 'unlivable' is required to circumscribe the domain of the subject" (1993, 3). Constraints generate both sanctioned and unsanctioned positions but uphold the former via a logic that repudiates the latter. Such a normative scheme would understand Jennifer Miller as having failed to materialize as a (human) subject. Instead, her deformation serves as the constitutive "outside" by which normality is constituted and regulatory norms are fortified (Butler 1993, 16). Her abject status locates her outside subjecthood. She is alive but not fully human.

The underlying problems in this operation, which affect all gay and lesbian and transgendered "subjects," are an Althusserian-influenced totalizing of ideology[8] and an overwillingness in Lacanian psychoanalysis to relegate irregular subjects to the "unrepresentable," a zone lacking symbolization and hence subjects. This is to mistake dominant ideology for all symbolization and to assume that what is unrepresented is unrepresentable. By contrast, Jennifer

Miller does not experience herself as abject, and she obviously claims subject-hood. She has not undergone a "psychotic dissolution" simply because she is no longer one-sex-identified. Nor does *she* see herself as the "living prospect of death."[9]

Despite her valuable identification of regulatory regimes that construct abjection, Butler details this operation *rhetorically* from an "inside" perspective. This limits the "imagination" of her theorization and contributes to the naturalization of a particular standpoint, which is then allowed to define abjection. Certainly, it can be argued that no person can exist totally outside dominant ideology, and therefore that the dominant ideology's abject is uninhabitable. However, given the coexistence of "other" discourses that rearticulate dominant terms from "other" positions (that dominant ideology would assign to the abject) a particular subject materialization may be considerably more complex than such a regulating discourse would suggest. Part of what dominant ideology expels via assignment to *its* abject is, in fact, *formative* counterdiscourse.[10]

Butler opposes (theoretically speaking) any claim to coherent identity.[11] Following Laplanche and Pontalis's theorization of fantasy as the staging and dispersion of the subject, in which the subject cannot be assigned to any one position, Butler asserts that the normative subject is produced not by the refusal to identify with the other, but rather through *identification with* an abject other (Butler 1993, 267, 112):

> A radical refusal to identify with a given position suggests that on some level an identification has already taken place, an identification that is made and disavowed, a disavowed identification whose symptomatic appearance is the insistence on the overdetermination of, the identification by which gay and lesbian subjects come to signify in public discourse. (Butler 1993, 113).

Likewise, Butler is careful to qualify the subversive potential of gender performativity. One cannot simply take on gender like one chooses clothing; this would imply a subject prior to gender. Rather, it is repetition in gender that forms the subject. Butler credits subversive rearticulation of the symbolic to the return of figures once repudiated (to the imaginary); this establishes a process of resignification rather than opposition and attributes contestation to the process of signification that inadvertently enables what it attempts to restrict (Butler 1993, 109). Although Butler allows for inexact repetitions, she is opposed to attributing any amendments to personal choice or deliberation:

> The practice by which gendering occurs, the embodying of norms, is a compulsory practice, a forcible production, but not for that reason fully determining. To the extent that gender is an assignment, it is an assignment which is never quite carried out according to expectation, whose addressee

never quite inhabits the ideal *s/he* is compelled to approximate. Moreover, this embodying is a repeated process. And one might construe repetition as precisely that which *undermines* the conceit of voluntarist mastery designated by the subject in language. (1993, 231)

Butler's work is outstanding for its deconstructions of identity and "natural" gender. However, her elucidation here seems more useful for understanding women's attempts to live up to an ideal—that is, their complicity with the maintenance of sexual difference—than for understanding feminist rejections of the ideal. For example, it better accounts for electrolysis as gender performativity ("the tacit cruelties that sustain coherent identity, cruelties that include self-cruelty") (Butler 1993, 115) than for Miller's refusal of electrolysis. It better explicates women's assumption of dominant norms for purposes of self-hatred than Miller's unconventional strength. Jennifer Miller's gendering cannot be explained simply as a failure to repeat. Certainly, the development of a beard on her body misses its conventional assignment; however, is not her decision to let the beard grow a choice (even if it is derived from a feminist ideology), and the subsequent (re)gendering (via the responses of others to her body) a result of her deliberate action (or inaction)? Does not Miller's bodily utterance alter the language of gender to some extent? Does not Gold's videotape reveal the boundary between symbolization and the "unrepresentable" real to be always in practice a fiction produced from a particular (dominant yet limited) point of view?

What I am suggesting by my discussion of Jennifer Miller in *Juggling Gender* is a salient temporality in subject formation. If indeed the subject is always a subject-in-process, then at any one point she is formed, being formed, and forming. Does not her formedness grant some subjectivity (however provisional), which she exercises even as cultural norms continue to interpellate her? My insistence on taking up marginal rather than (exclusively) dominant perspectives in theorizing subjectivity opens the way for *appreciating* a difference between a *failure* to repeat and a *refusal* to repeat.

In *OUTLAW* Leslie Feinberg, a transgender lesbian, describes her life as an everyday struggle. Feinberg is interviewed in a variety of meaningful settings. At the Pyramid Club, she refers to the female impersonators as sisters. At Liberty State Park in New Jersey, she criticizes people who assume the right to stare. At the Hudson piers, a Manhattan site notorious for transgenderist (and gay) gatherings and bashings, she explains that any place where transgenderists go becomes dangerous (for them). In her backyard, she explains that, to her, *butch* means butch on the street, an act of courage that earns one the right to engage in whatever acts she wants to in bed. At the gym, surrounded by workout machines and mirrors, she describes her self-image as a combination of how she sees herself and how the world sees her. In choosing the gym as an interview setting, Feinberg contributed to her media construction in a way transgenderists seldom are allowed to do. Rather than simply exposing the transgendered body for spectacle, Feinberg retains her subject position in an environment symbolic of self-empowerment.

Feinberg's testimony is solemn throughout *OUTLAW*. Only at rare moments does her enjoyment of life break through: in her exquisite "men's" suits, in scenes with her lover repotting plants and watching a home movie. When clips from *The Rocky Horror Picture Show* suggest a reprieve from her testimony of constant oppression, Feinberg reminds us that a mere movie is not going to liberate Eighth Street (in New York City, where the film was then playing midnights) from transgender bashing. Elsewhere, when Feinberg speaks of transgenderists reclaiming their histories, her smile is undercut by an edit to helicopters flying overhead in formation.

The pleasure in viewing *OUTLAW* derives from the complex collaboration of Feinberg's discourse and Alisa Lebow's disquisition. Using music (Danny Galton's "Funky Momma," for example), intertitles ("Suit and Tie Optional," for example), and extradiegetic imagery (a woman bodybuilder, for example), Lebow both underlines and adds ambiguity to Feinberg's analysis of transgender oppression. At one point Feinberg expresses disapproval and impatience with people who compare their childhood gender crossings with her lived experience. Such linkages erase the actual repression she risks when, for instance, she uses a public washroom. Lebow's inclusion of footage from the film *Yentl* at this point in the tape both demonstrates how transgenderism is often trivialized and also implies a continuum from feminist cross-dressing to transgenderism, which offers a conduit for viewer identification.

Lebow's video-making is most aggressive when she re-presents a scene of Feinberg appearing on the *Joan Rivers Show*, where Feinberg proclaims the need for transgenderists to name and speak for themselves. Through skillful editing, Lebow becomes Feinberg's co-conspirator. "I'm so sick of being psychologized. I'm so sick of being studied like a butterfly pinned to the wall," says Feinberg in voice-over as the face of a token authority figure, clinical sexologist Roger E. Peo, Ph.D., appears on the screen. Then Lebow audiocuts to sync sound as Peo begins, "I'm not in a position to judge and say this person should do this thing or that thing. What I try to do is . . ." On the original broadcast, the authority no doubt went on to state his opinion, but in the Lebow/Feinberg version his appraisal is excised. Smoothly but decisively, Lebow interrupts him with an audiovisual cut to Feinberg, who continues, now in sync sound: "All our lives, we've always seen ourselves refracted through other people's prisms. We're always hearing people analyze us, describe what our feelings are, what our thoughts are. How about talking about why Jesse Helms needs some therapy?"

OUTLAW begins with a discussion of Joan of Arc and ends with a dedication to Brandon Teena and Marsha P. Johnson. Brandon Teena (born Teena

Leslie Feinberg in Outlaw *(1994)*

Brandon but living as a male) was raped by two young men on Christmas Eve 1993 in Nebraska. Although Teena's face was injured and a hospital test confirmed recent vaginal penetration, his attackers were released after questioning. No arrests were made. One week later, on New Year's Eve, the same young men allegedly killed Teena. Martha Johnson, a drag queen veteran of the Stonewall rebellion, was found dead in the Hudson River (off the piers) after the 1992 New York City gay pride march. Although there were signs of resistance, Johnson's death was declared a suicide after a perfunctory police investigation. In addition to the outsider status guaranteed by their transgenderism, Teena and Johnson were working-class people. Like Feinberg, they lacked the protection of class privilege experienced by more acclaimed historical cross-dressers such as Radclyffe Hall, George Sand, and Gertrude Stein. It is significant to Feinberg that the powerful and persecuted Joan of Arc, who not only sported men's clothes but also passed as a man, was a peasant. That Feinberg could not know this as a child is a culpable suppression of (transgender) evidence. Gender and class are inseparable in all of these people and their expressions; we cannot know the meanings of their different transgenders without also knowing their class situations.

While claiming both transgenderism and homosexuality, Feinberg is careful to distinguish between them. During her interview at the Pyramid Club, she draws two intersecting circles on a blackboard and indicates her own position: within the intersection. *OUTLAW* reminds us that much of the violence enacted against gays and lesbians actually is directed at transgenderism.[12] Of course, as I remarked at the beginning of this essay, gender and sexual orientation have been intertwined historically by sexological discourse and homosexual appropriation of such discourse for self-coding. Transgenderism is attacked partly because it reads as homosexuality and vice versa. It is therefore important neither to collapse homosexuality and transgenderism nor to overlook their specific imbrications.

Eve Kosofsky Sedgwick argues in "How to Bring Your Kids Up Gay" that neither an essentialist nor a constructionist position guarantees safety for homosexual subjectivity. She locates a shift during the 1970s and 1980s from pathologizing adult homosexuality to pathologizing childhood gender crossing. The 1980 edition of the American Psychiatric Association's *Diagnostic and Statistical Manual* was both the first not to contain an entry for "Homosexuality" and the first to contain the entry "Gender Identity Disorder of Childhood." To Sedgwick, this *preventive* measure expresses the rage of parents, professionals, society at large, and even gays and lesbians at sissy boys and, to a lesser extent, butch girls. Ironically, she points out, the new psychoanalytic move to pathologize gender disorder while depathologizing sexual orientation is based on the recent theoretical move to distinguish gender and sex orientation (for example, the gender constructionist approaches of John Money and Robert Stoller) (Sedgwick 1993, 154–164). This makes it clear that the attempt by some homosexuals to pry apart gender and sexual orientation not only is inadequate but can fuel a reactionary discourse against those among us who cross gender. Therefore, any rejection of masculinity in lesbians or metaphoric feminization of the term *lesbian* warrants extreme caution.

Juggling Gender and *OUTLAW* re-present voices that contest the borders generally assumed to dominate symbolization and subject formation and problematize theory that situates its rhetorical point of view strictly within those borders. I understand gender and gender formation to be more flexible than the paradigm sexual binarism produces and to be continually influenced by social experience. By focusing on independent media, I call attention to alternative representations as well as alternative subjects.

NOTES

1. The videos discussed, *Juggling Gender* and *OUTLAW,* are distributed by Women Make Movies, 462 Broadway. Suite 500D, New York, NY 10013; telephone 212-925-0606; fax 212-925-2052; e-mail distdept@wmm.com.
2. For a wide-ranging discussion of differently sexed and gendered cultures, see Herdt 1994.

3. In *Juggling Gender*, gender often refers also to sex. Because of Miller's being perceived as one of the male sex, her constructed gender-sex expands beyond womanness.

4. Doane (1991, 17–32), drawing on Joan Riviere, has argued that womanliness *is* the masquerade of femininity. I complicate this in Straayer 1996, chapter 5.

5. The video foregrounds feminism over lesbianism. The extent to which the absence of lesbian sexuality is a by-product of the tape's focus, necessary for its feminist efficacy, and/or a self-conscious avoidance of the dangerous terrain of gender inversion explanations of homosexuality is difficult to determine.

6. The function of role model is important here because, as Butler (1993, 107) argues, the performative utterance has no valence unless it is repeated. Ultimately, Miller's rearticulation "exposes the norm itself as a privileged interpretation" (Butler 1993, 108) and serves as a model for *not* citing, *not* repeating assumed symbolic categories. In this way, I question the precision and efficacy of using the term *citation* (or *repetition*) to refer to both complicit and subversive acts.

7. See Echols 1989; Jagger 1983; and my discussion of motherhood in Straayer 1996, chapter 5.

8. The continued deployment of the repressive state apparatus should remind us that the ideological state apparatus is not as totalizing as it would have us believe.

9. Butler (1993, 98) says: "The breaking of certain taboos brings on the spectre of psychosis, but to what extent can we understand 'psychosis' as relative to the very prohibitions that guard against it? In other words, what precise cultural possibilities threaten the subject with a psychotic dissolution, marking the boundaries of livable being? To what extent is the fantasy of psychotic dissolution itself the effect of a certain prohibition against those sexual possibilities which abrogate the heterosexual contract? Under what conditions and under the sway of what regulatory schemes does homosexuality itself appear as the living prospect of death?"

10. For clarification, I want to stress that I am not taking up an imagined "other" position with respect to Butler. I am not promoting a humanist view of free will and individuality. I agree with Butler that language constrains subject formation. Nevertheless, I think that theoretical investigation should include the choice and responsibility within these limitations. To think of culture as *all* determining is neither accurate nor productive. Butler (1993, 97) *asks*: "Does not the refusal to concur with the abjection of homosexuality necessitate a critical rethinking of the psychoanalytic economy of sex?" Butler's focus here is sexual orientation, but I think she produces the same question regarding gender.

11. This includes those claims from the homosexual abject, whether gay, lesbian, sissy, butch, or femme (Butler 1993, 113). As she states, "Heterosexuality does not have a monopoly on exclusionary logics" (1993, 112).

12. Such violence is also directed at transgenderism among heterosexuals.

Gendering Genre

Jerry Mosher

Hard Boiled and Soft Bellied:
The Fat Heavy in Film Noir

Twitching and stigmatized, an unknown breed of men rose up before us.
—Raymond Borde and Etienne Chaumeton,
Panorama du Film Noir Américain

I didn't recognize you. You should lay off those candy bars.
—Marlene Dietrich to Orson Welles, *Touch of Evil*

In his introduction to the *Film Noir Reader*, Alain Silver states, "If observers of film noir agree on anything, it is on the boundaries of the classical period, which begins in 1941 with *The Maltese Falcon* and ends less than a score of years later with *Touch of Evil*" (1996, 11). The retroactive designation of these films as the "bookends" of film noir's classical period has been contested as too convenient or arbitrary, but many critics have made a persuasive case for the coalescence of classical film noir elements in *The Maltese Falcon*: its taut narrative, hard-boiled dialogue, femme fatale character, modern style and décor, and, especially, casting. No actor influenced film noir's development more than Humphrey Bogart as private detective Sam Spade, whose moral certitude was cut with inner turbulence and whose sexual escapades were undermined by ambivalence and guilt. Convincing arguments have also been made for the unraveling of these classical elements in the baroque *Touch of Evil* (1958), whose grotesquerie and dissipation so resolutely buried film noir conventions (which had begun to border on parody) that Paul Schrader, in his influential 1972 essay "Notes on Film Noir," deemed it "film noir's epitaph" (1972, 12).

What has not been addressed, however, is the fact that in both of these milestone films *the fat man steals the show*. When Warner Bros. asked a preview audience to name their favorite character in *The Maltese Falcon*, nearly all of the viewers answered, "the fat man" (Jones 1941). Among the film's stellar cast, only 285-pound Sydney Greenstreet received an Academy Award nomination. The sixty-one-year-old Greenstreet's sly portrayal of the articulate and menacing fat

Sidney Greenstreet with Humphrey Bogart in The Maltese Falcon *(1941). Warner Bros. Museum of Modern Art Film Stills Archive.*

heavy, aptly named Kasper Gutman, would prove to be a performance as iconic as that of Bogart. "To some acute Hollywood eye, Greenstreet represented a niche that needed to be filled," critic Stanley Kauffmann later noted. "There were other fat men in pictures, but not with that suavity or the depravity underneath the jolly smile" (1992, 154).

In May 1941, five months before Greenstreet's screen debut, Orson Welles had made his own unforgettable debut in *Citizen Kane.* The film's expressionistic style, investigative plot, complex chronology, and depiction of corrupted ideals would influence the American crime drama as much as *The Maltese Falcon* (Schatz 1981, 116–122).[1] Like Greenstreet, Welles would receive an Academy Award nomination for his portrayal of a greedy man driven to decadence in his futile search to recapture a mysterious and elusive ideal. The twenty-five-year-old Welles, cherubic but still relatively thin at the time, used makeup and padding to play a wide range of ages and sizes. Welles's appearance sometimes changed dramatically from one scene to the next, prophetically demonstrating the struggles he would have with weight for the rest of his life. Seventeen years later, in *Touch of Evil*, Welles weighed 350 pounds. In this film

Orson Welles in A Touch of Evil *(1958). Universal International. Museum of Modern Art Film Stills Archive.*

Welles took the fat heavy, which by 1958 had become a familiar and coveted role, to its logical extreme—he made him the protagonist. In interviews Welles denied it, insisting that his character, police chief Hank Quinlan, is "hateful" and Mexican investigator Mike Vargas (Charlton Heston) is the mouthpiece of the film's ideas (Bazin 1985, 204–205). Heston, however, knew Welles had the lead role from the start: "His part was the best part in the film . . . *Touch of Evil* is about the decline and fall of Captain Quinlan. My part is a kind of witness to this" (Delson 1985, 214).

The fat heavy's prominence in these bookends of film noir's classical period reveals the figure's importance within the film noir mythos. During the classical period, an unprecedented number of fat actors appeared in the crime drama; in the decade following Greenstreet's debut in *The Maltese Falcon*, new-comers Laird Cregar, Raymond Burr, William Conrad, Thomas Gomez, and Hope Emerson gained industry distinction playing fat heavies, and veteran fat actors such as Charles Laughton, Francis L. Sullivan, and Edward Arnold contributed some brilliant performances. The increasing number of fat men's roles in crime dramas can be partially attributed to the size consciousness of Dashiell Hammett, whose "thin man" and "fat man" characters appeared in numerous stories, novels, films, and radio programs from the 1930s through the 1950s.

MGM's lucrative screwball-detective series *The Thin Man*, based on Hammett's 1934 novel, starred William Powell and Myrna Loy in six films between 1934 and 1947. (The "thin man" was a murder victim in the first film, but the description became associated with Powell's suave detective.) Hammett's most famous fat man, Kasper Gutman in *The Maltese Falcon*, had been killed in the 1930 novel and in Warner Bros.' 1931 film adaptation, where he was played by the portly, fifty-one-year-old Dudley Digges.[2] In Warner Bros.' 1941 version, however, director/screenwriter John Huston preserved Greenstreet's fat man, perhaps sensing the allure of the role and Greenstreet's star-making performance. When Gutman and Joel Cairo (Peter Lorre) escape at the end of the film, it is implied that their quest for the falcon will continue.[3] Although a sequel did not materialize, the villainous pairing of the huge Greenstreet and the eccentric Lorre made such an impression that they appeared in eight more films together, establishing themselves as "the Laurel and Hardy of crime." The popularity of the fat man role also spawned a radio detective series called *The Fat Man* (billed as a Hammett "creation"), which aired on the ABC radio network from 1946 to 1950 and starred J. Scott Smart, who played the titular detective in a screen adaptation for Universal in 1951. Meanwhile, in 1934 crime writer Rex Stout created his fat detective Nero Wolfe, who was featured in dozens of novels, two screen adaptations (played by Edward Arnold in 1936's *Meet Nero Wolfe* and Walter Connolly in 1937's *The League of Frightened Men*), and several radio programs, including a 1950–1951 NBC series in which he was played by Greenstreet.

Greenstreet's popularity in *The Maltese Falcon* and subsequent Warner Bros. films like *Across the Pacific* (1942) and *Casablanca* (1942) was not lost on other studios, which promptly cast their own fat villains. The most immediately successful of these was six-foot-four, 320-pound Laird Cregar, whom Twentieth Century-Fox touted as their rival to Greenstreet. Cregar made his mark playing obsessive heavies in Fox's *I Wake Up Screaming* (released in November 1941, a few weeks after *The Maltese Falcon*) and Paramount's *This Gun for Hire* (1942). Fox quickly promoted Cregar to starring roles in *The Lodger* (1944) and *Hangover Square* (1945), both film noirish period pieces in which he played psychotic serial murderers. The stardom of Greenstreet and Cregar reveals how far the Hollywood studios were willing to bend in order to cultivate male stars during the manpower shortage of World War II. Thomas Schatz notes that during the war "there were frequent jokes about male stars being replaced by dogs (Lassie), horses (Flicka), kids (Margaret O'Brien, Baby Jean), and aging character actors (Charles Coburn and Barry Fitzgerald)" (Schatz 1997, 206). Cregar, however, desperately wanted to be thin enough to play leading romantic roles. He lamented, "I am, after all, a grotesque. That is, an actor who doesn't fit readily into parts. . . . I am too big, too tall, too heavy. I don't look like an actor" (Mank 1989, 201).[4] After completing *Hangover Square* in November 1944, Cregar undertook a crash diet and fat reduction surgery, which proved too stressful for his heart, killing him at the age of thirty-one. Greenstreet could sympathize; he remained under contract at Warner Bros. through the late 1940s and grew frustrated with the formulaic heavy roles he was often forced to play.

Industrial factors such as Greenstreet's groundbreaking performance, Hammett and Stout's popular fat characters, copycat casting, and the wartime manpower shortage undoubtedly contributed to the increased visibility of fat heavies in the 1940s, but they don't fully account for their powerful cultural resonance. Why, for instance, didn't Dudley Digges's portrayal of Gutman in Warner Bros.' 1931 version of *The Maltese Falcon* or Edward Arnold's fat heavy role in *The Glass Key* (a 1935 crime drama based on another Hammett novel) have as much cultural impact? Why did the 1940s and film noir kindle the explosive performances of so many fat heavies? Toward answering these questions, I first examine how America's cultural stigmatization of fat, which often discursively employed the nomenclature of crime, coincided with the development of hard-boiled fiction and crime films. I then analyze how characterizations of the fat heavy specifically functioned and evolved within film noir's visual and narrative economies. Throughout, I pay particular attention to Paul Schrader's periodizations of the historical entity called "film noir" to consider what is at stake in my own historicization of the fat heavy.

Criminalizing the Fat Body

The belief that the fat body is shameful, non-normative, and symptomatic of social deviance has been widely held since the late nineteenth century. Historian Peter N. Stearns argues that Americans' desire for a thin body at this time was largely compensatory (1997, 56–65). The rise of public opinion, facilitated by urbanism and communications technologies, fostered guilt about changing social mores. Stricter discipline of the body, therefore, was viewed as spiritual compensation for excessive consumerism, declining religious practice, and greater social freedoms. During World War I, the state had incentives to stigmatize fat citizens: it needed to conserve food to ensure the feeding of its soldiers, and it needed healthy bodies to fight its wars and produce its goods and materiel. Government officials such as Herbert Hoover, head of the U.S. Food Administration, suggested that obesity was treasonable. Hoover publicly boasted, "I eat as little as I can to get along," and advocated slogans such as "Do Not Help the Hun at Meal Time" (Schwartz 1986, 140). After the war, the rise of physical culture, which promoted diet and exercise regimens, and a "reducing craze" among the white middle classes (especially young women) contributed to the perception of obesity as a socially aberrant condition. But a single event did more than any of these things to crystallize the American public's association of "the fat man" with social deviance and crime.

On September 9, 1921, Hollywood ingenue Virginia Rappe died after attending a party in the San Francisco hotel room of 265-pound film comedian Roscoe "Fatty" Arbuckle.[5] The thirty-four-year-old actor was charged with manslaughter on the basis of sketchy evidence, which prompted tabloid rumors of sexual debauchery. After three trials Arbuckle was found "entirely innocent" and acquitted in April 1922, but film industry watchdog Will B. Hays nevertheless banned the scandal-ridden comedian from the screen. The public perception of fat actors was irrevocably altered; the jiggling physical excess long associated with Arbuckle's playful slapstick persona was now pathologized as a marker of sexual deviance and monstrous appetites.

This popular criminalization of fat was not lost on writers who created villains for fiction and film in the 1920s and 1930s. Hammett, who would become the most influential crime writer of this period, worked as a Pinkerton detective on the Arbuckle case, gathering information for the actor's defense attorneys. Hammett recalled seeing Arbuckle in a hotel lobby during his second trial: "His eyes were the eyes of a man who expected to be regarded as a monster but was not yet inured to it. I made my gaze as contemptuous as I could. He glared at me, went on to the elevator still glaring" (Johnson 1983, 34–35). Hammett biographer Diane Johnson notes that the Arbuckle case profoundly influenced his fiction: "Fatty stayed in Hammett's mind for years . . . when his daughters were big enough he talked to them about it, all the horrible details . . . Fat villains were to appear in his tales" (1983, 35).[6]

By the early 1940s, when Hammett's most famous fat man was being immortalized by Greenstreet on the nation's movie screens, medical researchers had begun to shift their conceptualization of obesity's origins from the metabolic to the psychological. During this same period, cinematic portrayals of crime as a "social problem" were transforming into film noir's individualized depictions of criminal addiction, sexual perversion, and emotional trauma. Both movements were influenced by the American importation of Freudian psychoanalysis. Group therapy approaches to dieting became popular in the postwar years, based on a growing literature of addiction and the 1940 founding of Alcoholics Anonymous. Instituting weigh-ins and social surveillance of obese citizens considered too undisciplined to help themselves, collective dieting reinforced the criminalization of fat in the public consciousness. TOPS (Taking Off Pounds Sensibly), the first national dieting group, was founded in Milwaukee in 1948. Its "Court of Weights and Measures" took the criminalization of fat to absurd lengths. In this court, the officiating judge was played by the group leader, the prosecuting attorney's role was assumed by the weight recorder, and the defense attorney was the defendant's "reducing pal" or sponsor. According to one account, "the defendant can almost never win an argument with the scales and avoid pleading guilty. However, past weight losses may be cited as extenuating circumstances . . . The sentence usually is a fine of five to ten cents for every pound gained" (Wyden 1965, 88–89).

The founding of TOPS had followed World War II and another round of food-rationing programs that stigmatized the obese for their failure to make necessary sacrifices. At Warner Bros., it was acceptable for the corpulent Greenstreet to play conspiratorial enemy spies in the war films *Across the Pacific* (1942) and *Background to Danger* (1943), but Greenstreet's U.S. Army colonel in the romantic comedy *Pillow to Post* (1945) is deemed too fat to qualify for dispatchment and is grounded stateside. The end of the war, however, did not end rationing or the war against fat. Food shortages continued through 1946 and black markets developed for rationed or price-controlled foods such as sugar, butter, and the best cuts of meat (Levenstein 1993, 95–96). Even after rationing had ended and economic recovery was in full swing, government leaders continued to characterize fat people as unpatriotic misanthropes (Schwartz 1986, 206). Fat had become public health enemy #1.

Creating the Iconic Fat Heavy

The creators of 1940s crime dramas exploited the expressionistic potential of bodies. Mobilizing the concept of "embodied deviance"—the belief that non-normative bodies evidenced social deviance and a failure to "measure up"—they frequently cast eccentric-looking actors such as the rotund Greenstreet, the moon-faced Lorre, and the bird-like Elijah Cook Jr., who played the criminal conspirators in *The Maltese Falcon*. In an iconic performance enabled by John Huston's skillful adaptation and direction, Greenstreet used his corpulence to subtly express Gutman's decadence. Gutman's habitat and hideout is a hotel suite; his spatial removal reflects both his social estrangement and his physical isolation from ordinary civilian life. The fat heavy's hideout, whether lavishly appointed (mimicking the penthouse suite of the modern corporation) or dark and subterranean (literally representing the criminal underworld) often serves as the crime film's physical and narrative center. Gutman's suite is the place around which *The Maltese Falcon*'s narrative swirls and always returns. His massive girth, frequently shot from low angles, establishes his power and presence—it is clear that the other characters must revolve around him.[7] The immobile fat heavy seamlessly fulfills Schrader's requirements of film noir style, in which "compositional tension is preferred to physical action. A typical film noir would rather move the scene cinematographically around the actor than have the actor control the scene by physical action" (1972, 11). Gutman never pulls a gun; rather, his body—and his knowledge—control the situation.

Gutman's primary activity is talking and listening; he does not involve himself in gunplay, fistfights, or other violent acts. (Instead, he drugs Spade, a decidedly passive-aggressive form of assault.) As such, he typifies what Wheeler Winston Dixon calls a "brain heavy," who from a distance devises schemes for his underlings to carry out and then impassively awaits and reviews the results (1990, 202–203). Only Gutman is capable of recounting the convoluted history of the Maltese falcon and surmising its whereabouts as he plots the actions of his minions, Joel Cairo (Lorre) and the "gunsel" Wilmer (Cook). In Dixon's typology, an "action heavy," on the other hand, is the underling who must do the brain heavy's dirty work and also take his punishment (1990, 203). In film noir, large, muscular actors such as Mike Mazurki, William Bendix, and Ted de Corsia usually play action heavies, but truly fat actors, whose size prohibits strenuous physical activity, play brain heavies. Action heavies tend to rely on brute force and rarely question orders or demonstrate initiative, whereas brain heavies may be decisive but as criminal "masterminds" tend to contemplate and brood.

The relationship between the isolated brain heavy and the action heavy who does his bidding, Dixon notes, is one of auditor and tale-teller (1990, 203). The brain heavy's auditory faculties are therefore highly developed and possess an erotic sensitivity; it often seems his greatest pleasure is derived from hearing the results of his machinations. It is thus not surprising that in their first meeting the aurally inclined Gutman quickly admits to Sam Spade that "I distrust a close-mouthed man" and "I'm a man who likes talking to a man who likes to talk." And how Gutman can talk! Greenstreet's voice—deep and mellow with just a trace of an English accent to suggest sophistication—is a versatile instrument capable of conveying intelligence, wit, and malevolence in the same breath. The fat actor who inhabits the role of the brain heavy typically is blessed with a deep, distinctive voice. His rich vocality serves to compensate for the weakness of his soft flesh, further establishing the primacy of his intellect.

Gutman's eloquence and exquisite taste in decor and clothes—usually double-breasted suits and silk robes, which he wears to drape and conceal his girth—are familiar cinematic markers of homosexuality (Corber 1997, 10). Combined with the fat heavy's embodied deviance and eccentricities, these fastidious characteristics often suggest a secret knowledge that is sexual; the fact that Gutman employs a "gunsel" who is "like a son" to him further telegraphs his homosexuality.[8] These familiar signifiers would continue to mark fat heavies in film noir. In *This Gun For Hire*, for example, Cregar plays a prissy villain who is afraid of violence and reads *Paris Nights* while nibbling on peppermints and lounging in silk pajamas; and in *The Big Clock* (1948), the sadistic, lip-curling Laughton is an erudite publishing magnate who keeps a mistress but appears to be more intimate with his jealous right-hand man, played by George Macready. In contrast, the six-foot-two, 230-pound Hope Emerson exhibits overly masculine traits: in *Cry of the City* (1948) she works as a masseuse in a seedy athletic club, applying therapeutic muscle to women she will eventually rob; and in *Caged* (1950) she is a cruel prison matron attracted to the women she brutally punishes.

The visibility of fat offers public clues about private conduct that only rarely is revealed diegetically in a scene involving eating. Customarily, private conduct—that is, *how the fat heavy got that way*—is left unseen and unspoken and must be deducted. What is hidden in the closet is *secret eating*, which sociologist Mildred Klingman calls "the secret of staying fat" (1981, 8). In film noir, visual clues often suggest that secret eating and secret sexuality reside in the same closet, the products of uncontrolled appetites.[9] Gutman's discomforting secret, hidden in the plain sight of his protruding belly, makes him duplicitous and unknowable. Greenstreet himself noted that he "enjoyed the subtlety necessary to get over the fact that while Gutman was saying one thing, he was usually thinking something entirely different" (1947, 123). The fat heavy's deep, measured vocality suggests control, but his girth reveals the self-indulgence of a man with a weakness for pleasure—and crime.

Gutman's unknowability functions like that of the femme fatale who typically lures film noir heroes to their ruin. Sexually deviant male characters in film noir are linked iconographically with the femme fatale, who displays a similar obsession with personal appearance, opulent decoration, and, especially, silk robes (Corber 1997, 10). Because Gutman inhabits a hotel suite and wears both formal attire and silk robes while receiving guests, one can never be sure whether he's conducting business or pleasure. The first time Spade calls on Gutman, the fat man is wearing a three-piece suit; after a few rounds of verbal sparring, Spade pretends to lose his temper and storms out. The second time Spade visits, Gutman appears more effeminate—wearing his silk robe—and this time his "seduction" of Spade is successful. At this point Gutman has the upper hand because he will recount the history of the Maltese falcon, which is a secret history: "not schoolbook history, not Mr. Wells's history, but history nevertheless." Combined with the fat man's other unspoken secrets, the exotic story is seductive enough to distract Spade while Gutman doctors his cocktail. As Spade contemplates the value of "the dingus" (symbol of phallic power), he slips into unconsciousness.

How could a fat man be allowed to get the best of Spade, one of the most secure and steadfastly masculine hard-boiled detectives? In Spade's code of behavior it is inexcusable to be duped by a woman or to be held at gunpoint by anyone for long. Yet he allows himself to be seduced and drugged by Gutman, for in many ways this fat man is his intellectual equal. Only among two men of equal standing can the instability (and homoerotics) of phallic power be unveiled and acknowledged. The unveiling of the dingus's history results in a stylistic rupture: a point-of-view shot of a blurry Gutman, indicating that Spade has finally lost (or given up) control. The shot illustrates Peter Lehman's assertion that "in the classical cinema, when fundamental assumptions about such things as masculinity and realism are critiqued, stylistic fissures occur within the text" (1993, 90). In order to function, the patriarchal ideology of masculinity must operate as an assumption; film noir's expression of anxieties about masculinity, therefore, is never direct. Its heroes' difficulty in maintaining masculinity, Richard Dyer notes, is tempered by "images of that which is *not* masculine and normal—i.e., that which is feminine and deviant—to mark off the parameters of the categories that they are unable actually to show" (1998, 115). Because the fat heavy so visibly exhibits embodied deviance and an uneasy incorporation of masculine and feminine characteristics, the role forces audiences to rethink their assumptions about masculine power and its representation.

The Postwar Fat Heavy

The Maltese Falcon typifies what Schrader calls "the private eye and lone wolf" phase of film noir, spanning the years 1941–1946. This first phase, he argues, is characterized by adaptations of Hammett and Raymond Chandler, glamorous stars and "classy" directors, studio sets and uniform lighting, and "more talk than action" (1972, 11). In addition, there is the wry humor displayed in Huston's *Maltese Falcon*, which seems to have more in common with 1930s detective films than with the gritty urban crime films that appeared after the war. The comedy that marked the series of detective films based on *The Thin Man* and S. S. Van Dine's Philo Vance novels disappeared in classical film noir, and survived only "in the verbal form of the wisecrack, which is grating rather than funny, and in the visual form of the grotesque, which is more repulsive than laughable" (Vernet 1993, 21). The sly, articulate fat heavy associated with Greenstreet (who had worked in theater as a character comedian for four decades prior to *The Maltese Falcon*) has more in common with the comic, verbose fat heavies played by the Irish-born Digges in the 1931 version and the pop-eyed Guy Kibbee in *City Streets* (1931) than with the violent, grotesque fat heavies who appeared after the war. Typical characterizations of the fat heavy in the 1930s were based on two popular models of fat representation that had prevailed for centuries: the fat clown and the fat authority figure. The "hilarious homicide" school of crime films emphasized the fat heavy's jolly and avuncular features, as reflected in the bumbling mannerisms of actors like Kibbee and Eugene Pallette. The "social problem" film relied on the perceived greed and moral corruption of the fat autocrat, whom Edward Arnold successfully played throughout the 1930s. In *The Maltese Falcon's* Kasper Gutman, Hammett—perhaps channeling his courtroom memories of the wealthy, menacing, yet childlike comedian Arbuckle—integrated the two models, but the brilliance of his characterization was not made apparent until Greenstreet's 1941 performance. Here was a heavy whom audiences had not seen before: jovial one minute and menacing the next, verbose but ultimately inscrutable.

Schrader's second phase of classical film noir, spanning 1945 through 1949, is the "postwar realistic period" of police procedure, political corruption, and crime in the streets, based more on contemporary news stories than hard-boiled fiction. "Proletarian" directors frequently shot these films on location at night with chiaroscuro lighting, using rugged protagonists and tawdry femme fatales (1972, 12). The fat heavy got rougher around the edges, too. By the end of the war Cregar was dead and Greenstreet was mired in stock villain roles at Warner Bros. Filling this vacuum and the increasingly realistic needs of the crime drama, a more brutal, less mannered fat heavy appeared after the war, played by hulking, gruff actors like Raymond Burr in *Desperate* (1947), *Raw Deal* (1948), and *Pitfall* (1948); Thomas Gomez in *Johnny O'Clock* (1947) and *I Married a Communist* (1949); William Conrad in *Sorry, Wrong Number* (1948) and *Cry Danger* (1951); and Hope Emerson in *Cry of the City* and *Caged*. These sweating, hot-tempered fat heavies exemplified the twitching, stigmatized, "unknown breed of men" described in Raymond Borde and Etienne Chaumeton's pioneering 1955 study of American film noir. (They also note that Emerson's butch masseuse in *Cry of the City* is "a real 'phallic' woman.")[10] Short on social grace, these heavies distrusted education and affectation and did not utter witty lines with an English accent, thereby approximating Hammett and Chandler's hard-boiled vision of a distinctly American criminal.

During this realistic phase, the typical film noir protagonist is not a suave detective but rather a seemingly ordinary guy who might have a salaried job, a wife, children, and a house in the suburbs. This protagonist, Paul Arthur notes, often attempts, "consciously or unconsciously, to escape expectations that constitute his social regime" (Arthur 1996, 95). In Andre De Toth's *Pitfall*, beleaguered insurance man Dick Powell complains to his wife, "I don't want to be an average American, backbone of the country." Fantasies of transformation motivate the white middle-class male to break out of rigid class stratifications. For Powell, there is nowhere to go but down: into the lower depths of forbidden sexuality and criminality, embodied in a sultry femme fatale (Lizabeth Scott) and a malevolent double (the 350-pound Burr, playing a creepy private investigator). The fat heavy's body visibly demarcates a place outside middle-class corporate culture, which after World War II increasingly privileged the Organization Man's lean body maintained by rigid self-discipline.

For the middle-class noir protagonist, the fat heavy incorporates both *the wish and the fear* of transformation: the fat heavy's power and ruthlessness, as well as his disregard for his own physical health, are both attractive and repulsive. Amid social pressure to keep fit and always look presentable within corporate culture, the protagonist harbors the secret wish *to just let go* and indulge every appetite. "Imprisoned in every fat man a thin one is wildly signalling to be let out," wrote British poet and essayist Cyril Connolly in 1944, during the height of wartime food rationing (Connolly 1981, 58). The noir protagonist's fantasy of transformation subverts this adage by suggesting the opposite: that inside every thin man lurks the boundless appetite of a fat man. Overindulgence in food, drink, drugs, sex, and violence—all discouraged by his former community—serves to rekindle the protagonist's tactile awareness of his own body and literally stigmatizes him as an outcast. (In *Pitfall*, Powell has a sexual affair with Scott and receives a black eye from Burr.) The consequences become apparent: once the appetites are unleashed, nothing satisfies—there is the endless, futile pursuit of "more." In the lesson of film noir, the rightness of Connolly's adage is restored: after doing time in the prison of the transgressive fat man, the ordinary thin man wildly signals to be let out. In *Pitfall* the potency Powell gains is not used to reject his rigid former environment, but rather to destroy his fat antagonist, who is the projection of his wishes and fears. The result, Arthur notes, is a "bourgeois cautionary tale": the noir protagonist's community may be stultifying, "but all attempts at change result in something worse than the original ills" (1996, 99).

The Fat Heavy's Epitaph

Schrader's third and final phase of classical film noir peaks between 1949 and 1953, "the period of psychotic action and suicidal impulse" in which the hero starts to "go bananas" and the psychotic killer often becomes an active protagonist (1972, 12). Now competing with television detective shows, film noir's final phase was marked by formal experimentation and a painful self-awareness, concluding in 1958 with *Touch of Evil*. In the film's most radical reversal, the criminal fat heavy is not only the protagonist; he is also a cop. The righteous, physically fit investigator Vargas (Heston) embodies what corrupt police captain Quinlan (Welles) might have been if his wife hadn't died, if he hadn't taken a bullet in the leg, if he hadn't hit the hooch, and if he hadn't gained 150 pounds. Face hidden in darkness, Quinlan first appears in a low-angle shot revealing his enormous belly emerging from a car. Quinlan's corpulence serves as a visual index of his spiritual disintegration; his size has made him unknowable to himself and a stranger to his own past, which includes a whore, Tanya (Marlene Dietrich), who no longer recognizes him. The meticulous mastermind figure that was still present in violent, postwar characterizations of the fat heavy is now absent. Roaming around town attempting to frame a suspect, Quinlan is unable to provide the spatial center held down by earlier brain heavies. Tanya's brothel, in fact, seems to be the closest thing to a spiritual or narrative center for the film and its spent protagonist—a place where he was once able to enjoy the use of his body.

To compensate for his game leg and distended paunch, Quinlan relies on a cane—a "penis extender" like Gutman's falcon—to maintain his sense of phallic power. The vulnerable guise of phallic power will again be unveiled, leading to the fat man's downfall. After strangling Uncle Joe Grandi (Akim Tamiroff), Quinlan forgets his cane, which Vargas will find and use as evidence to incriminate him. Tanya's final eulogy for Quinlan ("He was some kind of man") succinctly summarizes film noir's anxieties about masculinity. The men of film noir are revealed to be "some kind of man," but usually it is not the kind of man they had hoped to be. Welles himself would lose creative control of *Touch of Evil* and never again complete a feature film in the United States.

By 1960, the actors who had risen to prominence as fat heavies had, like Welles and film noir, succumbed to their own excesses or squeezed into the confines of television's small screen. Greenstreet died in 1954 and Emerson in 1960; a slimmer Burr starred in the TV series *Perry Mason* (1957–1966) and *Ironside* (1967–1975); Conrad spent the 1960s directing and producing before starring in the TV series *Cannon* (1971–1976) and *Jake and the Fatman* (1987–1992); and Gomez made infrequent appearances in film and television until his death in 1971. With classical Hollywood genres in decline, fat actors found little work in the youth-oriented counterculture pictures that dominated American film production, or even in the cycle of neo-noir films that began in the 1970s. The fat heavy was no longer larger than life in the cultural imaginary; he had been supplanted by the fat, domesticated proles atop the TV ratings in *The Honeymooners* (1952–1957), *All in the Family* (1971–1979), and *Roseanne* (1988–1997). In the last decades of the twentieth century, when medical experts were estimating that a majority of American adults were overweight, fat lost its aura of transgressive authority. It had become the domain of the masses.

NOTES

1. Schatz convincingly argues how *Citizen Kane* contributed to 1940s "American Expressionism" and fulfills Schrader's seven "recurring techniques" that characterize film noir.

2. The character Kasper Gutman did not appear in Warner Bros.' second adaptation of the novel, *Satan Met a Lady* (1936); its heavy, Madame Barabbas, was played by the matronly seventy-three-year-old actress Alison Skipworth.

3. In a February 1942 memo, Warner Bros. studio head Jack L. Warner requested that a story editor ask Hammett about writing a sequel to *The Maltese Falcon*. When Hammett demanded a $5,000 guarantee, the plan was dropped. See Behlmer 1985, 157–158.

4. Cregar gave his date of birth as July 28, 1916, but according to Mank, the actor's actual year of birth is 1913.

5. The twenty-five-year-old Rappe, who had passed out in Arbuckle's hotel room, was pregnant and suffered from venereal disease and peritonitis. She died four days later, having never accused Arbuckle of any wrongdoing. See Young 1994, 65–66.

6. In his introduction to the 1934 Modern Library edition of *The Maltese Falcon*, Hammett wrote that Gutman was based on a suspected spy he trailed in Washington, D.C., while working as a detective for the Pinkerton agency during World War I: "I never remember shadowing a man who bored me as much."

7. Greenstreet noted that "the cameraman helped me achieve the effect of fatness. To be sure, I'm not exactly a flyweight; I weighed 285 pounds at that time. But by bringing the camera near the floor and shooting up, they made me weigh about 350" (1947, 123).

8. In Hammett's novel, Gutman has a daughter, Rhea. She was dropped from Warner Bros.' screen adaptations, making Gutman's sexuality less ambiguous. Vito Russo notes that "since about 1915, bums and prisoners had used the German word *gansel* or *gosling*, corrupted to *gunsel*, for a passive sodomite, especially a young, inexperienced boy companion. From the mid-1920s it gradually came to mean a sneaky or disreputable person of any kind. By the 1930s it meant petty gangster or hoodlum." Such a word could thus pass Production Code restrictions while retaining its original underworld connotation (Russo 1987, 46–47).

9. For Laughton, Cregar, Burr, Gomez, and Emerson—all closeted homosexuals hiding behind marriages of convenience or romances fabricated by press agents—onscreen intimations of a secret sexuality reflected offscreen experience. They feared public disclosure while working in Hollywood, yet their more sexually suggestive performances may have been fueled by their wish for exposure. Laughton's wife, actress Elsa Lanchester, noted that the actor "seemed to need to be so secretive, all the while still wanting to be found out." See Callow 1987, 280. Cregar "was almost scandalously open about his sexual taste," much to the dismay of Fox production executive Darryl Zanuck. See Mank 1989, 219. Burr, who maintained a thirty-eight-year relationship with Robert Benevides, managed to sidestep several potential scandals. See Mann 2001, 313–314. Little has been published about the private lives of Gomez and Emerson, but their homosexuality was well known among Hollywood insiders. See Mann 2001, 135–136, 259.

10. First quote from Borde and Chaumeton 1996, 22. Second quote from Borde and Chaumeton 2002, 80.

Kathleen Rowe Karlyn

Comedy, Melodrama, and Gender: Theorizing the Genres of Laughter

> *If on the high dramatic plane it is the son who kills and robs, it is the wife who plays this role on the plane of comic Gallic tradition. She will cuck-old the husband, beat him, and chase him away.*
> —Bakhtin, *Rabelais and His World*, 243

Norman Jewison's 1987 film, *Moonstruck*, opens with an enormous moon hanging over the skyline of Manhattan, followed by a montage of shots of the "moonlit" city, from its bridges festooned with lights, to the Metropolitan Opera House, to a poster advertising Giacomo Puccini's opera, *La Bohème*. Within moments, the sky brightens and the streets awaken with the activity of the day. A truck marked "Metropolitan Opera" moves through the traffic, its path crossed by Loretta Castorini, a superstitious Italian American widow, walking to her job at a funeral parlor. The film concludes in the Castorini kitchen, where the newly expanded family is celebrating Loretta's engagement to Ronny and her mother Rose's reconciliation with her husband Cosmo. Panning across the grandfather's rowdy pack of dogs as it retreats into the parlor, the camera passes over a series of family portraits, until it rests finally on those of an aged couple, the matriarch and patriarch of the extended family gathered nearby.

These two scenes bracket *Moonstruck*'s thematic and formal tensions. Moving between darkness and daylight, death and life, the film repeatedly shifts from the pathos of romantic melodrama, most strongly represented by the story-within-the-story of the opera, to the irony and humor of romantic comedy, two of the genres most typically used to narrate fictions about women's lives. The film's musical score reinforces these tensions by playing the soaring melodies of Puccini against "That's Amore," a corny but charming popular song sung by Dean Martin ("When the moon hits your eye like a big pizza pie, that's *amore*"). *Moonstruck*'s interplay of romantic comedy and melodrama does not give equal weight to the two genres, however. After all, it is Dean Martin's voice that closes the film, as well as opens it, and Puccini's arias that are modulated into the schmaltzy pop style of "That's Amore." In the same way, the film uses romantic comedy to mirror, contain, and ultimately transform the melodramatic themes and motifs of *La Bohème*.[1] *Moonstruck* moves from the dying Mimi to the comic rebirth of the film's heroine Loretta; from Loretta's tears as opera spectator to the smiles and laughter of the film spectator; and from the opera's glorification of a romantic love based on woman's loneliness and pain to an alternative which, unlike most romantic comedy, refuses to make a woman's heterosexuality contingent on the symbolic death of her mother. Testing the values of melodrama against those of romantic comedy, the film argues finally for comedy.[2]

Romantic comedy might well rival melodrama as the narrative form most typically used to shape fictive accounts of women's lives. Yet feminist critics have been slow to direct much sustained attention to the genre.[3] For many women, the social contradictions of gender have been played out most compellingly in the narrative forms of melodrama (the sentimental and Gothic novels, the woman's weepie film, the television soap opera), which are centered on female suffering and tears. Although the study of melodrama has yielded ground-breaking feminist work, it has also reinforced feminist film theory's ambivalent but close relation to psychoanalysis, an interpretive paradigm that (despite its many variations) ties femininity to castration, pathology, and an exclusion from the symbolic. As a result, texts that might suggest less deterministic views of female subjectivity have not received the scrutiny they deserve. I am referring in particular to those that position women as subjects of a laughter that expresses anger, resistance, solidarity, and joy.

Traditionally, the genres of laughter associated with the social practice of carnival and the narrative structures of comedy have proven elusive and difficult to theorize. Humanist cultural criticism has neglected gender almost altogether in its studies of comedy and the carnivalesque. At the same time, feminists, with a few exceptions, have yet to fully investigate the potential of these forms to produce a theory that is not only explanatory but emancipatory. Such an investigation would not disavow melodrama but would place it within a wider range of cultural practices and genres as diverse as the television sit-com and the avant-garde, where women have made pointed use of the comic, the parodic, and the grotesque.

This essay takes a step in that direction by approaching the study of romantic comedy in terms of gender. Seeking, as Robin Wood advises, not the "what" of a genre but the "why," I locate one of the why's of romantic comedy in the ideological tension surrounding the "excessive" woman who "desires too much." Whereas the transgressive male finds his home in the heroic genres of what Mikhail Bakhtin has called "the high dramatic plane," the transgressive woman finds hers in the "lower" forms of melodrama and romantic comedy. But

whereas melodrama allows the transgressive woman to triumph only in her suffering, romantic comedy takes her story to a different end, providing a sympathetic place for female resistance to masculine authority and an alternative to
the suffering femininity affirmed by melodrama. Making fun of and out of
inflated and self-deluded notions of heroic masculinity, romantic comedy is
often structured by gender inversion, a disruption of the social hierarchy of male
over female through what might be called the *topos* of the unruly woman or the
"woman on top." When romantic comedy most fully realizes the potential of
this *topos*, it dramatizes a resistance to the law of Oedipus, a carnivalizing of
sexual identities and gender hierarchies that posits a new and more inclusive
basis for community than the social order it takes as its point of reference.

Comedy and the Feminine

An understanding of the transgressive woman's placement in romantic comedy
begins with her exclusion from the genres of the "high dramatic plane"—tragedy,
the epic, and genres associated with realism. It has become a critical commonplace that tragedy is an intrinsically "masculine" form, charting the progress of
the male hero on a quest through alien landscapes, war, corporate battlefields for
his Oedipal patrimony. While the term *tragedy* is most often used in connection
with historical periods centuries removed from our own, Hollywood has produced its own versions of the excessive, larger-than-life tragic hero in such figures as Charles Foster Kane and Michael Corleone of the *Godfather* saga.

The story of a woman with heroic aspirations, however, is rarely told
in a tragic form. As Carolyn Heilbrun has argued, women's lives can be narrated
only within the boundaries of heterosexual love, motherhood, and loneliness.
As a result, the female counterpart to the excessive male hero can rarely define
herself except as a *romantic* heroine, who is placed in relation to a man and
whose heroism is subordinated to that relationship. Her story must be "emplotted," to use historian Hayden White's term, in those genres oriented toward the
private sphere and the family: melodrama, which emphasizes loneliness and/or
motherhood (and is commonly considered debased or feminized tragedy), and
romantic comedy, which emphasizes love. *Moonstruck* casts all three of its
major female characters—Loretta, Rose, and Mimi—into stories that inter-
mingle loneliness and love, with Rose appearing in the motherhood plot as well.
It would seem that a man's presence, or conspicuous absence, keeps a woman's
desires, accomplishments, and failures in the proper perspective.

If tragedy is the most masculine of genres, the implications of gender
for comedy are less clear. What is the correspondence between the son who

"kills and robs in the high dramatic plane" and the wife who "plays this role" in the comic tradition? Why does changing the gender of the transgressive protagonist require a change in genre? And does the movement from tragic hubris to comic unruliness necessarily tame female transgressiveness?

Narrative comedy is notoriously difficult to define, let alone explain, and those theories that do exist diverge widely. Emerging from them are two apparently contradictory but closely related characteristics. The first, often a prelude to the second, is comedy's *antiauthoritarianism*—its attack on the Law of the Father and drive to level, disrupt, and destroy hierarchy, to contest the values tragedy affirms. Comedy breaks taboos and expresses those impulses that are outside social norms. Where comedy is, so are food, sex, excrement, blasphemy, usually presented obliquely enough to be socially acceptable. Comedy, in contrast, inflects the Oedipal story that underlies most narratives by shifting the son's guilt to the father. Youth (the small, the petty, and the powerless) triumphs over age (authority, repression, and the law), and the "happy ending" fulfills the son's transgressive desires. In one sense, comedy might be seen simply as staging a generational struggle between masculine forces to ensure the victory of the son. However, the weapons it deploys are also available to women and all oppressed people to express aggression and rage at the forces of the father.

Comedy's second tendency expresses an impulse toward *renewal* and *social transformation*. Emphasizing the second part of the Oedipal story, or the formation of the couple, this tendency finds its fullest expression in romantic comedy.[4] Male theorists, such as Northrop Frye, have often claimed too much virtue for this type of comedy, seeing its form as neutral rather than patriarchal. However, romantic comedy demands a place for women, both in its narrative and in its vision of a social order that is not only renewed but also, ideally, transformed. Romantic comedies such as *Moonstruck* that mock male heroism through gender inversion and female unruliness retain a strong element of antiauthoritarianism, and so combine both comedic tendencies, holding sentiment and skepticism in a balance that characterizes the most successful examples of the genre.

Sons and Fathers: Antiauthoritarianism in Comedian Comedy

Almost all comedic forms—from jokes to gags to slapstick routines to the most complex narrative structures—attempt a liberation from authority. Like carnival, comedy levels the lofty and erases distinctions, replacing the exalted hero of tragedy with one reduced to the level of Everyman, or lower. Comedy often mocks the masculinity that tragedy ennobles, as in the blockbuster 1990 film, *Home Alone*, and its 1992 sequel, *Home Alone 2*, which with their precocious little boy protagonists, exaggerate the comic male hero's infantilization.

Comedy's interest in the social, as opposed to tragedy's in the individual, aligns it with values that are conventionally associated with the feminine: community over separation, and the preservation of life rather than its sacrifice for principle or power. The very centrality of sex to the comedic agenda of renewing life opens up space for the presence of women that does not exist in the more masculine world of tragedy. Because sex is to comedy what death is to tragedy, the heterosexual couple that is a mainstay of Hollywood narrative film is also one of comedy's most fundamental conventions. In comedy, sex is not a means toward knowledge or transcendence of the self, as in tragedy, but part of a larger attack on repression and a means of connection within the space of family and the time of generation. Despite this apparent accord with the feminine, however, comedy in mainstream narrative film usually makes its case against the father with very little attention to the mother or daughter; it may show Oedipus to be a fool, but it still places him at the heart of the story. With a few exceptions, such as Mae West, the canon of (primarily U.S.) film comedy consists almost entirely of male directors and performers, from the Keystone Kops through Woody Allen, Eddie Murphy, and many more.

While some of these actors and directors have worked in romantic comedy, most of their films fall into a category Steve Seidman and others have described as "comedian" comedy and Stuart Kaminsky has called comedy "in the mode of the individual." Because "individual" usually means individual *male,* this kind of comedy might more aptly be described as "male-centered comedy," with male referring to an individual (Buster Keaton, Steve Martin), a couple (Laurel and Hardy, Dean Martin and Jerry Lewis), or entire troupe or ensemble (the Marx Brothers, Monty Python). Women have performed in comedian comedy since its earliest days, but until recently, their absence from the canon of comedian comedy, as well as the cultural and institutional reasons for that absence, have remained largely unexamined.

When comedian comedy mocks the heroic masculinity affirmed in serious drama, it often does so by creating a feminized, antiheroic male hero who appropriates the positive, anarchic, "feminine" principles comedy affirms. From Charlie Chaplin to Harpo Marx to Woody Allen to Danny DeVito, these figures are often small and feminine or androgynous in appearance, and positioned as feminine through their roles as underdogs. The films they appear in tend to emphasize their comic performance rather than a narrative trajectory to the altar; even if a bride exists in a romantic subplot, the son rather than unruly bride remains the primary agent of liberation.

Comedian comedy often compounds its erasure of the bride by directing its corrective laughter onto the matriarch, displacing hostility from the father onto the repressive, phallic mother. In such comedy, consistent with Freud's analysis of the joke, women do not stand as essential subjects in a drama of new social life but as fearsome or silly symbols of repression and obstacles to social transformation. The matriarch represents a dreaded domesticity and propriety. Her ranks include spinsters, dowagers, mothers-in-law, librarians, battle-axes, career women, and lesbians—women who serve as targets for the hatred of repression mobilized by comedy and especially by the infantile, regressive, and misogynistic male hero of the comedian comedy.

Sons and Brides: Renewal and Transformation in Romantic Comedy

Comedy celebrates excess not only for itself but because it paves the way for a community liberated from structures grown so rigid and unyielding that they threaten its very existence. Comedy that emphasizes this principle harnesses the genre's antiauthoritarian energy, and directs it toward creating a new vision of community based on the assumption that the renewal of both biological and social life depends on connection or relation to others. In this regard, comedy insists that community does not repress individual desire, but in fact represents its very fulfillment. *Romantic* comedy treats the social difference that impedes community as a matter of sexual difference, and so it builds the feminine into both the construction and the resolution of narrative conflict. The utopian possibilities of a new social order lie in the couple's victory over the obstacles between them, and in the child or new life implicit in their union. This utopianism is traditionally represented in the public ceremony of the wedding or feast. Few critics have surpassed Northrop Frye's insights into comedy's utopian dimension, Frye, in fact, can be credited with finding a profundity in romantic comedy, and in comedy itself, that had eluded earlier generations of critics.[5] For him, all narrative reworks a common story of community, struggle, and renewal; of birth, death, and rebirth. Comedy emphasizes the renewal element of the cycle. A world wilting under repressive law is liberated through a temporary movement into a dimension Bakhtin would call the carnivalesque, Victor Turner the liminal, and C. L. Barber the "green world" of festivity and natural regeneration.

In romantic comedy, this movement follows the remarkably tenacious pattern of New Comedy: "What usually happens is that a young man wants a young woman, that his desire is resisted by some opposition, usually paternal, and that near the end of the play some twist in the plot enables the hero to have his will" (Frye 1957, 163). The lovers are tested, and finally find themselves by retreating from the ordinary world, where their union seems impossible, to a "magical" place apart from everyday life, such as the moonlight island in *It Happened One Night* (1934), the cruise ship in *The Lady Eve* (1941), and the enchanting moments at the Metropolitan Opera and on the streets of New York City in *Moonstruck*. When the couple returns, their union, in Frye's words, "causes a new society to crystallize" around them. The family gathered at the end of *Moonstruck* represents just such a crystallization.

Within the overarching narrative structure of birth, death, and rebirth, every comedy contains a potential tragedy. But every tragedy can also be seen as an incomplete comedy. In the larger perspective of history, community, or even biology, the life and death of the individual are no longer tragic. By shifting the guilt to the father and allowing the victory of the son, comedy gets the last word, just as on the Greek stage a satyr play always concluded a trilogy of tragedies. Chaplin's comment that tragedy should be filmed in close-up and comedy in long shot is suggestive here.

There is much to fault about Frye's work. His assertions about comedy as wish-fulfilling fail to ask *whose* wishes; his impulse, and it is the impulse of a liberal humanism, is to seek a common ground of shared desire, rather than to investigate the divisions that make such common ground difficult if not impossible to achieve. Frye assumes too readily that desire in romantic comedy is the sole possession of the male hero, seeking a "bride to be redeemed." While this may be so in the Greek and Roman New Comedies, it is not true of Shakespearean comedy or such romantic film comedies as *Moonstruck*, with which it has much in common. As "women on top," female characters such as Loretta and Rose and the great heroines of classical Hollywood's romantic comedies are "women on top" who enjoy a dramatic weight comparable to that of the male hero in tragedy.

Nonetheless, Frye has much to offer feminist approaches to comedy. Like Fredric Jameson, he sees narrative as an epistemological category, a structure that gives meaning to those other phenomena that also contribute to comedy-performance, gags, jokes, laughter. By asserting the priority of narrative, Frye directs attention to the space, albeit limited, ensured for women in the comedic inflection of the Oedipal narrative. In addition, by asserting that comedy in effect contains tragedy, Frye implicitly reverses the hierarchy that has so long privileged tragedy: "The watcher of death and tragedy has nothing to do but sit and wait for the inevitable end; but something gets born at the end of comedy, and the watcher of birth is a member of a busy society" (170).

Melodrama and Romantic Comedy

Romantic comedy exists in the same kind of generic tension with melodrama that Frye finds between comedy and tragedy.[6] As *Moonstruck* suggests, romantic comedy usually contains a potential melodrama, and melodrama, like *La Bohème*, contains a potential romantic comedy. Melodrama depends on a belief in the possibility of romantic comedy's happy ending, a belief that heightens the pathos of its loss. Similarly, romantic comedy depends on the melodramatic threat that the lovers will not get together and that the heroine will suffer a fate like Mimi's—becoming a spinster, marrying the wrong man, suffering, even dying. In *Moonstruck*, we fear that Loretta will marry doltish Johnny rather than dashing Ronny. But while critics have exerted considerable effort to preserve the distinctions between drama on the high plane and others (such as melodrama), no such stakes are involved in preserving the distinction between melodrama and romantic comedy. Both forms are set squarely in the province of women—the private, the domestic, the home, or the heart. Both narrate the stories of "excessive" women who assert their own desire and whose stories are emplotted in narratives that depend on the ideology of heterosexual romance. Both use the deferral of sexual fulfillment not only to reinforce the fantasies of romance but also as plot devices to prolong narrative suspense. Both depend to varying degrees on the structure of gender inversion.

Important differences, of course, distinguish the forms. For my purposes, the most critical one concerns motherhood. Mothers and mother substitutes exist in some romantic comedies (*The Philadelphia Story*, *Bringing Up Baby*), but the heroine usually neither has nor is a mother. This absence can be explained by the genre's attention to the heroine's Oedipal passage to femininity, her acceptance of the terms of heterosexuality. To do so, she must reject the most important feminine identification of her life, her mother, in favor of an exclusive attachment to a man, a stand-in for her father. This rent between mother and daughter, ignored in our culture, is "the essential female tragedy," according to Adrienne Rich (1986, 237). Romantic comedy ironically allows its heroine to participate in its symbolic rebirth only by abdicating her literal connections with maternity, her bond to her mother and eventually to her own daughters. In *The Philadelphia Story* (1940), it is Tracy's relationship with her estranged father, not her mother, which is crucial; until she reconciles with him, she cannot complete the maturation into femininity signaled by her acceptance of her proper mate. Covering up the costs of a woman's heterosexuality with laughter and pleasure, romantic comedy tolerates, and even encourages, its heroine's short-lived rebellion because that rebellion ultimately serves the interest of the hero—testing his mettle and shaking him loose of his rigidity and other qualities he is better off without.

As *Moonstruck* suggests, the stronger the presence of women, the more a romantic comedy is likely to undercut or problematize the heterosexual couple. In *Bringing Up Baby*, for example, the aunt's position as bearer of social power reinforces the critique of conventional gender roles that runs through the film, culminating in its precarious resolution over a collapsing mountain of dinosaur bones. In the "working girl" comedies of the early 1930s, female roommates highlight the cost to women of leaving a female-centered community to become part of a heterosexual couple. In contrast to such comedies, melodrama not only teaches that a woman's lot under patriarchy is to suffer, but makes that suffering pleasurable. As Loretta says in *Moonstruck*, overwhelmed by Mimi's fate, "It's awful, beautiful, sad. She died."

Melodrama, like romantic comedy, ties a woman's rebellion to her refusal of the terms of heterosexuality. But unlike romantic comedy, it dooms her rebellion from the start. Exposing the male villainy repressed in romantic comedy—or shown as simple foolishness—melodrama takes up the story of the heroine for whom romantic comedy's happy ending never will be possible, or the story of what *follows* that happy ending. Because melodrama concerns the heroine who fails to resolve the Oedipal passage, it leaves the pre-Oedipal mother/daughter bond intact. It is no surprise, then, that under patriarchy the stories of such women are told in forms that guarantee their punishment. From *Mildred Pierce* (1945) to *Terms of Endearment* (1983), mothers and daughters caught up in each other's lives can only tear each other apart.

The melodrama *Stella Dallas* (1937) illustrates the structural relation between melodrama and romantic comedy and the place of the mother in each. Stella's story eventually encompasses all three "women's" narratives—love, motherhood and, finally, loneliness. The film begins in the love plot, where Stella's desire to cross the boundaries of class and gender by actively pursuing the boss's employee appears in the positive light of romantic comedy. As the film follows her story past love into motherhood and loneliness, it moves into melodrama. Here, the assertion of her desire takes on a tragic cast, as it begins to signify her transgressive refusal to submerge her own identity into that of her husband, as well as the impossibility of preserving that identity and being a "good mother" at the same time.

Through the daughter Laurel's story, the film allows the viewer to experience romantic comedy from the point of view—quite literally—of the mother, whose "death" is required to bring about its happy ending. In the film's most wrenching moment, the climax of Laurel's romantic comedy coincides with Stella's redemption in melodrama, after she has enacted the self-annihilation that ideology demands of mothers. Outside, excluded from her daughter's wedding, Stella watches Laurel, while Laurel watches only her new husband. With tears streaming down her face, radiant in her self-denial, Stella is banished from the occasion that in comedy stands above all for inclusiveness, renewal, and festivity.

Moonstruck Again

Moonstruck offers a very different version of the relations between mothers and daughters and the dynamics of romantic love. Whereas *Stella Dallas* ends as a melodrama, *Moonstruck* concludes as a romantic comedy—but one that comes close to having it both ways by intermingling the two forms. The film retains those elements of melodrama that are most positive from a feminist point of view—the recognition of masculine guilt and acknowledgment of women's suffering, the presence of the mother and the connection among women. It rewrites romantic comedy's "happily ever after" love story to include a serious dose of pain, from Mimi's to Rose's, reminding us that romantic comedy never tells the whole of a woman's story. But the film rejects one of the most crucial elements of melodrama, the suffering, victimized femininity represented by Stella and by Mimi in *La Bohème*. While retaining the couple as an emblem of the fulfillment of all desire, the film ironizes romantic love, especially when melodramatized by men. In addition, it places the couple in a community that subjects male authority to gentle but continual assault.[7]

Despite the immediate presence of melodrama in the film, *Moonstruck* is above all a comedy, and like most comedies, its conflicts and dilemmas are organized along the axis of life and death rather than the moral polarities of melodrama. Loretta speaks her first words of the film in a wry exchange with her boss about a corpse; Mamma Cammareri lies on her deathbed in Sicily; the grandfather socializes with his friends in a graveyard; Loretta and Ronny confess that they were "dead" before they met. Throughout, the film examines how to deal with life's pain, from broken hearts and broken dreams to mortality, arguing finally that such pain can be avoided only by avoiding life itself.

In *Moonstruck*, it is the men, more than the women, who retreat from life, because of fear, self-pity, or self-absorption. In so doing, they demonstrate a lack of self-knowledge that not only hurts the women who love them, but makes them prime subjects for comic critique. Cosmo's fear of death causes him to withdraw from Rose and take a mistress. Perry, the middle-aged professor, feels alive only when he sees himself through the eyes of young female students. Ronny hides in the inferno of his bakery. When he tells Loretta his life story, he rages like a villainous romantic hero of melodrama, while an adoring female employee weeps, saying, "He's the most tormented man I know. I'm in love with him." It is important to note from the outset that the film's comic critique of masculinity is made possible in part by its use of ethnicity, for foolish men who are Italian-American can more readily be made the subject of comedy than those (like the professor) who are WASP.

While male pain is played for comedy, female pain is not; and *Moonstruck*'s women are shown as having a clearer sense of their identity than the men do. That clarity and strength authorize the film's use of gender inversion, which it introduces in an early scene, when Johnny and Loretta witness the professor being humiliated in a restaurant by his date, a young female student. Johnny giggles, then tells Loretta that a man who cannot control his woman is funny. The remark signals Johnny's lack of self-awareness, but more important, it establishes a model of love—based on male dominance—that the film will eventually replace with another more appealing one. As a "woman on top," a characterization enhanced by the unruly star persona Cher brings to the part, Loretta challenges her father and the other men in her life. She dominates Johnny, and initiates the romance with Ronny, seeking him out, luring him from his cave, feeding him raw meat, and bringing him back to life. At the same time, by dramatizing the conflict between her desire for Ronny and her desire to remain independent, she exposes the contradictions lived by heterosexual women under patriarchy.

Cosmo's name means "world," but the social cosmos or community the Castorini family represents is organized around Rose, whose deadpan wisdom and clear-eyed perceptiveness contrast with the melodramatic suffering of the film's male figures. When she turns down Perry's invitation to a tryst, she tells him that she knows who she is, implying that he lacks a comparable degree of self-awareness. When she counters Cosmo's self-pitying speech with "Your life is *not* built on nothing. *Te amo*," she reminds him that the love that binds people together is not "nothing," but in fact all that there is. The prominence of Rose's story, and her intimacy with Loretta, displace romantic film comedy's conventional focus on the isolated heterosexual couple. Throughout the film the two women confide in each other, and their paths often cross. In this female-centered community, the crystallization of a new society does not occur until Cosmo capitulates to Rose, and Loretta does not have to give up her mother to get her man.

Not surprisingly, the moon is *Moonstruck*'s most important visual and thematic motif. Hanging over the film like the moon over the city is a sense of the mythic, the magic, the miraculous. The film is drenched in celestial imagery, from the moon itself to the stars and moons on the charm bracelet Cosmo gives Mona, the chandeliers at the Metropolitan Opera, the bags of "Sunburst Flour" piled next to Ronny in his dungeon bakery. Comparing himself to Orlando Furioso, a figure from Italian romance, Uncle Raymond sings, "Hey there, you with the stars in your eyes," and Ronny speaks of "storybook love" as having the unreal perfection of "stars and snowflakes." A familiar symbol of the feminine, the moon also suggests madness and the demonic, and it is accompanied by the masculine counterpart of the wolf, most comically rendered in the grandfather's pack of yapping dogs.

The grandfather has a privileged connection with the imagery of magic and romance. Observing the events that unfold with the same balance of engagement and detachment that the film asks of its viewers, he is the story's other Fool. Like Johnny, he is both puzzled and possessed of a naive wisdom. At one point he follows his dogs past a "No Trespassing" sign into a cemetery. This gentle act of transgression, of mixing death and life, is followed by another when the dogs dig up flowers and defecate on the new grave of his friend. For the grandfather, this is no sacrilege. The friend is dead (or "asleep," he says), and the dogs are alive. Where Cosmo surrounds death with the aura of melo-drama, the grandfather takes the attitude of the carnivalesque. He confronts death's inevitability as a fact of life, and worries only about threats to the liv-ing—for how Cosmo endangers the family by refusing to pay for Loretta's wed-ding. As Rose tells Cosmo, "No matter what you do, you're going to die, just like everyone else." She accepts this inevitability with a gaze as sober and direct as those of the old matriarch and patriarch of the family portraits.

To be moonstruck is to acknowledge the wolf within and the necessity of intense emotion, or howling at the moon. Melodrama is the generic equiva-lent of being moonstruck, and the film argues that it, too, must be given its place in the more utopian narratives of comedy. That place is most clearly occu-pied in the film by the opera *La Bohème*. Mimi epitomizes the suffering, pas-sivity, and self-denial of the melodramatic heroine, consumed by romantic love. The opera's music literally orchestrates the pathos of her story. Mirroring and inverting the film's play with genre, the opera contains a comic subplot based on the romances of Musetta, an unruly flirt. Musetta is spared Mimi's heartache and death, but she also does not experience the intensity of Mimi's passion, and takes second place dramatically and musically to her.

From its earliest moments, the film doubles the comic couple of Loretta and Ronny with the melodramatic couple of Mimi and Rodolfo. At the film's turning point, when Ronny and Loretta return home from the opera, they replay a scene they had just witnessed, only to a different end, coming together rather than separating as Mimi and Rodolfo do. Urging Loretta not to fight her desire for him, Ronny tells her, "We're here to ruin ourselves, and break our hearts, and love the wrong people." If Ronny appears still stuck in the mode of melo-drama, he is also arguing for the position of comedy, and the film resists the temptation to sentimentalize him or any of its male characters. By the end, Ronny has become a full-fledged romantic hero, but not until he has shown himself to be as much a fool as Cosmo and the professor. The very rhyming of his name with his clownish brother Johnny's shows that, at least initially, the two have more than a little in common. As a result, the film succeeds in exploit-ing comedy's double allegiance to anarchy and order, its centrifugal assault on authority, and its centripetal drive toward community.

In the broadest sense, *Moonstruck*'s message about finding life in social connection and embracing its totality is entirely conventional. That very con-ventionality, however, suggests that romantic comedy persists in part because it speaks to powerful needs to believe in the utopian possibilities condensed on the image of the couple—the yearning for friendship between men and women, and for moments of joy in relationships constrained by unequal social power.

Romantic comedy also offers an alternative to the passive and suffering heroines of melodrama. If Loretta finally submits to the same lunacy Mimi does when she agrees to "ruin herself" with Ronny, she differs from Mimi in one critical way: unlike Mimi, who lives and dies only to give Rodolfo a reason to sing, Loretta remains a woman on top. Where Mimi wastes away in isolation, Loretta will draw strength from the company of her mother and a community that extends beyond the individual couple. By giving centrality and weight to its women, *Moonstruck* not only demonstrates the flexibility of a popular and enduring narrative form, but takes a step toward more fully realizing its potential to foster new and more inclusive images of community.

NOTES

1. *La Bohème* tells the story of Mimi, a sickly seamstress, and Rodolfo, an impoverished artist. After a brief period of love, the couple quarrel and separate, Rodolfo returns to his bohemian friends, and Mimi dies. The opera represents the efforts of its composer Giacomo Puccini (1858–1924) to popularize the form by drawing its characters from ordinary life rather than heroic myths—in other words, to shift it from tragedy to melodrama.

2. Melodrama, like comedy, is a slippery term to define. For my purposes, I use it to refer to a set of narrative conventions loosely associated with the "woman's weepie" or television soap opera.

3. Among those who have are Mary Russo, Patricia Mellencamp, Lucy Fischer, Ramona Curry, and Pamela Robertson Wojcik.

4. This kind of comedy has been called by a number of names, most commonly "screwball comedy," when referring to films of the 1930s and 1940s. I prefer "romantic comedy" because, especially in its cinematic forms, it is deeply dependent on the thematics of romantic love.

5. Frye published his most ambitious book *Anatomy of Criticism* a little more than a decade before the social upheavals of the late 1960s. Charged with idealism and formalism, his work fell out of favor until thirty years later, when Fredric Jameson reclaimed it for its interest in the relation between art and social change.

6. See Neale and Krutnik (1990, 133–136) for a discussion of the relation between romantic comedy and melodrama.

7. Much recent comedy has been marked by an interest in melodrama similar to *Moonstruck*'s but from a point of view that sentimentalizes the male hero (for example, *Pretty Woman* [1993] and *Sleepless in Seattle* [1993]). These films tend to use melodrama in the service of a suffering, beleaguered masculinity.

Works Cited

Adams, Cindy. "She Played Every Scene as if She Were the Star." *New York Post*, April 26, 1995, 16.

Allison, Dorothy. Entry #3335. *The Columbia World of Quotations*. New York: Columbia University Press, 1996.

Anderson, Paul Thomas. *Magnolia: The Shooting Script*. New York: Newmarket Press, 2000.

Andrew, Geoff. *Stranger than Paradise: Maverick Film-makers in Recent American Cinema*. London: Limelight Editions, 1999.

Arbuthnot, Lucy, and Gayle Seneca. "Pre-text and Text in *Gentlemen Prefer Blondes*." In *Issues in Feminist Film Criticism*, edited by Patricia Erens, 112–125. Bloomington: Indiana University Press, 1990.

Arthur, Paul. "The Gun in the Briefcase; or, The Inscription of Class in Film Noir." In *The Hidden Foundation: Cinema and the Question of Class*, edited by David E. James and Rick Berg. Minneapolis: University of Minnesota Press, 1996.

Auerbach, Nina. *Romantic Imprisonment: Women and Other Glorified Outcasts*. New York: Columbia University Press, 1985.

Bakhtin, Mikhail. *Rabelais and His World*. Trans. Helene Iswolsky. Bloomington: Indiana University Press, 1984.

Bamber, Linda. *Comic Women, Tragic Men: A Study of Gender and Genre in Shakespeare*. Stanford: Stanford University Press, 1982.

Barthes, Roland. *Image—Music—Text*. Trans. Stephen Heath. New York: Hill and Wang, 1977.

Basnett, Susan. *Feminist Experiences: The Women's Movement in Four Cultures*. London: Allen and Unwin, 1986.

"Battle of Buna." *Life*, February 15, 1943, 17–29.

Baym, Nina. "Melodramas of Beset Manhood: How Theories of American Fiction Exclude Women Authors." *American Quarterly* 33.2 (Summer 1981): 123–139.

Bazin, Andre, Charles Bitsch, and Jean Domarchi. "Interview with Orson Welles." Trans. Terry Comito. In *Touch of Evil, Orson Welles, Director*, edited by Terry Comito. New Brunswick, N.J.: Rutgers University Press, 1985.

Beck, Marilyn, and Stacy Jenel Smith. "Just Call Pam Grier a 'Super Bad Momma.'" *L.A. Daily News*, June 22, 2001, n.p.

Behlmer, Rudy, ed. *Inside Warner Bros. (1935–1951)*. New York: Viking, 1985.

Benjamin, Walter. "On Some Motifs in Baudelaire." In *Illuminations*. New York: Schocken, 1969.

Benshoff, Harry, and Sean Griffin. *Queer Images: A History of Gay and Lesbian Film in America*. Lanham: Rowan & Littlefield, 2005.

Bensinger, Terralee. "Lesbian Pornography:The Re/Making of (a) Community." *Discourse* 15.1 (1992): 74.

Berger, John. *Ways of Seeing*. London: Penguin, 1972, 1979.

Bérubé, Allan. *Coming Out Under Fire: The History of Gay Men and Women in World War Two*. New York: Plume, 1991.

Biasin, Gian Paolo. *Montale, Debussy, and Modernism*. Princeton: Princeton University Press, 1989.

Bingham, Dennis. *Acting Male: Masculinities in the Films of James Stewart, Jack Nicholson, and Clint Eastwood*. New Brunswick: Rutgers University Press, 1994.

Bogle, Donald. *Brown Sugar*. New York: Da Capo Press, 1980.

Bondanella, Peter. *The Cinema of Federico Fellini*. Princeton: Princeton University Press, 1993.

Bone, Travis. "Diva Worship: Gay Men and Their Affinity for Strong Women." *Gay & Lesbian Times*, July 17, 2003.

Boone, Joel T. "The Sexual Aspects of Military Personnel." *Journal of Social History* 27 (March 1941): 113–124.

Borde, Raymond, and Etienne Chaumeton. *A Panorama of American Film Noir 1941–1953*. Trans. Paul Hammond. San Francisco: City Lights, 2002.

———. "Towards a Definition of Film Noir." Trans. Alain Silver. In *Film Noir Reader*, edited by Alain Silver and James Ursini. New York: Limelight Editions, 1996.

Boyd, Todd. "*Original Gangstas*." *Sight and Sound* 6, no. 10 (October 1996): 49–50.

Brandes, Stanley. "Like Wounded Stags: Male Sexual Ideology in an Andalusian Town." In *Sexual Meanings: The Cultural Construction of Gender and Sexuality*, edited by Sherry B. Ortner and Harriet Whitehead. Cambridge: Cambridge University Press, 1981.

———. *Metaphors of Masculinity: Sex and Status in Andalusian Folklore*. Philadelphia: University of Pennsylvania Press, 1985.

Braxton, Greg. "She's Back and Badder Than Ever." *L.A. Times* calendar section, August 27, 1995.

Brooks, Peter. *The Melodramatic Imagination*. New Haven: Yale University Press, 1995.

Brown, Jeffrey A. "Gender and the Action Heroine: Hardbodies and *The Point of No Return*." *Cinema Journal* 35, no. 3 (Spring 1996): 52–71.

Brunetta, Gian Piero. *Storia del cinema italiano. Dal neorealismo al miracolo economico 1945–1959*. Terzo volume. Roma: Riuniti, 1993.

Brunovska Karnick, Kristine, and Henry Jenkins, eds. *Classical Hollywood Comedy*. New York: Routledge, 1995.

Brunsdon, Charlotte. *Screen Tastes: Soap Opera to Satellite Dishes*. London and New York: Routledge, 1997.

Butler, Judith. *Bodies That Matter: On the Discursive Limits of "Sex."* New York: Routledge, 1993.

———. *Gender Trouble: Feminism and the Subversion of Identity*. New York: Routledge, 1990.

Byers, Jackie. *All that Heaven Allows: Re-reading Gender in 1950s Melodrama*. Chapel Hill: University of North Carolina Press, 1991.

Callow, Simon. *Charles Laughton: A Difficult Actor*. London: Methuen, 1987.

Carmago, Sandy. "'Mind the Gap': The Multi-Protagonist Film, Genre." *M/C : A Journal of Media and Culture* 5, no. 5 (2002). www.mediaculture.org.au/mc/0210/Carmago.html.

Carrano, Patrizia."Divismo." In *Schermi ed ombre. Gli italiani e il cinema del dopoguerra*, a cura di Marino Livolsi. Firenze: La Nuova Italia, 1988.

Carson, Diane, ed. *Multiple Voices in Feminist Criticism*. Minneapolis: University of Minnesota Press, 1994.

Case, Sue Ellen. *The Domain-Matrix : Performing Lesbian at the End of Print Culture*. Bloomington: Indiana University Press, 1996.

Castiglione, Baldesar. *The Book of the Courier*. Trans. Charles Singleton. Garden City: Anchor, 1959.

Chandler, Charlotte. *I, Fellini*. New York: Random House, 1995.

Chauncey, George, Jr. "Christian Brotherhood or Sexual Perversion? Homosexual Identities and the Construction of Sexual Boundaries in the World War One Era." *Journal of Social History* 19 (1985): 189–211.

Chiavola-Birnbaum, Lucia. *Liberazione della donna: Feminism in Italy*. Middletown: Wesleyan University Press, 1986.

Chodorow, Nancy. *The Reproduction of Mothering: Psychoanalysis and the Sociology of Gender*. Berkeley: University of California Press, 1978.

Clover, Carol. *Men, Women and Chain Saws: Gender in the Modern Horror Film*. Princeton: Princeton University Press, 1992.

Cohan, Steven. *Incongruous Entertainment: Camp, Cultural Value and the MGM Musical*, Durham: Duke University Press, 2005.

——. "Judy on the Net: Judy Garland Fandom and the 'Gay Thing' Revisited." In *Keyframes: Popular Cinema and Cultural Studies*. New York: Routledge, 2001.

——. *Masked Men: Masculinity and Movies in the Fifties*. Bloomington: Indiana University Press, 1997.

Cohan, Steven, and Ina Rae Hark, eds. *Screening the Male: Exploring Masculinities in Hollywood Cinema*. London and New York: Routledge, 1993.

Connolly, Cyril. *The Unquiet Grave: A Word Cycle by Palinurus*. Rev. ed. New York: Persea, 1981.

Cook, Pam. "Exploitation Films and Feminism." *Screen* 17, no. 2 (Summer 1976): 122–127.

Copjec, Joan. *Read My Desire: Lacan Against the Lacanians*. Boston: MIT Press, 1994.

Corber, Robert J. *Homosexuality in Cold War America: Resistance and the Crisis of Masculinity*. Durham: Duke University Press, 1997.

Costello, John. *Virtue Under Fire: How World War II Changed our Social and Sexual Lives*. Boston: Little, Brown, 1985.

Croce, Arlene. "Ginger Rogers," *New Yorker*, May 8, 1995, 71.

——. *The Fred Astaire and Ginger Rogers Book*. New York: Vintage, 1972.

Cruz, Omayra. "Between Cinematic Imperialism and the Idea of Radical Politics: Philippines Based Women's Prison Films of the 1970s." Paper delivered at Society for Cinema Studies Conference, Denver, CO, 2002.

Curry, Ramona. *Too Much of a Good Thing: Mae West as Cultural Icon*. Minneapolis: University of Minnesota Press, 1996.

Davis, Natalie Zemon. "Women on Top." In *Society and Culture in Early Modern France*. Stanford: Stanford University Press, 1975.

DeAngelis, Michael. *Gay Fandom and Crossover Stardom: James Dean, Mel Gibson, and Keanu Reeves*. Durham: Duke University Press, 2001.

de Cordova, Richard. *Picture Personalities: The Emergence of the Star System in America*. Urbana: University of Illinois Press, 1990.

De Lauretis, Tersea. *The Practice of Love: Lesbian Sexuality and Perverse Desire*. Bloomington: Indiana University Press, 1994.

Delson, James. "Heston on Welles." In *Touch of Evil, Orson Welles, director*, edited by Terry Comito. New Brunswick: Rutgers University Press, 1985.

D'Emilio, John. *Sexual Politics, Sexual Communities: The Making of a Homosexual Minority in the United States, 1940–1970*. Chicago: University of Chicago Press, 1983.

Denby, David. "San Fernando Aria." *The New Yorker* 75 (December 20, 1999): 102–103.

Dick, Leslie. Review of *Magnolia. Sight and Sound* 10, no. 4 (April 2000): 56–57.

Dillman, Joanne Clarke. "Twelve Characters in Search of a Television Text: *Magnolia* Masquerading as Soap Opera." *Journal of Popular Film and Television* 33, no. 3 (Fall 2005): 143–151.

Diones, Bruce. "Knockout." *New Yorker*, October 20, 1997.

DiPiero, Thomas. *White Men Aren't*. Durham: Duke University Press, 2002.

Diviso in due. Cesare Zavattini: cinema e cultural popolare. Edited by Pierluigi Ercole. Reggio Emilia: Edizioni Diabasis, 1999.

Dixon, Wheeler Winston. "Archetypes of the Heavy in the Classical Hollywood Cinema." In

Beyond the Stars: Stock Characters in American Popular Film, edited by Paul Loukides and Linda K. Fuller. Bowling Green: Bowling Green State University Popular Press, 1990.

———. *Experimental Cinema: The Film Reader.* London and New York: BFI, 2002.

Doane, Mary Ann. "Film and the Masquerade: Theorizing the Female Spectator." In *Femmes Fatales: Feminism, Film Theory, Psychoanalysis.* New York: Routledge, 1991.

———. *The Desire to Desire: The Women's Films of the 1940s.* Bloomington: Indiana University Press, 1994.

———. "Woman's Stake: Filming the Female Body." *October* 17 (Summer 1981).

Doherty, Thomas. *Projections of War: Hollywood, American Culture, and World War II.* Rev. ed. New York: Columbia University Press, 1999.

Doty, Alexander. *Flaming Classics: Queering the Film Canon.* New York: Routledge, 2000.

———. *Making Things Perfectly Queer: Interpreting Mass Culture.* Minneapolis: University of Minnesota Press, 1993.

———. "Queer Theory." In *Film Studies: Critical Approaches*, edited by John Hill and Pamela Church Gibson. Cambridge: Oxford University Press, 1998.

Dunye, Cheryl. "Cheryl Dunye." In *What It Is, What It Was!: The Black Film Explosion of the '70s in Words and Pictures*, edited by Gerald Martinez, Diana Martinez, and Andres Chavez. New York: Hyperion (Miramax), 1998.

Dworkin, Andrea. Entry # 18138. In *The Columbia World of Quotations.* New York: Columbia University Press, 1996.

Dyer, Richard. "Don't Look Now—The Male Pin-Up." *Screen* 23, nos. 3/4 (September–October 1982).

———. *Gays and Film.* London: British Film Institute, 1980.

———. *Heavenly Bodies.* New York: St. Martins, 1986.

———. *Now You See It: Studies on Lesbian and Gay Film.* London: Routledge, 1990.

———. *Only Entertainment.* New York: Routledge, 1992.

———. "Resistance Through Charisma: Rita Hayworth and *Gilda*." In *Women in Film Noir*, rev. ed., edited by E. Ann Kaplan. London: British Film Institute, 1998.

———. *Stars.* London: BFI, 1979.

Easthope, Anthony. *What A Man's Gotta Do: The Masculine Myth in Popular Culture.* Boston: Unwin Hyman, 1990.

Ebert, Alan. "Pam Grier: Coming into Focus." *Essence*, January 1979.

Ebert, Roger. "*Magnolia*." *Chicago Sun-Times* (January 7, 2000): C2.

———. "*Mars Attacks!*" *Chicago Sun Times*, 1996. Online. www.suntimes.com. (accessed February 12, 2003).

Eberwein, Robert. "'As a Mother Cuddles a Child': Sexuality and Masculinity in World War II Combat Films." In *Masculinity: Bodies, Movies, Culture*, edited by Peter Lehman. New York and London: Routledge, 1991, 149–166.

———. *Sex Ed: Film, Video, and the Framework of Desire.* New Brunswick, N.J.: Rutgers University Press, 1999.

Echols, Alice. *Daring to Be Bad: Radical Feminism in America 1967–1975.* Minneapolis: University of Minnesota Press, 1989.

Eells, George. *Ginger, Loretta and Irene Who?* New York: G. P. Putnam, 1976.

Eimer, David. "Reborn." *The Independent*, March 8, 1998.

Faludi, Susan. *Backlash: The Undeclared War Against American Women.* New York: Doubleday, 1991.

Farber, Stephen. "Pam Grier," *Moviegoer*, May 1983.

Farmer, Brett. "The Fabulous Sublimity of Gay Diva Worship," *Camera Obscura* 59 (2005): 165–194.

Ferguson, Mary. *Images of Women in Literature.* Boston: Houghton Mifflin, 1977.

Fischer, Lucy. *Cinematernity: Film, Motherhood, Genre.* Princeton: Princeton University Press, 1996.

———. *Designing Women: Cinema, Art Deco and the Female Form.* New York: Columbia University Press, 2003.

————, and Marcia Landy. "'Dead Again' or A-Live Again: Postmodern or Postmortem?" *Cinema Journal* 33, no. 4 (Summer 1994): 3–22.

————. "Sometimes I Feel Like a Motherless Child: Comedy and Matricide." In *Comedy/Cinema/Theory*, edited by Andrew Horton. Berkeley: University of California Press, 1991, 60–78.

Forward, Susan, and Buck Craig. *Betrayal of Innocence: Incest and its Devastation*. London: Penguin, 1978.

Freud, Sigmund. *Beyond the Pleasure Principle*. Trans. James Strachey. New York: Norton, 1961.

————. "The Ego and the Id." In *The Complete Psychological Works of Sigmund Freud*. Vol. 19. London: Hogarth, 1969.

————. *General Psychological Theory*. Ed. Philip Rieff. New York: Simon and Schuster, 1991.

————. "Inhibitions, Symptoms and Anxiety." In *The Complete Psychological Works of Sigmund Freud*. Vol. 20. London: Hogarth, 1969.

————. *Jokes and their Relation to the Unconscious*. Trans. and ed. James Strachey. New York: Norton, 1960.

————. "Mourning and Melancholia." In *The Complete Psychological Works of Sigmund Freud*. Vol. 14. London: Hogarth, 1969.

————. "The Uncanny." In *The Complete Psychological Works of Sigmund Freud*. Vol. 17, London: Hogarth, 1969.

Freydberg, Elizabeth Hadley. "Sapphires, Spitfires, Sluts, and Superbitches: Aframericans and Latinas in Contemporary American Film." In *Black Women in America*, edited by Kim Marie Vaz. Thousand Oaks and London: Sage Publications, 1995.

Frye, Northrop. *Anatomy of Criticism: Four Essays*. Princeton: Princeton University Press, 1957.

Fuqua, Joy. "'Can You Feel It, Joe?': Male Melodrama and the Feeling Man." *Velvet Light Trap* 38 (Fall 1996): 28–38.

Fuss, Diana. *Essentially Speaking*. New York: Routledge, 1990.

Gabbard, Krin. "Black Angels in America: Millennial Solutions to the 'Race Problem.'" In *Black Magic: White Hollywood and African American Culture*. New Brunswick, N.J.: Rutgers University Press, 2004.

————. *Black Magic: White Hollywood and African American Culture*. New Brunswick, N.J.: Rutgers University Press, 2004.

————. "John Wayne." In *Men and Masculinities: A Social, Cultural, and Historical Encyclopedia*, edited by Michael Kimmel and Amy Aronson. Santa Barbara: ABC-Clio, 2004: II, 819–821.

————. and Glen O. Gabbard. *Psychiatry in the Cinema*. Chicago: University of Chicago Press, 1987.

Gilmore, David. "Introduction: The Shame of Dishonor." In *Honor and Shame and the Unity of the Mediterranean*, edited by David Gilmore. Washington, D.C.: American Anthropological Association, 1987.

————. *Manhood in the Making: Cultural Concepts of Masculinity*. New Haven: Yale University Press, 1990.

Giovannini, Maureen J. "Woman: A Dominant Symbol within the Cultural System of a Sicilian Town." *Man: The Journal of the Royal Anthropological Institute* 16, no. 3 (November 1981): 408–426.

Gledhill, Christine, ed. *Home is Where the Heart Is: Studies in Melodrama and the Woman's Film*. London: The British Film Institute, 1987.

Godard, Jean-Luc. Entry #25138. In *The Columbia World of Quotations*. New York: Columbia University Press, 1996.

Golden, Daniel."Pasta or Paradigm: The Place of Italian-American Women in Popular Film." *Explorations in Ethnic Studies : The Journal of the National Association of Interdisciplinary Ethnic Studies* (1978): 3–10.

Gramaglia, Mariella. "1968: Il venir dopo e l'andar oltre del movimento femminista." In *La questione femminile in Italia dal '900 ad oggi*, edited by G. Ascoli et al., Milano: Franco Angeli Editore, 1979.

Grapes, Bryan J. *Child Abuse.* San Diego: Greenhaven, 2001.

Green, Philip. *Cracks in the Pedestal: Ideology and Gender in Hollywood.* Amherst: University of Massachusetts Press, 1998.

Greenstreet, Sydney. "The Role I Liked Best." *Saturday Evening Post*, February 22, 1947, 123.

Greer, Germaine. *The Change: Women, Aging and the Menopause.* New York: Random, 1993.

Grier, Pam. "Pam Grier." In *What It Is, What It Was!: The Black Film Explosion of the '70s in Words and Pictures*, edited by Gerald Martinez, Diana Martinez, and Andres Chavez. New York: Hyperion (Miramax), 1998.

Grignafini, Giovanna. "Female Identity and Italian Cinema of the 1950s." In *Off-Screen: Women and Film in Italy.* London: Routledge, 1988.

Grosz, Elizabeth. *Volatile Bodies: Toward a Corporeal Feminism.* Bloomington: Indiana University Press, 1994.

"Guadalcanal," *Life*, March 1, 1943, 68.

Guerrero, Ed. *Framing Blackness: The African American Image in Film.* Philadelphia: Temple University Press, 1993.

Gundle, Stephen. "Fame, Fashion and Style: The Italian Star System." In *Italian Cultural Studies: An Introduction*, edited by David Forgacs and Robert Lumley. Oxford: Oxford University Press, 1996.

Halberstam, Judith. *Female Masculinity.* Durham: Duke University Press, 1998.

Hankin, Kelly. "A Rebel Without a Choice?: Femme Spectatorship in Hollywood Film," *Velvet Light Trap* (1998): 3–18.

———. "*Badass Supermama* Meets *Foxy Brown*." In *The Girls in the Back Room: Looking at the Lesbian Bar.* Minneapolis and London: University of Minnesota Press, 2002.

Hansen, Miriam. *Babel and Babylon: Spectatorship in American Silent Film.* Cambridge, Mass.: Harvard University Press, 1994.

Haskell, Mary. *From Reverence to Rape: The Treatment of Women in the Movies.* 2nd ed. Chicago: University of Chicago Press, 1987.

Heilbrun, Caroline G. *Writing a Woman's Life.* New York: Ballantine, 1988.

Herdt, Gilbert, ed. *Third Sex, Third Gender.* New York: Zone, 1994.

Hoberman, J. *Midnight Movies.* New York: Perseus, 1991.

———. "New Jack Prairie." *Village Voice*, n.p.

Holmund, Chris. *Impossible Bodies: Femininity and Masculinity at the Movies.* London: Routledge, 2002.

———. "Latinas in La La Land." In *Impossible Bodies: Femininity and Masculinity at the Movies.* London and New York: Routledge, 2002.

———. "Nouveaux Westerns for the 1990s: Genre Offshoots, Audience Reroutes." In *Impossible Bodies: Femininity and Masculinity at the Movies.* London and New York: Routledge, 2002.

Holub, Renate. "Towards a New Rationality? Notes on Feminist and Current Discursive Practices in Italy." *Discourse* 4 (Winter 1981–1982): 89–107.

hooks, bell. *Black Looks: Race and Representation.* Boston: South End Press, 1992.

Howe, Desson. "*Above the Law.*" *Washington Post*, April 8, 1998. Online. www.washingtonpost.com. (accessed February 12, 2003).

Hunt, Dennis. "Pam Grier Is Shedding Her Redundant Image." *Los Angeles Times*, May 27, 1994.

Jacobson, Mark. "Sex Goddess of the '70s." *New York*, May 19, 1975.

Jagger, Alison M. *Feminist Politics and Human Nature.* Totowa: Rowman and Allanheld, 1983.

Jeffords, Susan. *Hard Bodies: Hollywood Masculinity in the Reagan Era.* New Brunswick: Rutgers University Press, 1993.

Johnson, Diane. *Dashiell Hammett: A Life.* New York: Random House, 1983.

Johnson, Thomas, and David Fantle. "Coffy Time." *Outré* 9 (1997): 63–64.

Johnston, Claire, ed. *Dorothy Arzner: Towards a Feminist Cinema*. London: British Film Institute, 1975.

———. "Femininity and the Masquerade in *Anne of the Indies*." In *Jacques Tourneur*, edited by Claire Johnston and Paul Willemen. Edinburgh Film Festival, 1975.

Jones, Carlisle. "Unstarred Star of British Stage a Hit in Films." *New York Herald Tribune*, September 28, 1941. Sydney Greenstreet biographical file, Margaret Herrick Library, Academy of Motion Picture Arts and Sciences.

Jones, Kent. "Kent Jones Tours P.T. Anderson's *Magnolia*." *Film Comment* 36, no. 1 (January–February 2000): 38–39.

Julius, Marshall. *Action! The Action Movie A–Z*. Bloomington and Indianapolis: Indiana University Press, 1996.

Kael, Pauline. "The Current Cinema." *New Yorker*, February 23, 1981.

Kaminsky, Stuart. *American Film Genres*. 2nd ed. Chicago: Nelson Hall, 1985.

Kaplan, E. Ann. *Women and Film: Both Sides of the Camera*. London and New York: Routledge, 1983/2000.

———. *Motherhood and Representation: The Mother in Melodrama and Popular Culture*. London and New York: Routledge, 1992. New edition, 2002.

———, ed. *Feminism and Film*. New York and Oxford: Oxford University Press, 2000.

Kauffmann, Stanley. Interviewed in *Round Up the Usual Suspects: The Making of Casablanca—Bogart, Bergman, and World War II*, by Aljean Harmetz. New York: Hyperion, 1992.

Kincaid, Jamaica. "Pam Grier: The Mocha Mogul of Hollywood." *Ms.* 1975.

Klingman, Mildred. *The Secret Lives of Fat People*. Boston: Houghton Mifflin, 1981.

Knutsvik, Geir Stenar. "Pam Grier: An Actiondronning Vender Tilbake." *Z* 64 (1998): 8–11.

Koestenbaum, Wayne. *The Queen's Throat: Opera, Homosexuality and the Mystery of Desire*. New York: Vintage, 1993.

Koppelman-Cornillon, Susan. *Images of Women in Fiction: Feminist Perspectives*. Bowling Green: Bowling Green University Press, 1973.

Krutnik, Frank. *In a Lonely Street: Film Noir, Genre and Masculinity*. London: Routledge, 1991.

Kuhn, Annette. *Cinema, Censorship and Sexuality 1909–1925*. London and New York: Routledge, 1988.

Landy, Marcia. *Italian Films*. Cambridge: Cambridge University Press, 2000.

Lang, Robert. *Masculine Interests: Homoerotics in Hollywood Film*. New York: Columbia University Press, 2002.

Lazzerini, Marcello. *Mastroainni e gli allegri 'ragazzi' di Castiglioncello*. Firenze: Loggia de' Lanzi, 1999.

Leab, Daniel. *From Sambo to Superspade*. Boston: Houghton Mifflin, 1976.

Lederman, Marie Jean. "Dreams and Vision in Fellini's *City of Women*." *Journal of Popular Film and Television* 9, no. 3 (Fall 1981): 114–122.

Lehman, Peter, ed. *Masculinity: Bodies, Movies, Culture*. New York and London: Routledge, 1991.

———. *Running Scared: Masculinity and the Representation of the Male Body*. Philadelphia: Temple University Press, 1993.

Leonardi, Susan, and Rebecca Pope. *The Diva's Mouth: Body, Voice, Prima Donna Politics*. New Brunswick: Rutgers University Press, 1996.

Levenstein, Harvey. *Paradox of Plenty: A Social History of Eating in Modern America*. New York: Oxford University Press, 1993.

Levy, Emanuel. Review of *Magnolia*. *Variety* 377 (December 13/19, 1999): 105–106.

Lipsitz, George. "Genre Anxiety and Racial Representation in 1970s Cinema." In *Refiguring American Film Genres*, edited by Nick Browne. Berkeley, Los Angeles, London: University of California Press, 1998.

Lott, Tommy. "A No-Theory Theory of Black Cinema." In *Representing Blackness*, edited by Valerie Smith. New Brunswick, N.J.: Rutgers University Press, 1997.

Lugowski, Charles. "'A Treatise on Decay': Leftist Critics and Queer Readings in Depression-Era U.S. Film." In *Looking Past the Screen: Case Studies in American Film History and Method*, edited by Jon Lewis and Eric Smoodin. Durham: Duke University Press, 2007.

Luhr, William. "John Wayne and *The Searchers*." In *The Searchers: Essays and Reflections on Ford's Classic Western*, edited by Arthur M. Eckstein and Peter Lehman. Detroit: Wayne State University Press, 2004, 75–90.

———. "Mutilating Mel: Martyrdom and Masculinity in *Braveheart*." In *Mythologies of Violence in Postmodern Media*, edited by Christopher Sharrett. Detroit: Wayne State University Press, 1999, 227–246.

Lumley, Robert. *States of Emergency: Cultures of Revolt in Italy from 1968 to 1978*. London: Vers, 1990.

Machiavelli, Niccolò. *The Prince*. Trans. Peter Bondanella and Mark Musa. Oxford: Oxford University Press, 1979.

Major, Wade. "Jackie Speaks." *Boxoffice* 133, no. 11 (November 1997): 28.

Mank, Gregory William. *The Hollywood Hissables*. Metuchen: Scarecrow Press, 1989.

Mann, William J. *Behind the Screen: How Gays and Lesbians Shaped Hollywood, 1910–1969*. New York: Viking, 2001.

Marrone, Gaetana. "Memory in Fellini's *City of Women*." In *Perspectives on Federico Fellini*, edited by Peter Bondanella and Cristina Degli Esposti. New York: G. K. Hall & Co., 1993.

Mastroianni, Marcello. *Mi ricordo, sì, io mi ricordo*, a cura di Francesco Tatò. Milano: Baldini & Castoldi, 1997.

Mask, Mia. "Divas of the Silver Screen: Black Women in American Film 1950–2000." Ph.D. diss., New York University, 2001.

Mayne, Judith. "Caged and Framed: The Women-in-Prison Film." In *Framed: Lesbians, Feminists, and Media Culture*. Minneapolis and London: University of Minnesota Press, 2000.

———. *Directed by Dorothy Arzner*. Bloomington: Indiana University Press, 1994.

McCarthy, Todd. "*Posse*." *Variety* 351, no. 1 (May 3, 1993): 40.

McGee, Mark Thomas. *Fast and Furious: The Story of American International Pictures*. Jefferson and London: McFarland & Co., 1984.

McHugh, Kathleen. "'Sounds That Creep Inside You': Female Narration and Voiceover in the Films of Jane Campion." *Style* 35, no. 2 (Summer 2001): 193–218.

Mellen, Joan. *Women and their Sexuality in the New Film*. New York: Horizon Press, 1974.

Mellencamp, Patricia. *High Anxiety: Catastrophe, Scandal, Age, and Comedy*. Bloomington, Indiana University Press, 1992.

———. "Situation Comedy, Feminism and Freud." In *Studies in Entertainment*, edited by Tania Modleski. Bloomington: Indiana University Press, 1986, 80–95.

Menninger, William. *Psychiatry in a Troubled World: Yesterday's War and Today's Challenge*. New York: Macmillan, 1948.

Millett, Kate. *Sexual Politics*. Garden City: Doubleday, 1970.

Milliken, Christie. "Fair to Feminism? Carnivalizing the Carnival in Fellini's *City of Women*." *Spectator* (Spring 1990): 28–45.

Mims, Sergio Alejandro. "1970–1975: Le phénoméne de la 'Blaxploitation,'" *Cinémaction, Le Cinéma noir américain*: 123–129.

Modleski, Tania. *Loving With a Vengeance: Mass-Produced Fantasies for Women*. New Haven: Shoestring Press, 1982.

———. "Time and Desire in the Woman's Film." *Cinema Journal* 23, no. 3 (Spring 1984): 19–30.

———. "The Search for Tomorrow in Today's Soap Operas: Notes on Feminine Narrative Form." *Film Quarterly* 33, no. 1 (Autumn 1979): 12–21.

Monti, Raffaele. *Bottega Fellini. La città delle donne: progetto, lavorazione, film*. Roma: DeLuca Editore, 1981.

Mulvey, Laura. *Visual and Other Pleasures*. Bloomington: University of Indiana Press, 1989.

———. "Visual Pleasure and Narrative Cinema." Reprinted in *Feminism and Film*, edited by E. Ann Kaplan. New York and Oxford: Oxford University Press, 2000, 34–47.

Nardini, Gloria. *Che Bella Figura! The Power of Performance in an Italian Ladies' Club in Chicago*. Albany: State University of New York Press, 1999.

Nash Kelvinator Advertisement, *Time*, May 1944, inside cover.

National Research Council, *Psychology for the Fighting Man: What You Should Know about Yourself and Others*. Washington: Infantry Journal, 1943.

Neale, Steve. *Genre and Hollywood*. London and New York: Routledge, 2000.

———. "Masculinity as Spectacle." *Screen* 24, no. 6 (November–December 1983).

———, and Frank Krutnik. *Popular Film and Television Comedy*. New York: Routledge, 1990.

Negrón-Muntaner, Frances. "Jennifer's Butt." *Aztlán: A Journal of Chicano Studies* 22, no. 2 (Fall 1997): 181–194.

"New Picture." Review of *This Is the Army*, *Time*, August 16, 1943, 93–94.

Norton, Andrew, ed. *Comedy/Cinema/Theory*. Berkeley: University of California Press, 1991.

Null, Gary. *Black Hollywood: The Negro in Motion Pictures*. Secaucus: Citadel Press, 1975.

O'Healy, Àine. "Unspeakable Bodies: Fellini's Female Grotesques." *RLA: Romance Languages Annual* 4 (1992): 325–329.

Olsen, Mark. "Singing in the Rain." *Sight & Sound* 10 (March 2000): 26–28.

Ottoson, Robert L. *American International Pictures: A Filmography*. New York and London: Garland, 1985.

"Pam Grier Is Sinister and Sexy in *Something Wicked This Way Comes*." Press book, *Something Wicked This Way Comes*. Walt Disney Productions, 1983.

Pellerin, Dominique. "*Holy Smoke*: Un Symbolisme excessif," *Séquences* 208 (May–August 2000): 46–47.

Penley, Constance. *Feminism and Film*. New York and London: Routledge, 1988.

"Picture of the Week," *Life*, February 8, 1943, 24–25.

Pinsker, Sanford. *The Schlemiel as Metaphor: Studies in Yiddish and American Jewish Fiction*. Rev. and enlarged ed. Carbondale: Southern Illinois University Press, 1991.

Pitkin, Donald S. "Italian Urbanscape: Intersection of Private and Public." In *The Cultural Meaning of Urban Space*, edited by Robert Rotenberg and Gary McDonogh. Westport: Bergin & Garvey, 1993.

Radicalesbians, "The Woman Identified Woman." In *Radical Feminism*, edited by Anne Koedt, Ellen Levine, and Anita Rapone. New York: Quandrangle, 1973.

Reich, Jacqueline. *Beyond the Latin Lover: Marcello Mastroianni, Masculinity, and Italian Cinema*. Bloomington: Indiana University Press, 2004.

Reid, Mark. *Redefining Black Film*. Berkeley, Los Angeles, Oxford: University of California Press, 1993.

Rhines, Jesse A. *Black Film, White Money*. New Brunswick, N.J.: Rutgers University Press, 1996.

Rich, Adrienne. *Of Woman Born: Motherhood as Experience and Institution*. New York: W. W. Norton and Co., 1986.

Rickenbacker, Eddie. "Pacific Mission [Part I]," *Life*, January 25, 1943, 20–27, 90, 92, 94–96, 99–100.

Rickey, Carrie. "Little Sheba's Comeback." *Village Voice*, March 4–10, 1981.

Rictor, Norton. "A Critique of Social Constructionism and Postmodern Queer Theory," "Gender Nonconformity," June 1, 2002. www.infopt.demon.co.uk/socia104.htm

Robertson, Pamela. *Guilty Pleasures: Feminist Camp from Mae West to Madonna*. Durham: Duke University Press, 1996.

———. "'The Kinda Comedy That Imitates Me': Mae West's Identification with the Feminist Camp." *Cinema Journal* 32, no. 2 (1993): 57–72.

Robinson, Cedric. "Blaxploitation and the Misrepresentation of Race." *Race & Class* 40, no. 1 (1998): 1–12.

Rodowick, David. *The Difficulty of Difference Psychoanalysis, Sexual Difference and Film Theory*. London and New York: Routledge, 1991.

Roeder, George H., Jr. *The Censored War: American Visual Experience of World War Two*. New Haven: Yale University Press, 1993.

Rosen, Marjorie. *Popcorn Venus: Women, Movies and the American Dream*. New York: Avon Books, 1973.

Ross, Irwin. "Sex in the Army." *American Mercury* 53 (December 1941): 661–669.

Rowe, Kathleen. *The Unruly Woman: Gender and the Genres of Laughter*. Austin: University of Texas Press, 1995.

Russo, Mary. "Female Grotesques: Carnival and Theory." In *Feminist Studies, Critical Studies*, edited by Teresa De Lauretis. Bloomington: Indiana University Press, 1986, 213–229.

Russo, Vito. *The Celluloid Closet: Homosexuality in the Movies*, Rev. ed. New York: Harper and Row, 1987.

Salvo, Patrick. "Pam Grier: The Movie Super-Sex Goddess Who's Fed Up with Sex and Violence." *Sepia* 25, no. 2 (February 19, 1976): 48–54.

Schatz, Thomas. *Boom and Bust: American Cinema in the 1940s*. Berkeley and Los Angeles: University of California Press, 1997.

———. *Hollywood Genres: Formulas, Filmmaking and the Studio System*. Philadelphia: Temple University Press, 1981.

———. *Hollywood Genres: Formulas, Filmmaking, and the Studio System*. New York: McGraw-Hill, 1981.

Scheman, Naomi. "Missing Mothers/Desiring Daughters: Framing the Sight of Women." *Critical Inquiry* 15 (1988): 63–89.

Schickel, Richard. "Magnolia." *Time* (December 12, 1999): 37.

Schrader, Paul. "Notes on Film Noir." *Film Comment* 8, no. 1 (Spring 1972): 8–13.

———. *Schrader on Schrader*. New York: Faber and Faber, 2004.

Schubert, Lawrence. "Still Foxy After All These Years." *Detour Magazine*, August 1998.

Schwartz, Hillel. *Never Satisfied: A Cultural History of Diets, Fantasies and Fat*. New York: The Free Press, 1986.

"Second Chain." *Time*, July 5, 1943, 96.

Sedgwick, Eve Kosofsky. *Epistemology of the Closet*. Berkeley: University of California Press, 1992.

———. *Tendencies*. Durham: Duke University Press, 1993.

Seidman, Steve. *Comedian Comedy: A Tradition in Hollywood Film*. Ann Arbor: UMI Research Press, 1981.

Sheldon, Caroline. "Lesbians and Film: Some Thoughts." In *Gays and Film*, edited by Richard Dyer. London: British Film Institute, 1984.

Shohat, Ella, and Robert Stam. *Unthinking Eurocentrism: Multi-Culturalism and the Media*. London and New York: Routledge, 1994.

Silver, Alain. "Introduction." In *Film Noir Reader*, edited by Alain Silver and James Ursini. New York: Limelight Editions, 1996.

Silverman, Kaja. *Male Subjectivity at the Margins*. London and New York: Routledge, 1992.

Simpson, Mark. *Male Impersonators: Men Performing Masculinity*. New York: Routledge, 1994.

Sims, Yvonne Denise. "From Mammies to Action Heroines: Female Empowerment in Black Popular Culture." Ph.D. diss., Bowling Green State University, August 2000.

Singer, Ben. "Female Power in the Serial-Queen Melodrama: The Etiology of an Anomaly." *Camera Obscura* 22 (1990): 91–129.

Singleton, John. "Singular Filmmaker John Singleton Greets Comeback Queen Pam Grier." *Interview*, June 1996.

Smith, Patricia Juliana. "Divas." In www.glbtq.com, edited by Claude Summers, 2002.

Smith, Paul. *Clint Eastwood: A Cultural Production*. Minneapolis: University of Minnesota Press, 1993.

Smith, Valerie. *Not Just Race, Not Just Gender*. New York and London: Routledge, 1998.

Smith-Shomade, Beretta E. "Rock-a-Bye, Baby!": Black Women Disrupting Gangs and Constructing Hip-Hop Gangsta Films." *Cinema Journal* 42, no. 2 (Winter 2003): 25–40.

Sontag, Susan. *Against Interpretation*. New York: Delta, 1967.

Spinazzola, Vittorio. *Cinema e pubblico. Lo spettacolo filmico in Italia 1945–1965*. Roma: Bulzoni, 1985.

Stacy, Paul H., and Virginia Hale. "*Fort Apache, the Bronx*: Saints, Sinners and Symbols." *Literature/Film Quarterly* 14, no. 1 (January 1986): 53–57.

Staiger, Janet. "Film Noir as Male Melodrama: The Politics of Film Genre Labeling." Paper delivered on July 25, 2006, at The Centre for Cultural Inquiry. University of Auckland (New Zealand).

———. *Interpreting Films: Studies in the Historical Reception of American Cinema*. Princeton: Princeton University Press, 1992.

Stearns, Peter N. *Fat History: Bodies and Beauty in the Modern West*. New York: New York University Press, 1997.

Steichen, Edward. *The Blue Ghost*. New York: Harcourt Brace, 1947.

Steinhem, Gloria. *Moving Beyond Words: Age, Race, Sex, Power, Money, Muscles*. New York: Simon & Schuster, 1994.

Straayer, Chris. *Deviant Eyes, Deviant Bodies: Sexual Re-Orientations in Film and Video*. New York: Columbia University Press, 1996.

Stryker, Susan, and Stephen Whittle, eds. *The Transgender Studies Reader*. New York: Routledge, 2006.

Studlar, Gaylyn. *In the Realm of Pleasure: Von Sternberg, Dietrich, and the Masochistic Aesthetic*. New York: Columbia University Press, 1988.

———. *This Mad Masquerade: Stardom and Masculinity in the Jazz Age*. New York: Columbia University Press, 1996.

"Synopsis." *Coffy*, Press book, American International Pictures, 1973.

Tasker, Yvonne. *Spectacular Bodies: Gender, Genre, and the Action Cinema*. London and New York: Routledge, 1993.

———. *Working Girls: Gender and Sexuality in Popular Cinema*. London and New York: Routledge, 1998.

Taves, Brian. *The Romance of Adventure: The Genre of Historical Adventure Movies*. Jackson: University of Mississippi Press, 1993.

"Term of Endearment." *People* 49, no. 3 (January 26, 1998).

Thom, Rene. *Structural Stability and Morphogenesis: An Outline of a General Theory of Models*. Reading: W. A. Benjamin, 1975.

Turner, Victor. "Frame, Flow and Reflection: Ritual and Drama as Public Liminality." In *Performance in Postmodern Culture*, edited by Michel Benamou and Charles Caramello. Milwaukee: University of Wisconsin Press, 1977, 33–55.

Turner, William. *A Genealogy of Queer Theory*, Philadelphia: Temple University Press, 2000.

Vernet, Marc. "Film Noir on the Edge of Doom." In *Shades of Noir*, edited by Joan Copjec. London: Verso, 1993.

Villarejo, Amy, and Matthew Tinkcom. *Keyframes: Popular Cinema and Cultural Studies*. London: Taylor and Francis, 2001.

Weber, Samuel. *The Legend of Freud*. Minneapolis: University of Minnesota Press, 1982.

White, Patricia. *The Uninvited*. London and New York: Routledge, 1999.

Wiegman, Robyn. "Feminism, 'TheBoyz,' and Other Matters Regarding the Male." In *Screening the Male: Exploring Masculinities in Hollywood Cinema*, edited by Steven Cohan and Ina Rae Hark. London and New York: Routledge, 1993, 173–193.

Willemen, Paul, and Jim Pines, eds. *Questions of Third Cinema*. London: British Film Institute, 1990.

Williams, Linda. *Playing the Race Card*. Princeton and Oxford: Princeton University Press, 2001.

————. "Something Else Besides a Mother." In *Home is Where the Heart Is: Studies in Melodrama and the Woman's Film*, edited by Christine Gledhill. London: The British Film Institute, 1987, 299–325.

Willis, Sharon. *High Contrast: Race and Gender in Contemporary Hollywood Film*. Durham: Duke University Press, 1997.

Wills, Gary. *John Wayne's America*. New York: Touchstone, 1997.

Wittson, C. H., H. I. Harris, W. A. Hunt, P. S. Solomon and M. M. Jackson. "The Neuropsychiatric Selection of Recruits," *American Journal of Psychiatry* 99 (March 1943): 639–650.

Wollen, Peter. "The Hermeneutic Code." In *Readings and Writings*. London: Verso, 1982.

Wood, Robin. "Ideology, Genre, Auteur." *Film Comment* 13, no. 1 (1977): 46–51.

Wyden, Peter. *The Overweight Society*. New York: William Morrow, 1965.

Young, Robert, Jr. *Roscoe "Fatty" Arbuckle: A Bio-Bibliography*. Westport: Greenwood Press, 1994.

Zavattini, Cesare. *Diario cinematografico*. Ed. Valentina Fortichiari. Milano: Bompiani, 1979.

Contributors

Robert T. Eberwein is Emeritus Distinguished Professor of English at Oakland University in Rochester, Michigan. His most recent publications are *The War Film* (Rutgers University Press, 2004) and *Armed Forces: Masculinity and Sexuality in the American War Film* (Rutgers University Press, 2007).

Lucy Fischer is Distinguished Professor of Film Studies and English at the University of Pittsburgh, where she serves as director of the Film Studies Program. She is the author of seven books: *Jacques Tati* (1983), *Shot/Countershot: Film Tradition and Women's Cinema* (1989), *Imitation of Life* (1991), *Cinematernity: Film, Motherhood, Genre* (1996), *Sunrise* (1998), *Designing Women: Art Deco, Cinema, and the Female Form* (2003), and *Stars: The Film Reader* (co-edited with Marcia Landy, 2004.) She is presently at work editing two additional books: *American Cinema of the 1920s: Themes and Variations* (forthcoming, Rutgers University Press) and *Teaching Film* (co-edited with Patrice Petro, Modern Language Association).

Krin Gabbard teaches cinema studies, comparative literature, and cultural studies at the State University of New York at Stony Brook. His most recent books are *Hotter Than That: The Trumpet, Jazz, and American Culture* (Faber and Faber, 2008) and *Black Magic: White Hollywood and African American Culture* (Rutgers University Press, 2004).

Chris Holmlund is a professor of cinema studies, women's studies, and French at the University of Tennessee, where she chairs the Cinema Studies Program. She is the author of *Impossible Bodies* (Routledge, 2002), editor of *American Cinema of the 1990s: Themes and Variations* (forthcoming, Rutgers University Press), and co-editor (with Justin Wyatt) of *Contemporary American Independent Film: From the Margins to the Mainstream* (Routledge, 2005) and (with Cynthia Fuchs) *Between the Sheets, In the Streets: Queer, Lesbian, Gay Documentary* (Minnesota University Press, 1997). She is currently working on a book on *Stars in Action* (for BFI/Palgrave Macmillan).

E. Ann Kaplan is Distinguished Professor of English and comparative literary and cultural studies at Stony Brook University, where she also founded and directs The Humanities Institute. She is past president of the Society for Cinema and Media Studies. Kaplan has written many books and articles on topics in cultural studies, media, and women's studies, from diverse theoretical perspectives including psychoanalysis, feminism, postmodernism, and post-colonialism. She has given lectures all over the world and her work has been translated into six languages. Her recent books include *Trauma and Cinema: Cross-Cultural Explorations* (co-edited with Ban Wang in 2004) and *Trauma Culture: The Politics of Terror and Loss in Media and Literature* (Rutgers University Press, 2005). She is working on two new book projects, *Public Feelings, Memory, and Affective Difference: Contemporary Visual Culture* and *The Unconscious of Age: Screening Older Women.*

KATHLEEN ROWE KARLYN is the author of *The Unruly Woman: Gender and the Genres of Laughter* (University of Texas Press, 1995). She has published articles on feminist theory, cultural studies, and film and television genres in *Screen, Cinema Journal, Genders, Feminist Media Studies*, and other journals and anthologies. Her current project, *Unruly Girls, Unrepentant Mothers*, is a companion to her first book and examines mothers and daughters in the context of girl culture and feminism's third wave.

DAVID LUGOWSKI is an associate professor of English and film studies and director of Communication Studies at Manhattanville College. He has published on queer theory, censorship, international filmmakers, and world cinema in such venues as *Cineaste, Cinema Journal, Arizona Quarterly, Senses of Cinema*, and *The Encyclopedia of Documentary Film*, and anthologies including *Film and Sexual Politics, American Cinema of the 1930s: Themes and Variations*, and *Looking Past the Screen: Case Studies in American Film History and Method.*

WILLIAM LUHR is a professor of English and film at Saint Peter's College and is currently completing a book on *Film Noir* for Wiley-Blackwell. His recent books include *Thinking About Movies: Watching, Questioning, Enjoying*, 3rd ed. (co-authored, Wiley-Blackwell, 2008) and *The Coen Brothers' Fargo* (Cambridge University Press, 2004)

PATRICIA MELLENCAMP is Distinguished Professor Emeritus, at the University of Wisconsin—Milwaukee, currently residing on the coast of Northern California (imitating Jessica Fletcher in *Murder, She Wrote*). Her current book project is titled *Ordinary Mysticism: On Death, Dating, and Aging*. Unlike Jessica, she is looking for a publisher. Since 2003, in addition to writing, her time has been devoted to her private life—getting married in her sixties, becoming a grandmother, and traveling around the world. Motorcycling, flying, and golfing are recent interests—think Rosalind Russell as Amelia Earhart and Katherine Hepburn in *Pat and Mike*—and then age them by thirty or more years.

JERRY MOSHER is an assistant professor in the Department of Film and Electronic Arts at California State University, Long Beach. He has published essays on the fat body and media culture in the anthologies *Bodies Out of Bounds: Fatness and Transgression, The End of Cinema As We Know It: American Film in the Nineties, Where the Boys Are: Cinemas of Masculinity and Youth, From Hobbits to Hollywood: Essays on Peter Jackson's* Lord of the Rings, and *A Family Affair.*

JACQUELINE REICH is an associate professor of Italian and comparative literary and cultural studies at SUNY Stony Brook, where she directs the Cinema and Cultural Studies Undergraduate Program. She is the author of *Beyond the Latin Lover: Marcello Mastroianni, Masculinity, and Italian Cinema* (Indiana University Press,

2004), and co-editor of *Re-viewing Fascism: Italian Cinema, 1922–1943* (Indiana University Press, 2002). She is presently at work on a book-length study on body-building, nation formation, and visual culture in twentieth-century Italian and American culture.

CHRIS STRAAYER is an associate professor and former chair of the Department of Cinema Studies at New York University, author of the influential *Deviant Eyes, Deviant Bodies: Sexual Re-Orientation in Film and Video* (Columbia University Press, 1996), essays in books such as *Masculinity: Bodies, Movies, and Culture*, edited by Peter Lehman (Rutgers University Press, 2001), and *Women in Film Noir, 2nd Edition*, edited by E. Ann Kaplan (British Film Institute, 1999), and articles in journals such as *Jump Cut, Afterimage, Camera Obscura*, and *Screen*.

Index

Monti, Raffaele, 60n10

Moonstruck (1987), 155–156, 157, 160, 161, 162, 163, 163–167; use of *La Bohème* in, 156, 164, 166

Moore, Demi, 92n1

Morrisey, Paul, 21

Morrison, Marion. *See* Wayne, John

Motherhood and Representation (Kaplan), 20

"Mourning and Melancholia" (Freud), 86

Mr. Smith Goes to Washington (1939), 41

Multiple Voices in Feminist Criticism (Carson, Dittmar, and Welsch, eds.), 22

Mulvey, Laura, 2, 17–19, 21, 23, 25, 36, 97

musical (film genre), 10, 43

Nardini, Gloria, 59n3

Nashville (1975), 41

National Council on Child Abuse and Family Violence, 33

Nazzari, Amedeo, 53

Nazzari, Totò, 53

Neale, Steve, 2, 23, 27, 75n2

neorealism, 52

New Jack City (1991), 71

New Queer Cinema: A Critical Reader (Aaron, ed.), 27

New University Community (NUC), 15

"Notes on Film Noir" (Schrader), 141

Notes on a Scandal (2006), 80

Now You See It (Dyer), 26–27, 99

obesity, criminalization of, 145–147

object relations psychology, 32

Objective, Burma! (1945), 118–119

Ocean's Thirteen (2007), 80

Olsen, Mark, 40, 44

Operation Pacific (1951), 5

Oprah, 79

Original Gangstas (1993), 63, 69, 70, 71, 72, 74–75

Our Dancing Daughters (1928), 7

OUTLAW (1994), 123, 133–136. *See also* Feinberg, Leslie

Oxenberg, Jan, 21

Pallette, Eugene, 151

Pangborn, Franklin, 109

Paris Is Burning (1991), 109

patriarchy, 30; in *Magnolia*, 30–31

Pelosi, Nancy, 80

Penley, Constance, 2

Peters, Bernadette, 103

Philadelphia Story, The (1941), 162

Pickford, Mary, 17, 88, 89

Pillow to Post (1945), 147

Pines, Jim, 22

Pinsker, Sanford, 52

Pitfall (1948), 151, 152

Polley, Sarah, 80

Popcorn Venus (Rosen), 17

Posse (1993), 63, 69, 71, 72

poststructuralism, 19

Powell, William, 144

Practices of Love (de Lauretis), 26

Prelude to a Kiss (1992), 7

Pretty Woman (1993), 167n7

Primrose Path (1940), 103, 107

prison films, 64, 65; lesbian plots in, 66

psychoanalysis, 18, 19, 21, 27–28; master narratives' reliance on analogies in speculating on film, 95. *See also* Freud, Sigmund

Psychology for the Fighting Man, 112–113

Puccini, Giacomo, 167n1

Queen, The (2006), 80

Queen Christina (1933), 10

queer studies, 9–10, 16, 26–27, 28, 95, 97–98; debates about categories employed in, 27; use of the term *queer*, 99–101

Questions of Third Cinema (Willemen and Pines, eds.), 22

race, and cinema, 16, 22–23

Rain (1932), 7

Randall, Tony, 24

Rapper, Irving, 109

Rather, Dan, 92n1

Raw Deal (1948), 151